THIRD EDITION

The Politics of Gun Control

SUNY, College at Cortland

CQ PRESS

A Division of Congressional Quarterly Inc.
Washington, D.C.

CQ Press
1255 22nd Street, N.W., Suite 400
Washington, D.C. 20037

Phone, 202-729-1900
Toll-free, 1-866-4CQ-PRESS (1-866-427-7737)

www.cqpress.com

Printed and bound in the United States of America

07 06 05 04 03   5 4 3 2 1

LIBRARY OF CONGRESS CATALOGING-IN-PUBLICATION DATA

Spitzer, Robert J.
    The politics of gun control / by Robert J. Spitzer.— 3rd ed.
        p.   cm.
Includes bibliographical references and index.
ISBN 1-56802-905-5 (pbk. : alk. paper)
1. Gun control—United States.   I. Title.
HV7436.S68   2004
363.3'3'0973—dc21

2002009916
CIP

To Ted Lowi,
Mentor, Friend, Bon Vivant

and to the memories of
Bill Spitzer (1921–1996)
and
Ed Artinian (1936–1997)

and
to my wonderful Tess

Contents

Preface

THIS PROJECT BEGAN in classic academic style. Almost two decades ago, a colleague contacted me to inquire about my interest in writing a chapter for a policy issues book. I was offered a choice of topics and settled on gun control, in large part because I knew little about the topic aside from what I read in the occasional newspaper article. One of the joys of academic life is the opportunity to examine and research subjects for the sheer pleasure of exploration. So it was with gun control. Since that time, I have continued to accumulate materials, write articles, and reflect on the singular nature of the gun debate, as well as the continuing need for analytical writing on this subject.

One interesting phenomenon I observed through the research process was the almost frantic yet very conscious penchant of a few writers on the gun issue to embrace, or run away from, ideological labels. The polemical undergrowth of the gun issue is certainly one reason for such proclamations, as is the penchant for ad hominem rather than substantive argumentation; yet such proclamations are unusual in scholarly literature, and I was trained to let arguments and facts speak for themselves. Declaratory statements by some lawyers and writers that they were good liberals, or not members of various gun associations, seemed anxious efforts to protest too much. Nevertheless, in the spirit of such personal declarations, let me state for the record that I am, as of this writing, a member of the National Rifle Association and the Brady Coalition (formerly Handgun Control, Inc.). These memberships have been edifying for me in that they have helped provide a keener view of the gun issue from the trenches on each side.

Three key cultural shocks have shaped the politics of gun control since the second edition of this book was published in 1998. The first was the April 1999 shooting at Columbine High School in Littleton, Colorado, which resulted in the murder of twelve students and one teacher, and the suicide of the two student perpetrators. That shocking event, in turn, led to the first significant legislative effort to alter existing federal gun laws since 1994. It also spawned a short-lived but dramatic mass movement in favor of stricter gun laws that culminated in the Million Mom March in May 2000.

The second event was the 2000 elections. On the Democratic side, the two main contenders for the nomination, Vice President Al Gore and former senator Bill Bradley, both made gun control an important component of their campaigns, talking openly about subjects that had been taboo since the 1960s—gun registration and gun licensing. On the Republican side, Texas governor George W. Bush paid less attention to the gun issue, but as president he has stood squarely with those who oppose stronger gun laws, closely following the agenda of the National Rifle Association on matters ranging from the interpretation of the Second Amendment to the conduct of foreign policy.

The third event was the terrorist attack of September 11, 2001. Foreign policy crises often push domestic issues to the side, but the domestic political dynamics that have swirled around the gun issue for decades proceeded unabated. Terrorism left its mark on the issue, as critics noted with bitter irony the ease with which alleged Middle Eastern terrorists acquired guns in the United States. A London-based organization allegedly linked to Middle Eastern extremists, Sakina Security Services, actually advertised on its Web site an invitation to practice sniper skills at a target range located somewhere in the United States. And in a less dramatic turn of events, handgun sales shot up in the aftermath of September 11th. The Federal Bureau of Investigation reported that it performed 455,000 more background checks for handgun purchases in the six months after September 11th than during the same period a year earlier (although gun sales then dropped off sharply in 2002). That some Americans instinctively reach for a gun in times of crisis is an important part of the American gun story. These three events underscore the import of this new edition.

I wish to acknowledge the advice, assistance, and thoughtful comments of several SUNY Cortland colleagues and friends, including Seth Asumah, Bruce Atkins, Frank Burdick, James Clark, Deb Dintino, Herb Haines, Hubert Keen, Carol McPhee, Peg Murphy, Loretta Padavona, Tom Pasquarello, Len Ralston, Tim Shannon, Judson Taylor, and Don Wright. Two Cortland colleagues read significant portions of the original manuscript. My particular thanks to Craig Little and Jerry O'Callaghan. John Mearsheimer of the University of Chicago also offered crucial suggestions and advice. I was very grateful for the opportunity to work with Chatham House's then-publisher, the no-nonsense Ed Artinian, and one of its former editors, Chris Kelaher, on the original edition. And as always, I thank Bill and Jinny Spitzer, and my wonderful wife, Teresa.

In recognition of the completion of this third edition, I wish to thank Mark Prus and Kathleen Burke, both highly skilled economists at SUNY Cortland, and Ted Bolen, Katharine Miller, Clare Williams, and Rachel Hegarty of Chatham House/Seven Bridges Press. I am excited at the prospect of working with this book's new publisher, CQ Press, which has recently acquired Chatham House. My special thanks to CQ's Brenda Carter, James Headley, and Charisse Kiino. I also wish to acknowledge Gail Popa, Jason Popa, and Skye Wilson, who enjoys seeing her name in print, and who is also the Queen of Everything.

Introduction

THE FUROR OVER gun control has raged across the American landscape for decades, with a sustained intensity and intractability found among few other issues. Despite all that has been written on the subject, no comprehensive political and policy analysis on gun control exists, even though the gun debate is precisely a political dispute over the proper scope and consequences of government policy.

At its heart, the gun debate is a question about the relationship between the citizen, the state's power to regulate, and the maintenance of public order. All these relationships come together under the public policy umbrella and are thus amenable to a policy analysis that has as its central question: should gun possession and use be significantly regulated? In raising this question, I am less concerned with the efficacy of each and every regulatory alternative, although most receive treatment here, than with the regulation principle as it applies to the gun issue. This is no esoteric exercise; every political dispute over some new effort to regulate guns invokes broader questions of government regulation.

The regulatory question is given coherence and context within a larger framework of policy analysis. Far from being an idiosyncratic issue that defies generalized analysis, the gun issue fits into a broader policy pattern, labeled social regulatory policy, that provides considerable predictive and explanatory power for the observed political trends.

This framework provides the organizational pattern for the analysis in this book. Chapter 1 lays out primary traits of the gun controversy, its social and cultural roots, and the social regulatory policy framework. Chapter 2 is devoted exclusively to the meaning, interpretation, and consequences of the Second Amendment to the Constitution, the much-cited yet little understood right to bear arms. The talismanic quality of the Second Amendment extends its importance beyond the narrow, arcane confines of constitutional and legal interpretation. The Constitution frames political rights, but constitutional imagery and symbolism frame political discourse.

Chapter 3 digests the wide-ranging arguments concerning the criminological consequences of guns and gun control in society. Most gun analysis and debate concentrate on the links between guns and crime. Yet any such analysis is incomplete unless it incorporates suicidal, accidental, and self-defense questions as well.

Chapter 4 turns to the political patterns that spring from, and are indeed typical of, social regulatory policy. Needless to say, gun politics has been dominated by one giant player, the National Rifle Association. Yet other, emergent political forces have deprived the NRA of its monopoly control in recent years, including a well-organized opposition led by the Brady Center to Prevent Gun Violence (formerly known as Handgun Control, Inc.). Serving as background for this struggle has been a surprisingly constant public disposition favoring control and an enduring party split.

Chapter 5 focuses on the key national institutions—Congress, the presidency, and the federal bureaucracy—that have been, at best, unwilling participants in the furious gun debate. The surprising finding that all three institutions have behaved contrary to conventional views of these institutions loses its surprise within the social regulatory framework.

Chapter 6 brings together the separate policy strands of the other chapters to synthesize the policy dilemma and to propose a new way to approach the gun issue. This chapter draws on international relations theory to assess the arguments of gun control supporters and opponents and to propose a new way to achieve political accommodation, despite enduring hostility and mutual suspicion. The idea that political accommodation can be reached between hostile, intransigent opponents unwilling to give ground, much less negotiate, is a difficult and unwieldy phenomenon in American politics, but a commonplace one in international relations.

Only two elements of the gun debate do not receive detailed attention here. Except for some discussion in the final chapter, gun policy at the state level receives relatively little attention. To be sure, much that is important has happened at state and local levels, but this book is consciously about national policymaking. A systematic treatment of state policy efforts could easily consume a volume larger than this one. In addition, I provide no comparative analysis with gun policies in other nations. This, too, is an important subject, but the differences between the American case and that of most other developed nations are sufficiently great, and the depth of analysis required is sufficiently imposing, that I chose to bypass this analysis. Even with these two editorial decisions, anyone approaching national gun policy in America has her or his hands more than full.

CHAPTER 1

Policy Definition and Gun Control

I come from a State where half the folks have hunting and fishing licenses. I can still remember the first day when I was a little boy out in the country putting a can on top of a fencepost and shooting a .22 at it. I can still remember the first time I pulled a trigger on a .410 shotgun because I was too little to hold a .12 gauge. . . . This is part of the culture of a big part of America. . . . I live in a place where we still close schools and plants on the first day of deer season, nobody is going to show up anyway. . . . We have taken this important part of the life of millions of Americans and turned it into an instrument of maintaining madness. It is crazy.

—**President Bill Clinton, comments at 30 November 1993 signing ceremony for the "Brady bill"**

THE CONTROVERSY OVER gun control revolves around two related questions of government authority: does the government have the right to impose regulations; and, assuming the existence of such a right, should the government regulate guns? It is perfectly obvious that numerous gun control regulations already exist, from the national to the local level. Indeed, gun control opponents are quick to point out that thousands of gun laws exist throughout the country, a fact usually quoted to underscore their belief that such regulation is futile. A pamphlet produced by the National Rifle Association (NRA) mentions "an estimated 20,000 local, state, and federal firearms laws," the vast majority of which are local codes.[1] Gun control opponents also argue that further gun restrictions could impinge on constitutional rights and the innate rights of the citizenry in a free nation. Before proceeding with these key questions, we must begin with the role and purpose of government regulation.

Regulation, Public Order, and Public Policy

The fundamental purpose of government—indeed, its first purpose—is to establish and maintain order. As many political thinkers have noted, human existence before the establishment of governments was chaotic and anarchic. Writing in the seventeenth century, the British political theorist Thomas Hobbes in his *Leviathan* noted that life in such a "state of nature" was "solitary, poor, nasty, brutish, and short." The only "law" in this situation was that of self-preservation, when one could expect only the "war" of "every man, against every man." To stave off such an anarchic condition, people formed governments, to which citizens traded some of their freedom, including the "freedom" to kill or be killed, in exchange for the order of civil society. In such a "civil state," according to Hobbes, "there is a power set up to constrain those that would otherwise violate their faith."

Writing several decades after Hobbes, the British political thinker John Locke in his *Of Civil Government* concurred, noting that "God hath certainly appointed government to restrain the partiality and violence of men. I easily grant that civil government is the proper remedy for the inconveniences of the state of nature." That we in America largely take the value of order for granted is a testament to the remarkable stability of American life.[2] Order is not the only priority for government, of course, since democratic nations value freedom and the protection of basic rights as well and must continually strive to strike an appropriate balance between these values.[3] Nevertheless, order is the first purpose of government because without order there can be no freedom in society (aside from the "freedom" of anarchy to which Hobbes and Locke referred). As the political scientist Samuel Huntington once noted, "men may, of course, have order without liberty, but they cannot have liberty without order."[4] And, as James Madison wrote to Thomas Jefferson in 1788, "It is a melancholy reflection that liberty should be equally exposed to danger whether the Government have too much or too little power."

The maintenance of public order by governments occurs through public policy, defined most simply as "whatever governments choose to do or not to do."[5] The close link between order and public policy is underscored by the interesting semantic fact that "policy" has the same linguistic root as "police."[6] Note the link between the two in this definition of public policy offered by the British constitutionalist William Blackstone in 1769: "the due regulation and domestic order of the kingdom, whereby the inhabitants of the State, like members of a well-governed family, are bound to conform their general behavior to the rules of propriety, good neighborhood, and good manners, and to be decent, industrious, and inoffensive in their respective stations."

The techniques or tools of public policy take many forms, from the dispensing of benefits to strict regulation of individual conduct. Yet basic questions of public order usually involve direct regulation—power exercised by the government "for the protection of the health, safety, and morals of their citizens."[7] Beyond the simple maintenance of order, "government is the guarantor of the public good. Ideally, this is achieved as government regulates private functions to maximize public welfare."[8] The regulation of individual conduct may include that considered harmful to others, such as driving under the influence of alcohol, or conduct considered immoral, such as gambling or prostitution.[9]

This returns us to the question of the regulation of firearms. (In this analysis, "guns" and "firearms" are treated as synonymous.) The fierce and protracted debate over gun control raises a variety of issues about individual behavior and the role of the government. Nevertheless, the gun debate at its core turns on a single, central question of public policy as it relates to both order and personal conduct: *should gun possession and use be significantly regulated?* This central question of public policy guides the organization of this book.

Guns and Regulation

Why has gun control been such a difficult, controversial, and intractable issue in American politics? The first answer is because of the nature of regulation. Whenever the government seeks to apply its coercive powers directly to shape individual conduct, the prospect of controversy is great, especially in a nation with a long tradition of individualism. According to the policy analyst Theodore J. Lowi, when the likelihood of government coercion[10] is immediate—that is, when the behavior of individual citizens is directly affected, as in the case of regulation—the prospect of controversy is high. When the likelihood of government coercion is remote—that is, when the primary purpose of the policy in question is, say, to provide benefits rather than regulate individual conduct—the prospect of controversy is low. Examples of policies where government coercion is low include public works projects (construction of roads, harbors, buildings, etc.) and subsidies to farmers (labeled "distributive"; see figure 1.1, p. 5). Government can influence behavior by providing these benefits, but the primary emphasis is on the awarding of benefits, not the shaping of conduct.

In addition to immediate coercion, regulatory policy shares a characteristic that fans the flames of political controversy: it seeks to control individual conduct. When the government imposes highway safety regulations, pure food and drug requirements, cable television rates, criminal laws, or laws regulating abortions, it is regulating the conduct of individuals (not only individual citizens, but individual companies or other entities). Because of these direct consequences to individuals, regulatory policies are more controversial than policies that seek to shape the "environment of conduct," such as fiscal and monetary policy, the progressive income tax, and welfare programs. Even though these latter policies (labeled "redistributive"; see figure 1.1) affect individual citizens, the policies themselves are designed to shape broad classes or groups of people—the poor, certain categories of wage earners, homeowners—or even the entire society.[11] Thus the hand of government is less directly felt by the individual citizen than policy designed to regulate the conduct of individuals. The fourth and least controversial form of policy is that for which government coercion is remote and seeks to shape the environment of conduct. Labeled "constituent" policy (see figure 1.1), examples include policies pertaining to the administration of the government, the budgeting process, and the civil service.

Figure 1.1 summarizes the relationship between these four kinds of policies. Among the four, regulatory policy is the most likely to spawn controversy. Immediate coercion applied to individual conduct usually involves specific rules or sanctions with accompanying punishments, such as fines or imprisonment. The other kinds of policies are progressively less likely to include such specific and individually felt sanctions, as reflected in the numerical rank ordering in figure 1.1.[12]

We can make an even finer distinction within the category of regulatory policy by distinguishing between two primary types of regulation: economic regulation and social regulation.[13] Economic regulation dates back to the late nineteenth century when the national government began to become involved with the regulation of elements of the nation's economy. The first modern regulatory agency, the Interstate Commerce Commission (ICC), was created in 1887 to regulate railroad rates, control prices affecting consumers, require the publication of rail rates, and bar collusive practices.[14] Economic regulation accelerated in the twentieth century, incorporating a wide variety of business, market, and economic sectors.

Social regulation dates back many decades. Government, usually at the state level, has long been concerned with the regulation of prostitution, marriage and polygamy, alcohol consumption, and the like. Nevertheless, social regulation greatly expanded at the national level in the 1960s. It differs from economic regulation in that it is less concerned with narrow economic questions and more concerned with broader issues of public safety, health, or morals. The focus is social relationships, not economic transactions. According to political scientists Raymond Tatalovich and Byron Daynes, social regulatory policy is "the exercise of legal authority to affirm, modify, or replace community values, moral practices, and norms of interpersonal conduct."[15] Examples of such issues cited by Tatalovich and Daynes include abortion, crime control, women's rights, pornography, school prayer, gay rights, civil rights, affirmative action, and gun control. As this laundry list suggests, these issues are among the most controversial facing American society. Some social regulation is especially controversial and may provoke even greater controversy than economic regulation, for the fundamen-

Applicability of coercion

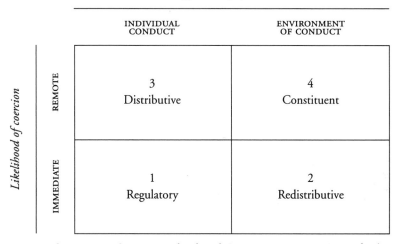

FIGURE 1.1   Government Coercion and Political Controversy among Types of Policy

Note: 1 = most controversial; 4 = least controversial.

tal reason that it is concerned with values. Moral issues often inspire even stronger feelings than economic issues.[16]

While government involvement in some social regulatory policies predates the 1960s (notably crime control), considerable governmental and societal interest has been focused on these issues in recent decades as the federal government has moved into this area, spawning intense, even explosive political antagonisms. The political characteristics of gun control conform closely to this characterization. But why is gun control an issue of social regulation? Or, to rephrase the question, what is it about gun control that provokes such sharp, deeply held feelings? What values underlie guns?

The Gun Controversy

In order to understand the dynamics of the gun issue, we need to begin with the admittedly narrow common ground of opponents and proponents. Despite the enormous differences that separate gun control advocates and opponents, they do share a few common assumptions:

1. The primary and unique purpose of firearms is to provide an efficient means of destruction of people, animals, and objects. While some may admire firearms for aesthetic, artistic, sporting, or other qualities,

no one can dispute this central purpose of firearms. Indeed, they evolved from the pressures of war during the Middle Ages.[17] Other objects in society cause great destruction, of course, from knives to automobiles, but these objects exist or were created to serve other purposes.[18] Knives, for example, serve a nearly infinite variety of other purposes; automobiles exist for the primary purpose of transporting people and commodities across vast expanses. That injury, destruction, or death arise from these or other objects is incidental, or at least secondary to the primary and necessary purpose for which they exist. The same cannot be said for firearms, so they are distinctive for this reason alone.

2. Existing gun laws have at best limited effects in curtailing gun-related deaths and injuries nationwide. Gun control advocates argue that the relative ineffectiveness of gun laws lies with their weakness and the problem of jurisdiction. The vast majority of gun laws exist at state and local levels, and states and cities with tougher gun laws find them at least partly neutralized by the ease with which guns can be transported from areas with weak gun laws. Stronger and more inclusive federal laws could address this problem—whether they could succeed is a separate question—but existing federal regulation is considered both limited and weak, although some gun control opponents find even existing law too restrictive. Gun control opponents argue that government simply cannot succeed in such regulation either for practical reasons—that is, too many Americans already own weapons—or because stronger laws would violate fundamental American values, beliefs, and practices.

3. Although gun ownership has been gradually declining, guns still permeate American society. From 1959 to 1993, an average 47 percent of American homes (from a low of 43 percent in 1972 to a high of 58 percent in 1983) reported having a gun in the house. A 1997 National Institute of Justice study concluded that as of 1994, 35 percent of households had at least one gun, and that 44 million Americans owned 192 million firearms. A 1999 federal government study found that 36 percent of American households had at least one gun.[19] Thus, whatever one's view on gun regulation, any effort by government to alter gun ownership and use patterns significantly must be prepared to cope with the ubiquity of guns.[20]

4. Part of America's social and cultural tradition includes an identifiable "gun culture," a phrase popularized by historian Richard Hofstadter in his "America as a Gun Culture."[21] Many gun control proponents decry America's long association with, and affection for, the gun; gun

control opponents for the most part embrace and celebrate the connections between guns and America's heritage. Regardless of one's personal or political feelings about guns, however, the gun culture is an undeniable component of American history and the gun debate.[22]

Despite this common ground, those who square off over gun control disagree on nearly everything else. Indeed, they cannot agree on the interpretation of laws and court cases about guns, on the validity of comparisons between the United States and other democratic nations (nearly all of which have stricter gun laws than those of the United States), or even on the effects of gun control on such basic issues as crime and public safety. Of course, many issues in American politics provoke sharp disagreement. Abortion, for example, provokes at times even greater passion than gun control. Yet, unlike gun control, those on opposing sides of the abortion question can at least agree on how abortions are performed, the desirability of avoiding unwanted pregnancies as a way to avoid the problem of abortion entirely, and the consequences of varying degrees of government regulation. Their disagreement turns primarily on the normative question of whether various restrictions should be imposed. Those on opposing sides of the gun debate cannot even agree on the basics.

The Gun Culture

To return to an earlier question: why such strong feelings over relatively simple metal-and-wood objects that do nothing more than propel small bits of metal at high speeds? The first answer is obvious: in recent years, more than 30,000 Americans have been killed annually as the result of the homicidal, accidental, and suicidal use of guns; in all, Americans wielding guns intimidate, wound, and kill hundreds of thousands every year.[23] These actions disrupt American lives, inflame public sentiment, and interrupt the societal concept of ordered liberty. While the absence of guns would not end violence and mayhem in America, the presence and easy availability of guns magnify the violent strain in the American character, multiplying its deadly consequences. These concerns are the ones typically expressed by gun control advocates.[24]

The second answer is both less obvious and more important. It is the just-mentioned American gun culture. This phrase usefully summarizes the long-term sentimental attachment of many Americans to the gun, founded on (1) the presence and proliferation of guns since the earliest days of the country; (2) the connection between personal weapons ownership and the country's early struggle for survival and independence, followed by the country's frontier experience; and (3) the cultural mythology that has grown up about the gun in both frontier and modern life, as reflected in books, movies, folklore, and other forms of popular expression.

Not all Americans, by any means, embrace this gun culture, and most who do acknowledge in some respect the destructive consequences of weapons. Yet these concerns are counterbalanced by strong personal feelings about guns. Beyond this, the gun culture is generally recognized, rightly or wrongly, as a key component of the American mythic tradition.[25] A recent study by historian Michael Bellesiles has argued that the modern gun culture is founded largely on myth. Contrary to the typical image of prolific gun ownership by frontier Americans who were reputedly excellent marksmen, Bellesiles found in his study of probate records (records of property inherited after death) that "gun ownership was exceptional in the eighteenth and nineteenth centuries" and that "at no time prior to 1850 did more than a tenth of the people own guns." In his subsequent award-winning but controversial book, Bellesiles argued that, aside from being relatively rare, gun ownership was more often disdained than admired in America, and that relatively few Americans possessed the marksmanship skills so often attributed to them in folklore. These arguments are supported by the facts that early guns were expensive, cumbersome, difficult to operate, unreliable, and made from materials (mostly iron) that deteriorated rapidly even with regular maintenance. Further, he argued that gun ownership and use became widespread only after the Civil War, in part because gun manufacturers such as Samuel Colt developed advertising campaigns that deliberately romanticized the attachment to guns, and because technological improvements made guns cheaper, more reliable, easier to use, and more durable.[26] Regardless of its origins, the American gun culture as it exists today contains at least two elements that have survived since the country's early history: the hunting/sporting ethos and the militia/frontier ethos.

The Hunting/Sporting Ethos

The first of these elements sprang from a time when the U.S. was an agrarian, subsistence nation existing in a hostile environment. Hunting game was one source of food for American settlers (although domesticated animals were almost certainly a far more important food source than game), just as it was a method for protection from animal predators, including bears, panthers, and wolves, although mounting evidence indicates that wolves posed no direct threat to humans. In addition, the growing market for furs encouraged hunting and trapping as a source of income. Noting the connection between shooting skills, survival, and the acquisition of these skills as a "rite of passage" for boys entering manhood, one colonial observer commented that "a well grown boy at the age of twelve or thirteen years, was furnished with a small rifle and shot-pouch.

He then became a fort soldier, and had his port-hole assigned him. Hunting squirrels, turkeys and raccoons, soon made him expert in the use of his gun."[27] For at least some Americans, guns were a necessity of everyday life for reasons of subsistence alone. That they were used for self-protection from Native Americans and other hostiles is equally evident. The role of guns as a mark of maturity is one that lingers to this day.[28]

As American society evolved, becoming more urban and more developed, the necessity for and practice of hunting declined. In fact, the practice of carrying arms declined along the nation's eastern coast as settlements grew. Even "during the colonial period, the urban areas were relatively free of the consistent use of firearms."[29] Yet the hunting tradition survived, especially in rural areas. So, too, did the element of competitive/sport shooting, a form of recreation also dating back to the country's earliest days. Such competitions occurred in part to improve shooting skill and aim, for despite the much-vaunted reputation of the American sharpshooter, even during the Revolution the sharp-shooting reputation exceeded actual American shooting skills. According to one observer, shooting matches in the country's early history were "the major sport of America."[30] While the accuracy of this claim is questionable, some shooting matches certainly occurred.

Today, about 14 million persons identify themselves as hunters (among those sixteen years of age and older, representing about 6 percent of the country's population).[31] Based on a study of hunters by Stephen Kellert of the Yale School of Forestry and Environmental Studies, the reasons for hunting vary, but the primary motivations include procurement of food, pursuit of sport, and the desire to commune with and participate in nature.[32] Beyond a mere activity, hunting survives as a central component of the gun culture. According to a variety of studies, the decline in hunting first predicted in the 1960s has resulted from and is continuing primarily because of the decline in farming and rural populations and changing social attitudes. Indeed, some predict that the "hunting heritage" may disappear entirely by the middle of the twenty-first century.[33]

The Militia/Frontier Ethos

The second tradition, the militia/frontier ethos, has more direct political antecedents and consequences. Early Americans had to rely on their wits and skills to protect themselves and their families from hostile Native Americans and foreign armies. Necessity dictated that anyone capable of carrying and using a weapon (excluding blacks and, for the most part, women) participate in local defense. Neither the budget nor the manpower existed to maintain a full-time army, so the armed citizen-soldier bore this responsibility. Nor did the government have the resources to arm its citizens; in fact, from the earliest days of the colonies, able-bodied men were pressed, even required, not only to serve but to provide their own arms and ammunition, since the colonies' very survival depended on these citizen militias. The mother country was little help, either. Even though the colonies were under British rule, England only began to send troops to America in the 1740s.[34]

As is well known, citizen-soldiers serving in state-based militias fought and won American independence against what was considered the finest standing army in the world (more is said about this in chapter 2). Yet by the 1790s, the many drawbacks of citizen militias accelerated the reliance on volunteer units and a professional, full-time army. The death knell of the citizen militia was its abysmal performance in the War of 1812, after which it ceased to play any active role in national defense.[35] Despite this fact, the militia tradition has survived.

Closely related to the militia tradition is the frontier tradition, which linked westward movement with weaponry. Just as the Pennsylvania-Kentucky style rifle was closely associated with the American colonial and revolutionary experience,[36] nineteenth-century firearms became readily identifiable symbols of westward expansion. The principal enemies of westward-moving settlers, said to be outlaws and Indians, necessitated an armed citizenry ready and willing to use their Winchesters, Smith & Wessons, Remingtons, and Colts to defend hearth and home at a time when allegedly the only reliable justice came from the barrel of a gun. "Men who wanted to hold their own against all comers carried their law with them—a Colt peacemaker, slung from their belt or in an arm-pit holster."[37] Axiomatic expressions such as "the guns that won the West" and "arm[s] that opened the West and tamed the wild land" typify what in actuality is a romanticized and wildly exaggerated assessment of the importance of guns in the settling of the West. Indeed, some have gone so far as to claim that "the American experiment was made possible by the gun."[38]

These characterizations can be faulted for ignoring the central role of homesteaders, ranchers, miners, tradesmen, businessmen, and the generalized movement of "civilization," to label it thus, across the western plains. The so-called taming of the West was in fact an agricultural and commercial movement, attributable primarily to ranchers and farmers, not gun-slinging cowboys.[39] In fact, the six-shooter and rifle played relatively minor roles in the activities of all these groups—even the cowboys. According to Richard Shenkman,

> The truth is many more people have died in Hollywood westerns than ever died on the real frontier. . . . In the real Dodge City, for instance, there were just five killings in 1878, the most homicidal year. . . . In the most violent year in Deadwood, South Dakota, only four people were killed. In the worst year in Tombstone, home of the shoot-out at the OK Corral, only five people were killed. The only reason the OK Corral shoot-out even became famous was that town boosters deliberately overplayed the drama to attract new settlers.[40]

Even in the most violence-prone towns, the western cattle towns, vigilantism and lawlessness were only briefly tolerated.[41] In his sweeping history of the West, the historian Ray Allen Billington noted that local businesspeople and other leaders quickly pushed for town incorporation in order to establish local police forces, which were supported by taxes levied against local bars, gambling establishments, and houses of prostitution. Prohibitions against carrying guns were strictly enforced, and there were few homicides. The gun "disarmament" that was routinely practiced in newly formed western towns was well understood as a sign of civilization and an improvement in public safety. Ironically, such measures provoke more political heat and outrage in the twenty-first century than in the nineteenth century. The western-style shoot-outs glorified in countless books and movies were literally "unheard of."[42]

In the most violent cow towns of the old West—Abilene, Caldwell, Dodge City, Ellsworth, and Wichita—a total of forty-five killings were recorded between 1870 and 1885, and only six of these killings were from six-shooters; sixteen killings were by police. Outside populated areas, cowboys and other range riders who carried six-guns almost never used them in Hollywood-style gunfights or to enforce some brand of western justice. As cowboy experts Joe B. Frantz and Julian E. Choate observed, "the six-shooter has been credited with use entirely disproportionate with the facts."[43]

Even western outlaws illustrate the extent to which myth has replaced fact with respect to guns and lawlessness. Many studies of the famed western outlaws demonstrate that "they were few, inconspicuous, and largely the invention of newspaper correspondents and fiction writers." Moreover, "the western marshall [was] an unglamorous character who spent his time arresting drunks or rounding up stray dogs and almost never engaging in gun battles."[44] Most of the killing that took place on the frontier involved the wars between the U.S. Cavalry and those Native Americans who rebelled against harsh and duplicitous treatment at the hands of whites.[45]

The hunting/sporting and militia/frontier views converge to produce a certain mythical elevation of the gun. This mythologizing parallels, indeed draws strength from, the broader mythologizing of the American frontier tradition. As American cultural analyst Richard Slotkin observed:

> The Myth of the Frontier was developed by and for an America that was a colonial offshoot of Europe, agrarian in economy, localistic in politics, tentative as to nationality, and relatively homogeneous in ethnicity, language, and religion; yet the Myth has been most thoroughly and impressively set forth in the ninety years that followed the closing of the Wild West, in and for an America that is a preeminent world power, urban-centered and fully industrialized, centralized in government, and heterodox in culture.[46]

This veneration of guns, with all its attendant symbolism and mythology, drives a powerful and deeply felt belief that guns are not only an integral part of, but a force responsible for, America as it exists today. While the percentage of Americans who aggressively embrace this tradition and consider it applicable to modern life is relatively small, the myths composing the gun culture survive and thrive in major elements of mass culture.

For example, one can hardly count as coincidence the fact that the very first feature film, *The Great Train Robbery*, sent moviegoers ducking for cover when an outlaw in the 1903 film aimed his six-gun at the camera and fired. From that day to this, the admittedly ambivalent relationship between movies and guns has nevertheless helped cultivate America's gun tradition, as have other forms of mass culture.[47]

The Modern Gun Culture

In contemporary society, the gun culture revolves around those who continue to own and use guns for legitimate hunting, sporting, and related purposes—although there are those who would include urban street gangs, gun-toting criminals, and other antisocial individuals and groups in this category. Modern social science has carefully identified the core of those who continue to promote a legitimate gun culture, based on both practice and attitude (these qualities are discussed in greater detail in chapter 4).

Those who compose and support the active gun culture are overwhelmingly white males, live in rural areas (especially in the South), are likely to be Protestant, and are from "old stock" (that is, have ancestors who came to this country longer ago than the more recent immigrant waves). Naturally, they are highly likely to own and use guns. Conversely, those for whom the gun culture carries the least appeal are likely to be females, from larger metropolitan areas, from the Northeast, and from more recent immigrant descent. Despite impressions to the contrary, levels of education and income bear little relation to the gun attachment.[48] Those most likely to embrace and carry on the gun tradition are socialized early in their lives by other family members into patterns of gun ownership and use.[49]

Having explored the basis of deep-seated feelings about guns, and therefore about gun control, we return to the contemporary political debate. That debate incorporates two features: stridency and immobility.

Policy Gridlock

The political pattern typifying the gun debate is one in which repetitive political scenarios play themselves out with great fury but astonishingly little effect. The cycle of outrage, action, and reaction usually begins with the sensational and the horrific.

Outrage

The first modern gun regulation, New York State's Sullivan law, was enacted in 1911 in reaction to an attempt to murder New York City Mayor William Gaynor.[50] The shooting deaths of Senator Robert F. Kennedy and the Reverend Martin Luther King Jr., both in 1968, were more recent instances when public outrage over deaths from guns prompted a significant political reaction—passage of the federal Gun Control Act of 1968.

In the 1980s and 1990s, highly publicized incidents of senseless mass slaughter and urban gang violence (with the latter often related directly or indirectly to drugs) again fanned the flames of public outrage. In 1989, for example, a man named Patrick Purdy opened fire with an AK–47 assault rifle on an elementary school playground in Stockton, California, killing five children and wounding thirty-three others. In 1991, a man using a semiautomatic pistol fired into a crowded cafeteria in Killeen, Texas, killing twenty-two people in the worst peacetime massacre of its kind in American history.[51] In 1999, two boys shot and killed twelve students and one teacher at Columbine High School in Littleton, Colorado, a crime that shocked the nation.

Action

Building on popular outrage, gun control proponents pressed for stronger gun laws in Congress and many state legislatures, meeting with some success. In the early 1990s, for example, states enacted laws that banned the sale and possession of assault rifles, barred those under the age of eighteen from possessing handguns, and held parents criminally liable for the gun-related actions of their children. In 1993 and 1994, Congress enacted new federal gun control laws (see chapter 5). After the Columbine massacre, national outrage pushed the U.S. Senate to approve the first new federal gun control measure since 1994 (the bill eventually died in the House of Representatives).

Reaction

Anti-gun-control forces, spearheaded by the National Rifle Association (NRA), have fought all of these efforts. These forces were mostly successful in blocking gun control measures in the states and at the federal level in the 1970s and 1980s, but toward the end of the 1980s, public sentiment shifted more strongly toward gun control, and the NRA's political inflexibility and stridency began to make more enemies than friends. As a consequence, the political fulcrum began to shift in favor of gun control proponents, spearheaded by Handgun Control, Inc. (HCI).

Still, the net policy change has been, for the most part, marginal, even in the states. A major federal battle revolved around the so-called Brady bill (named after gun control supporter and former White House Press Secretary James Brady, who was critically wounded in the 1981 attempt to assassinate President Reagan), which as enacted in 1993 imposed a five-day waiting period and background checks for handgun purchases. Most agree that the Brady law is an extremely modest, even marginal effort at regulation.[52] Yet the political struggle over this law has been nothing less than furious.

The key policy question for the moment is not whether these policies are wise or prudent, but whether wise or rational policy is likely to result from this outrage-action-reaction cycle. Do sensational killings exemplify a larger problem, or are they simply extreme cases? If the latter, do they provide adequate justification for stricter gun laws? While good policy may result, it surely cannot be attributed to a sound process in a policy sense.

The outrage-action-reaction cycle is symptomatic of the fundamental value conflict at the heart of the gun issue. As policy analyst Thomas R. Dye notes, "policy analysis is not capable of resolving value conflicts."[53] Yet the machinery of politics cannot abandon its pursuit of better policy simply because of its degree of political difficulty. What policy analysis can do is formulate its best analysis of the issue and use that analysis both to instruct and to provide a basis for reasonable policy prescription. Theodore J. Lowi frames this effort as

> develop[ing] a political science of policy analysis. . . . Political science may best make its pro rata contribution to good government on the basis of its ability to help define what government is . . . and to evaluate the significance and impact of each form of government action *on the political system itself.* (Emphasis in original.)[54]

Lowi's first step, to "define what government is," translates for our purposes to a definition of "what gun control is." The social regulatory policy formulation provides the necessary theoretical tool for addressing this question. Lowi's second step, to "evaluate the significance and impact" of policies on the political system, constitutes the other analytical component of this book. It serves to bring together policy options and political realities, as reflected in the central question posed at the start of this chapter: should gun possession and use be significantly regulated?

Social Regulatory Policy Analysis

As discussed earlier, social regulatory policies seek to apply governmental authority in a direct and immediate way to shape individual actions in the realm of values, morals, and norms. As with other forms of government regulation, this shaping is usually accomplished by the enactment of specific rules accompanied by specific sanctions or penalties.

According to social regulatory policy theory, certain distinctive political patterns and characteristics are associated with social regulatory issues. These patterns are observable among the major elements of the political process, including the political behavior of the courts, interest groups, the presidency, political parties, Congress, public opinion, federal agencies, and intergovernmental relations. The specific predicted patterns include the following:

1. The *courts* provide a key avenue for definition and change of the issue.
2. *Single-issue groups* are prevalent in the politics of the issue, and they behave in an absolutist, polarizing fashion; that is, they are singularly strident, they seek and defend extreme positions, and they are reluctant to compromise.
3. *Presidential leadership* plays a relatively marginal role and operates primarily on a symbolic level.
4. The *political parties* generally seek to exploit differences over social regulatory policy, with Republicans using such issues to mobilize conservatives and Democrats seeking to mobilize liberals.
5. *Congress* is more heavily involved in this kind of issue than the president, but it tends to support the status quo, often following the lead of state legislatures instead of setting the course for the states.
6. It is difficult to rally and to mobilize *public opinion* behind change; at the same time, for change to occur, it must be linked to, and draw support from, social/community norms and values.
7. Federal *government agencies* exercise limited control and jurisdiction over the issue, and the agencies are buffeted by political winds from Congress, the president, and interest groups.
8. *Federalism* defines the structure and politics of the issue. That is, unlike many issues on which the federal government has become the primary actor, state and local governments continue to operate with a high degree of autonomy and control, even in the presence of federal regulations.[35]

The rest of the book relies on these predicted patterns to organize and explain the politics surrounding the gun control issue. The next chapter examines constitutional and legal issues, converging on court rulings and the much discussed but poorly understood Second Amendment to the Constitution.

CHAPTER 2

The Second Amendment: Meaning, Intent, Interpretation, and Consequences

> A well regulated Militia, being necessary to the security of a free State, the right of the people to keep and bear Arms, shall not be infringed.
> —**Second Amendment, U.S. Constitution**

ANY CONSIDERATION OF the gun control debate inevitably turns to questions of the Constitution and the law. That the two are inextricably linked is illustrated by this quotation from the constitutional scholar Lucilius Emery:

> The greater deadliness of small firearms easily carried upon the person, the alarming frequency of homicides and felonious assaults with such arms, the evolution of a distinct class of criminals known as "gunmen" . . . are now pressing home the question of the reason, scope, and limitation on the constitutional guaranty of a right to keep and bear arms.[1]

That Emery raised this issue in 1915 underscores the long and important connection between the gun debate and the Second Amendment.

In the more public debate surrounding gun control, the Second Amendment is constantly invoked, especially by gun control opponents.[2] To pick a simple example from publications of the National Rifle Association (NRA), its October 1993 issue of *American Hunter* contained thirty-four references to the Second Amendment or the ownership of guns as a constitutionally protected right. Its November 1993 issue of the *American Rifleman* contained fourteen such references. In 1998, the NRA created a new publication, the *American Guardian,* devoted entirely to the NRA's political and legal priorities. Two years later, the magazine was renamed *America's First Freedom* (another reference to the Second Amendment). Various polls have reported that most Americans believe that the Second Amendment protects an individual's right to own weapons. A 1995 *U.S. News & World Report* poll reported that 75 percent of Americans believe that "the Constitution guarantees you the right to own a gun."[3]

The Second Amendment warrants detailed treatment for two reasons. First, it is essential as a matter of public policy to know what the law does and does not allow, because public policy springs from and is defined by law. Specifically, does the Second Amendment pose any obstacles to gun controls? If so, what are they? If not, why is the Second Amendment so often cited as a barrier to gun control?

Second, an understanding of the Second Amendment and its consequences is essential precisely because it is a touchstone of the gun debate. In American political discourse, claims to rights abound. Some rights, such as free speech and religious freedom, are indeed cornerstones of American life, springing directly from the Bill of Rights. Yet Americans claim a bevy of other rights as well. Some, such as the right to privacy, are deemed to arise from the Bill of Rights, even though privacy is not actually mentioned there. Other rights claims are far less supported, among them the right to smoke, the right to drive, the right to drink (but not drink and drive), and the right to burn leaves in one's yard. The constitutional scholar Mary Ann Glendon has labeled this phenomenon "rights talk," a reference to "our increasing tendency to speak of what is most important to us in terms of rights, and to frame nearly every social controversy as a clash of rights."[4] This singularly American habit is founded in our historical tendency to view law as the preeminent vehicle for articulating American values, enshrining political legitimacy, and emphasizing individual rights. Rights language is "universal, inalienable, inviolable." Rights claims tend to be absolutist; thus, this kind of debate "heightens social conflict, and inhibits dialogue"; it erodes mutual respect and elevates the individual at the expense of social responsibility.[5] As Glendon notes, these attributes describe the gun control debate as well.

The purpose of this chapter is to assess the meaning and consequences of the Second Amendment. (Because this book is principally concerned with federal gun issues, the chapter does not deal with state court rulings or Second Amendment–like provisions found in many state constitutions.)[6] Only after this assessment can we judge the abundant "rights talk" surrounding the gun control debate. Following up on the social regulatory policy analysis introduced in chapter 1, we would expect the courts to provide a key avenue for definition and change of the issue.

In order to clarify the meaning and consequences of the Second Amendment, we examine (1) the circumstances and thinking that led to its insertion in the Bill of Rights, (2) its interpretation by the courts, and (3) its connection to the modern gun control debate. In order to accomplish this, we examine political and constitutional history leading up to and including the federal period, incorporating the thinking of the authors of the Bill of Rights; pertinent court cases; and the writings of Bill of Rights and Second Amendment specialists, including standard legal reference works. We then discuss the theories of those who take issue with the verdict of history and law. Above all, the reader should remember that claims to constitutional legitimacy hold special importance in American politics. Sometimes, the claim is even more important than the fact.

Historic Roots

As discussed in chapter 1, firearms possession (whether common or rare) was a part of colonial and frontier life. Settlers found it necessary to band together to provide for mutual defense from foreign armies and hostile Native Americans. This reliance on part-time militias, instead of on a regular, professional standing army was based on two facts of life. First, the emerging American nation did not possess the manpower or resources to raise, finance, supply, or maintain a large professional army. Second, Americans shared a profound mistrust of standing armies. This suspicion stemmed from their knowledge of and experiences with standing armies in European history, where with depressing regularity professional armies had subverted or overthrown civilian governments and deprived people of basic rights.

The British Heritage

Great Britain had recently experienced such turmoil. For thirteen years in the middle of the seventeenth century, professional military forces under the control of Oliver Cromwell ruled England. The country was, in the words of the great British historian Thomas Babington Macaulay, "governed by the sword" in that "the civil power" was "subjected to military dictation." Under Cromwell's standing army, "the King had been murdered, the nobility degraded, the landed gentry plundered, the Church persecuted."[7]

Only a few years after Cromwell, King James II, a devout Catholic, promoted the cause of "papism" by filling the leading ranks of the army with Catholics, to the exclusion of Protestants. James's oppressive practices in the cause of advancing Catholicism, including the threat of a swelling Catholic-led army that might overwhelm local Protestant militias (controlled by local landed gentry), eventually led to his overthrow and replacement by William of Orange, an event dubbed the Glorious Revolution of 1688.

Thereafter, Parliament enacted the British Bill of Rights in 1689, in which various grievances against James II were enumerated, including that he "did endeavor to subvert and extirpate the Protestant Religion and the Laws and Liberties of this Kingdom. . . . By causing several good Subjects, being Protestants, to be disarmed at the same Time when Papists were both armed and employed contrary to Law." The right defined in Article VII of this document was "that the Subjects which are Protestants may have Arms for their Defence suitable to their Conditions, and as allowed by Law."[8] The law to which this sentence referred stipulated that firearms could be owned only by the nobility, wealthy landowners, and members of the militia executing their duty to defend the country. As historian Lois Schworer noted of Article VII, "Englishmen did not secure to 'ordinary citizens' the right to possess weapons."[9] This provision from the British Bill of Rights is cited as the forerunner of America's Second Amendment, although there is no direct evidence that it served as the model for the Second Amendment.[10]

Foreshadowing the American experience, the British recognized the superior fighting capabilities of standing armies, but for political and historical reasons they found it necessary to pay the militia its due. In Macaulay's words, the British "were forced to acknowledge that, dangerous as it might be to keep up a permanent military establishment, it might be more dangerous still to stake the honour and independence of the country on the result of a contest between plowmen officered by Justices of the Peace, and veteran warriors led by Marshalls of France. In Parliament, however, it was necessary to express such opinions with some reserve; for the militia was an institution eminently popular."[11]

These important episodes in British history revealed the actual and feared mischief of standing armies of which British subjects in America were keenly aware. They also underscored the government's connection of firearms ownership and regulation with militia/military service.[12]

The Colonial Heritage

The mistrust of standing armies was a pervasive sentiment during the revolutionary period[13] and was directly related to the bearing of arms by citizens. James Lovell wrote in 1771 that "the true strength and safety of every commonwealth or limited monarchy, is the bravery of its freeholders, its militia. By brave militias they rise to grandeur; and they come to ruin by a mercenary army." In 1776 Samuel Adams wrote that a "standing army, however necessary it may be at sometimes, is always dangerous to the liberties of the people." Samuel Seabury characterized the standing army as "the monster." George Washington observed that "mercenary armies . . . have at one time or another subverted the liberties of almost all the Countries they have been raised to defend." At the same point, however, John Adams spoke bluntly to one American general when he said, "We don't choose to trust you generals, with too much power, for too long [a] time."

In this way, the reliance on the citizen-soldier became synonymous with the revolutionary spirit.[14] The Virginia Declaration of Rights, written in 1776, said that "standing armies, in time of peace, should be avoided, as dangerous to liberty." The other states copied Virginia's wording.[15]

Sentiments favoring the militia as more compatible with democratic values were buttressed by the public myth prevailing at the time concerning the military effectiveness of militias. What the political scientist Clinton Rossiter labeled "the Cincinnatus complex" was the belief that no professional army could fight as effectively as a citizen militia.[16] This and related sentiments were reflected in the political thought of such philosophers as Francois-Marie Voltaire, Francois Quesnay, Anne-Robert-Jacques Turgot, and Jean-Jacques Rousseau. As was true in Britain, military reality would prove this politically popular myth to be hollow indeed.[17]

Not only had the Americans inherited the mistrust of standing armies from the British, but that mistrust was, ironically, magnified by the behavior of British troops on American soil. American outrage over the behavior of British troops found specific expression in the Declaration of Independence, wherein Thomas Jefferson complained that "He [the King] has kept among us, in Times of Peace, Standing Armies, without the consent of our Legislatures. He has affected to render the Military independent of and superior to the Civil Power." The 1776 Declaration also complained that the British were "quartering large Bodies of Armed Troops among us" and "protecting them, by a mock Trial, from Punishment for any Murders which they should commit on the Inhabitants of these States." The British only compounded these grievances and suspicions by "transporting large armies of foreign mercenaries [Hessians] to compleat the works of death, desolation, and tyranny." Not surprisingly, the British also took any and every opportunity to seize American weapons and ammunition.

As a consequence, American prosecution of the Revolutionary War relied for the most part on citizen militias that, according to the historian Merrill Jensen, were really "fourteen armies: the thirteen state militias and the Continental Army."[18] While the reliance on militias was politically satisfying, it proved to be an administrative and military nightmare. State detachments could not be easily combined into larger fighting units; soldiers could not be relied on to serve for extended periods, and desertions were common; officers were elected, based on popularity rather than experience or training; discipline and uniformity were almost nonexistent.[19] Commander-in-Chief George Washington defended the militia in public, but he made his real sentiments brutally clear in correspondence with Congress:

> To place any dependence upon Militia, is, assuredly, resting upon a broken staff. Men just dragged from the tender Scenes of domestick life; unaccustomed to the din of Arms; totally unacquainted with every kind of military skill,

which being followed by a want of confidence in themselves, when opposed to Troops regularly train'd, disciplined, and appointed, superior in knowledge and superior in Arms, makes them timid, and ready to fly from their own shadows . . . if I was called upon to declare upon Oath, whether the Militia have been most serviceable or hurtful upon the whole; I should subscribe to the latter.[20]

At a later point, Washington said of the militias that they "come in, you cannot tell how; go, you cannot tell when, and act, you cannot tell where." Despite the militia handicap, America did of course win its independence, owing to the durability of the core group of soldiers composing the Continental Army that maintained the force's continuity as militias came and went; the size of its force (more than 400,000 men participated during the course of the war); the adoption of tactics appropriate to American terrain; the assistance of the French; British difficulties related to distance and supply; and the American "home court advantage."

The Constitution

America's first constitution, the Articles of Confederation (1777–89), reflected suspicion not only of standing armies but also of a strong national government. The Articles specifically granted sovereignty to the states and severely limited the power of Congress. Formulated and adopted during the Revolution, the Articles placed the primary burden of national defense on the states, stipulating that "every state shall always keep up a well regulated and disciplined militia, sufficiently armed and accoutred" (Article VI) and that Congress's military powers could only be exercised by a vote of nine of the thirteen states (Article IX). No specific provision was made for a national standing army.

These and other shortcomings of the Articles led to the Federal Convention of 1787 and the adoption of the modern Constitution. The military issue was resolved by recognition of both the militia and a standing army, and it split powers between the national government and the states. In Article I, section 8, Congress was given the power to "raise and support armies," to "provide and maintain a Navy," and to finance and regulate both. In an important departure from the Articles, Congress would now have key authority over the state militias, as it could "provide for calling forth the Militia" in order "to execute the Laws of the Union, suppress Insurrections and repel Invasions"; and it could "provide for organizing, arming, and disciplining, the Militia, and for governing such Part of them as may be employed in the Service of the United States." On the other hand, the states retained some control, as the Constitution reserved "to the States respectively, the Appointment of the Officers, and the Authority of training the Militia according to the discipline prescribed by Congress." In addition, the president would serve as commander-in-chief of the military forces, including the militia (Article II, section 2).

The founders recognized the long-standing mistrust of standing armies[21] but accepted the reality that the militia was no substitute for a trained professional force controlled by the national government. Those at the Constitutional Convention of 1787 who feared too much federal control over the military won two key concessions: control over the militias was divided between the states and the federal government, and militia mobilization by Congress could occur only under the three circumstances listed above.

The overriding necessity for an effective fighting force was keenly felt in the country's early history, as it faced not only hostile European and indigenous forces on all sides but threats from internal rebellion. As colonial historian Max Farrand noted, "Shays's rebellion [January 1787] had taught a much needed lesson. It was not sufficient to place the state militia under some central control. The central government must be empowered to maintain an efficient army and navy to protect the states against internal disorders, as well as against external dangers."[22]

Reflecting the prevailing political view of the time, George Mason also spoke for many at the Constitutional Convention when he said during debate that "he hoped there would be no standing army in time of peace, unless it might be for a few garrisons. The Militia ought therefore to be the more effectually prepared for the public defence."[23] James Madison said that "as the greatest danger to liberty is from large standing armies, it is best to prevent them by an effectual provision for a good Militia."[24] At the same time, Madison and Edmund Randolph recognized that the states had often neglected their militias, making them unreliable unless the federal government could impose uniformity and discipline. Mason attempted to codify the warning against the liberty-eroding tendencies of standing armies when he proposed (unsuccessfully) an amendment to Article I, section 8, to add the phrase "That the Liberties of the People may be the better secured against the Danger of regular Troops or standing Armys in time of Peace," preceding "To provide for organizing arming & disciplining the Militia."[25]

Many of the issues raised during the Constitutional Convention arose in state ratifying conventions. During the Virginia ratifying convention in 1788, Edmund Randolph (also a delegate to the federal convention) said, "With respect to a standing army, I believe there was not a member in the federal convention who did not feel indignation at such an institution."[26] From a distance of two decades, founder Gouverneur Morris reflected the contrary sentiment in a singularly blunt fashion when he wrote in 1815:

> An overweening vanity leads the fond many . . . to believe or affect to believe, that militia can beat veteran troops in the open field and even play of battle.

This idle notion, fed by vaunting demagogues, alarmed us [the founders] for our country, when in the course of that time and chance . . . she should be at war with a great power. . . . To rely on militia was to lean on a broken reed.[27]

Defenders of the new Constitution sought to assuage fears and counter criticisms in the *Federalist Papers*. In *Federalist* No. 24, Alexander Hamilton argued that it would be a mistake to restrict or ban standing armies in times of peace, citing constant threats the young nation faced along its vast frontiers and the necessity of allowing Congress appropriate latitude to meet variable but persistent military threats. In No. 25, Hamilton argued forcefully that standing armies were naturally superior on the battlefield, the Revolutionary War notwithstanding, and were similarly superior in dealing with civil unrest (No. 28). Further, Hamilton noted in No. 29 that the federal government must have the power to impose uniformity on the militias in order for them to be effective and efficient. Both he and Madison dismissed the fear that a standing army would deprive the states of their sovereignty or citizens of their liberties. To "those who prophesy the downfall of the State governments," Madison in No. 46 computed that the United States could at the time raise at best an army of 30,000 men—a force that could be opposed by state militias totaling a half-million men.

The Bill of Rights

The adoption of the Constitution codified the dual militia-standing army military system, but it did not resolve the nagging question of federalism; that is, the new Constitution not only countenanced a national standing army but gave the federal government vast new power over the militia. Anti-Federalists were extremely concerned that this power might be used not only to undercut the effectiveness and independence of state militias (for example, by federal government refusal to organize, arm, or train them—although Federalists asserted that the states would retain such powers if the federal government failed to act), but to gut state power entirely. Convention delegate and Anti-Federalist Luther Martin predicted nothing less than the demise of the states if the Constitution were adopted with federal control of militias included:

They [supporters of the Constitution] said, that . . . if the militia was under the control and the authority of the respective States, it would *enable* them to *thwart* and *oppose* the general [federal] government. . . . If after having retained to the general government the great powers already granted, and among those, that of *raising* and *keeping* up regular troops without limitations, the *power* over the *militia* should be *taken away* from *the States*, and also given to the general government, it ought to be considered as the last *coup de grace* to the *State gov-*

ernments; that it must be the most convincing proof, the advocates of this system design the *destruction* of the State governments.[28]

These fears found voice in several state ratifying conventions, most particularly that of Virginia, where the Anti-Federalist cause found no more eloquent champion than the revolutionary firebrand Patrick Henry. Profoundly suspicious of the concentrated federal governmental power provided in the new Constitution, Henry spoke for many who preferred a weak national government and strong states when he asked, "Have we [in Virginia] the means of resisting disciplined armies, when our only defence, the militia, is put into the hands of Congress?" Henry sought assurance that "with respect to your militia, we only request that, if Congress should refuse to find arms for them, this country may lay out their own money to purchase them."[29] Setting an example for other states,[30] the Virginia convention passed this wording, modeled on Virginia's Declaration of Rights of 1776, when it ratified the Constitution:

> That the people have a right to keep and bear arms; that a well-regulated militia, composed of the body of the people trained to arms, is the proper, natural, and safe defence of a free state; that standing armies, in time of peace, are dangerous to liberty, and therefore ought to be avoided, as far as the circumstances and protection of the community will admit; and that, in all cases, the military should be under strict subordination to, and governed by, the civil power.[31]

In short, "the advocates of state sovereignty wished the main reliance to be upon militia, while their opponents [Federalists] saw the need for an effective standing army."[32] The central question giving rise to the Second Amendment was whether congressional authority over state militias could eclipse that of the state governments and whether this new federal military power (over both the militia and the federal-controlled professional army) might be used to abrogate state sovereignty and power. While this might seem like an arcane or irrelevant issue to modern Americans, it went to the very core of the dispute over the new Constitution of 1787.

The pressure for a Bill of Rights to limit federal authority became all but irresistible. On 8 June 1789, Madison introduced in the House of Representatives of the First Congress a proposed list of rights to be added to the Constitution. Drawn heavily from Virginia's 1776 Declaration of Rights, the list included this, to be inserted in Article I, section 9 (a section of the Constitution that lists several limits on the federal government, and that followed the section dealing with military matters): "The right of the people to keep and bear arms shall not be infringed; a well armed, and well regulated militia being the best security of a free country: but no person religiously scrupulous of bearing arms, shall be compelled to render military service in person." As reported out of House committee on 28 July, the amendment said: "A well regulated militia, composed of the body of the people, being the best security of a free State, the right of the people to keep and bear arms shall not be infringed, but no person religiously scrupulous shall be compelled to bear arms." On 24 August the House passed this wording: "A well regulated militia, composed of the body of the People, being the best security of a free State, the right of the People to keep and bear arms, shall not be infringed, but no one religiously scrupulous of bearing arms, shall be compelled to render military service in person." This and the other amendments then went to the Senate, where the final wording of what became the Second Amendment emerged: "A well regulated militia, being necessary to the security of a free State, the right of the people to keep and bear arms, shall not be infringed."[33]

The sparse debate over the Second Amendment in the First Congress dealt with a few familiar questions, all concerning military matters: whether the amendment wording should codify the right of conscientious objectors to opt out of military service for religious reasons; the relationship between militias, standing armies, and liberty; the need to subordinate the military to civilian authority; and the military unreliability of the militia as compared with a professional army.[34] To judge by the brief debate about and modest wording changes in the amendment's four versions above, the basic sentiment was held throughout—*that citizens have a constitutionally protected right to serve in state militias when called into service by, and in defense of, state and country.* The aim was to ensure the continued existence of state militias as a military and political counterbalance to the national army, and more broadly to national power (the federalism question). Southerners in particular were very concerned about maintaining state militias to suppress slave rebellions, because they were doubtful that a national government dominated by northern interests would be willing to commit federal troops and supplies to keep African Americans in the bondage of slavery. All of the debate over the Second Amendment dealt with military questions. As Elbridge Gerry said during congressional debate,

> What, sir, is the use of a militia? It is to prevent the establishment of a standing army, the bane of liberty. . . . Whenever government mean to invade the rights and liberties of the people, they always attempt to destroy the militia, in order to raise an army upon their ruins. This was actually done by Great Britain at the commencement of the late revolution.[35]

Thus, the Second Amendment is founded on *federalism*, balancing powers between the federal government and the states; and *military necessity*, developing a political compromise between politically popular militias and a politically unpopular but militarily necessary national professional army. Most believed that the nation's very survival had to involve the entire adult male population. Absent from this extended history is any connection between the Second Amendment and any personal use of weapons, for purposes including hunting, sporting, recreation, or even personal protection (a matter already addressed by common law in the eighteenth century).[36] Its purpose, like that of the Bill of Rights as a whole, was to place limits on the federal government and strike a balance between national power and state power.

The Militia Transformed

Soon after the ratification of the Bill of Rights in 1791, Congress moved ahead to establish rules and procedures governing the militias. Titled "An Act more effectively to provide for the National Defence by establishing an Uniform Militia throughout the United States," the Uniform Militia Act of 1792 (I U.S. Stat. 271) defined the nation's militia (in keeping with American militia tradition) as "every free able-bodied white male citizen of the respective states" between the ages of eighteen and forty-five.

Also in keeping with the militia tradition, the militiamen were legally obligated to provide their own weapons, ammunition, and accoutrements: "That every citizen so enrolled . . . shall . . . provide himself with a good musket or firelock, a sufficient bayonet and belt, two spare flints, and a knapsack, a pouch with a box therein to contain not less than twenty-four cartridges . . . each cartridge to contain a proper quantity of powder and ball."[37] It is not hard to understand why the Second Amendment was so careful to protect the right to keep and bear arms when militiamen, by law and tradition, bore the burden of arming themselves. Indeed, even though the Constitution said that Congress bore responsibility for arming the militia (Article I, section 8), Madison "observed that 'arming' as explained did not extend to furnishing arms." Rufus King elaborated that arming meant providing "for uniformity of arms," including "authority to regulate the modes of furnishing" them.[38]

In the two years following the passage of the Uniform Militia Act, all fifteen states passed their own laws to bring their militia systems into line with federal guidelines. Both the wisdom of and fears prompting the militia system seemed borne out in the country's first few years. Some key battles with Native Americans were successfully won with militia forces in 1794, and the Whiskey Rebellion of the same year was suppressed with a militia force of 15,000.[39] In 1794, Georgia militiamen literally faced federal troops with weapons loaded and aimed in a dispute over the treatment of the Creek and Cherokee peoples. A dispute over the Alien and Sedition Acts of 1798 nearly precipitated a similar encounter between federal troops and the Virginia militia in 1798.

Despite these events, it was already clear by the close of the eighteenth century that the militias were impractical, if not obsolete. Almost without exception, the states failed to implement the terms of the Uniform Militia Act. The system of fines imposed to impel men to arm and uniform themselves, and to ensure that they showed up for drill, failed to achieve these objectives. Neither the states nor the federal government took much interest in continuing universal militia training and service, although the social structure of the militia system continued for decades.[40] Indeed, the "history of the state militias between 1800 and the 1870s is one of total abandonment, disorganization, and degeneration." Instead, the government relied on its professional army and elite corps of volunteers, called the select (later "organized") militias.[41] The reputation of the citizen militias suffered a final, crippling blow as the result of their terrible performance in the War of 1812. According to military historians Donald M. Snow and Dennis M. Drew, this conflict shattered the illusion that general militias were militarily effective and reliable. The War of 1812 revealed militias to be "generally ineffective"; any successes were the result of "overwhelming odds or the incompetence of the adversary," factors that help to explain why this conflict was "the closest thing to a decisive military defeat the United States has ever suffered." The American forces' "unpreparedness" and "amateur military leadership" was "a national disgrace."[42] As the political historian Stephen Skowronek noted in his important study of the evolving military system of the nineteenth century: "By the 1840s the militia system envisioned in the early days of the republic was a dead letter. Universal military training fell victim to a general lack of interest and administrative incompetence at both the federal and state levels."[43] Thus, subsequent references to the militia pertained to the select militia, not to the system of universal male service with which the country began. The idea of universal militia service would persist, however, since Congress retained the theoretical power to mobilize such a force; more important, it persisted as part of the political symbolism surrounding the Second Amendment.

No significant legal changes occurred until the start of the twentieth century. In a 1901 message to Congress, President Theodore Roosevelt called for long-overdue legal change, saying that "our militia law is obsolete and worthless."[44] In 1903 Congress passed the Militia Act, which legally separated the "organized [also known as volunteer or select] militia, to be known as the National Guard," from the "reserve militia," also called the unorganized militia, even though the unorganized militia had by now been discarded as a viable military entity, for the simple reason that fighting could no longer be given over to untrained amateurs. The balance of the act provided for federal arming, training, and drilling of the National Guard. It made no provision whatsoever for the unorganized militia.[45]

In 1916, Congress passed the National Defense Act, which mandated that the National Guard would be organized in the same method as the "Regular Army." It also placed state Guards under federal guidelines.[46]

Thus, from 1903 onward, America's active militia in law was the National Guard, which though now under federal regulation, is still trained by the respective states.[47] Congress retained for itself the theoretical option of calling up the reserve militia—all able-bodied men from seventeen to forty-five[48]—but America's now substantial regular army, plus the National Guard, constituted formidable and ample military forces to meet national needs. Any gaps in those needs have been met in modern times by the military draft rather than by activation of the old-style militia.

In sum, the possession of firearms referred to in the Second Amendment comes into play only at such time as (1) the unorganized militia is activated by a state or the federal government, a practice effectively abandoned before the Civil War;[49] and (2) the government fails to provide weapons for that force. Thus the Second Amendment has been rendered essentially irrelevant to modern American life, as is the prospect of, say, National Guard troops from New York and Pennsylvania squaring off against each other, weapons at the ready, along state borders.[50]

Supreme Court Rulings

The Second Amendment has generated relatively little constitutional law. In four instances, however, the Supreme Court has ruled directly on this amendment.

In the first case, *U.S.* v. *Cruikshank*, 92 U.S. 542 (1876), William Cruikshank and two other defendants were charged with thirty-two counts of depriving blacks of their constitutional rights, including two claiming that the defendants had deprived blacks of firearms possession, in violation of the Force Act of 1870. Speaking for the Court, Chief Justice Waite wrote:

> The second and tenth counts are equally defective. The right there specified is that of "bearing arms for a lawful purpose." This is not a right granted by the Constitution. Neither is it in any manner dependent upon that instrument for its existence. The Second Amendment declares that it shall not be infringed; but this . . . means no more than that it shall not be infringed by Congress. This is one of the amendments that has no other effect than to restrict the powers of the National Government.[51]

The Court in this case established two principles that it (and most other courts) have consistently upheld: that the Second Amendment simply does not afford any individual a right to bear arms free from government control; and that the Second Amendment is not "incorporated," meaning that it pertains only to federal power, not state power (this is what the Court meant when it referred to the Second Amendment not being "infringed by Congress"). Admittedly, the Supreme Court did not begin to incorporate parts of the first ten amendments (that is, use the wording of the due process and equal protection clauses of the Fourteenth Amendment to extend parts of the Bill of Rights to the states) until 1897.[52] But the Court has never accepted the idea of incorporating the entire Bill of Rights,[53] and it has never incorporated the Second Amendment, despite numerous opportunities. In other words, the courts have continued to treat the Second Amendment differently from most of the rest of the Bill of Rights.

Ten years later, the Court ruled in *Presser* v. *Illinois*, 116 U.S. 252 (1886), that an Illinois law that barred paramilitary organizations from drilling or parading in cities or towns without a license from the governor was constitutional. Herman Presser challenged the law after he was arrested for marching and drilling his (armed) fringe group, *Lehr und Wehr Verein*, through Chicago streets. In upholding the Illinois law, the Court reaffirmed that the Second Amendment did not apply to the states (citing *Cruikshank*).[54] Speaking for a unanimous Court, Justice Woods went on to discuss the relationship between the citizen, the militia, and the government:

> It is undoubtedly true that all citizens capable of bearing arms constitute the reserved military force or reserved militia of the United States as well as of the States; and, in view of this prerogative . . . the States cannot, even laying the constitutional provision in question out of view, prohibit the people from keeping and bearing arms, so as to deprive the United States of their rightful resource for maintaining the public security, and disable the people from performing their duty to the General Government. But, as already stated, we think it clear that the sections under consideration do not have this effect.

The Court then went on to ask whether Presser and his associates had a right to organize with others as a self-proclaimed and armed military organization, against state law. No, the Court answered, since such activity "is not an attribute of national citizenship. Military organization and military drill and parade under arms are subjects especially under the control of the government of every country. They cannot be claimed as a right independent of law." In other words, militias exist only as defined and regulated by the state or federal government, which in Illinois at the time was the 8,000-member Illinois National Guard (as the Court noted in its decision). To deny the government the power to define and regulate militias would, according to the Court, "be to deny the right of the State to disperse assemblages organized for sedition and treason, and the right to suppress armed mobs bent on riot and rapine." Thus, the Presser case confirmed the understanding that the right to bear arms came into play only in connection with the formation and conduct of the militia, as formed and regulated by the government. The Court emphatically rejected the idea that citizens could create their own militias, much less that the Second Amendment protected citizens' rights to own weapons for their own purposes.

In 1894, the Supreme Court unanimously ruled in *Miller* v. *Texas*, 153 U.S. 535 (1894), that a Texas law "prohibiting the carrying of dangerous weapons" did not violate the Second Amendment. Again, the Court said that the right to bear arms did not apply to the states. The Court ruled similarly in *Robertson* v. *Baldwin*, 165 U.S. 275 (1897).[55]

The final Supreme Court case in this sequence, and the only one handed down after the Court began the process of incorporation, is *U.S.* v. *Miller*, 307 U.S. 174 (1939). The Miller case was founded on a challenge to the National Firearms Act of 1934, which regulated the interstate transport of various weapons. Jack Miller and Frank Layton were convicted under the 1934 act of transporting an unregistered 12-gauge sawed-off shotgun (having a barrel less than 18 inches long) across state lines. They challenged the act's constitutionality by claiming that it was a violation of the Second Amendment and that it represented an improper use of the commerce power. The Court turned aside these claims and ruled that the federal taxing power could be used to regulate firearms and that firearm registration was constitutional. Beyond this, the Court was unequivocal in saying that the Second Amendment must be interpreted by its "obvious purpose" of assuring an effective militia as described in Article I, section 8, of the Constitution (to which the Court referred in its decision). Speaking for a unanimous court, Justice McReynolds wrote:

> In the absence of any evidence tending to show that possession or use of a "shotgun having a barrel of less than eighteen inches in length" at this time has some reasonable relationship to the preservation or efficiency of a well regulated militia, we cannot say that the Second Amendment guarantees the right to keep and bear such an instrument. Certainly it is not within judicial notice that this weapon is any part of the ordinary military equipment or that its use could contribute to the common defense.

Thus, the Court stated that citizens could possess a constitutional right to bear arms only in connection with service in a government-organized and -regulated militia. In addition, it affirmed the constitutional right of Congress, as well as the states, to regulate firearms. Most of the rest of the decision is an extended discussion of the antecedents of the Second Amendment. Justice McReynolds cited various classic works, colonial practices, and early state laws and constitutions to demonstrate the importance of militias and citizen-armies to early America as the explanation for the presence and meaning of the Second Amendment.

Critics of this case have on occasion taken the wording quoted above to mean that the Court would protect under the Second Amendment the ownership of guns that do bear some connection with national defense. Such an interpretation is foolish on its face because, first, such reasoning would justify the private ownership of such militarily useful weapons as bazookas, howitzers, and even tactical nuclear weapons. Second, the Court decision states that possession of such weapons as sawed-off shotguns could only be allowed under existing law if that possession were connected with militia service. Because the two men charged under the 1934 law obviously did not have the gun for the purpose of, or while they were serving under, an organized militia, their prosecution and conviction were justified; the Second Amendment would only apply in the context of militia service. And as *Presser* clearly stated, citizens may not create their own militias independent of the government. Ironically, sawed-off shotguns can and do have some military value.[56] Remembering that the Court's point in this case arose from the challenge to the National Firearms Act (the source of the Court's definition of a sawed-off shotgun[57]), its remedy lay in the failure of Miller and Layton to claim any credible connection to Second Amendment–based militia activities. The Second Amendment has received brief mention in two other Supreme Court cases, *Adams* v. *Williams*, 407 U.S. 143 (1972; the comment on the Second Amendment was in a dissenting opinion) and *Lewis* v. *U.S.*, 445 U.S. 95 (1980), when the court specifically cited the 1939 *Miller* case to uphold gun regulations as long as there was some "rational basis" for them.[58] Both of these cases support the logic of the earlier four.

Other Court Rulings

These Supreme Court cases represent an unbroken line to current Court thinking—one followed by lower courts. Challenges to gun regulations and related efforts to win a broader interpretation of the Second Amendment (including efforts to incorporate the Second Amendment) have been uniformly turned aside, with a single exception. In no fewer than thirty-seven cases since *U.S.* v. *Miller*, federal courts of appeal "have analyzed the Second Amendment purely in terms of protecting state militias, rather than individual rights."[59] Of those, the Supreme Court has declined to hear appeals in the fifteen instances when such appeals were made, thus letting the lower court rulings stand. The inescapable conclusion is that the Supreme Court has settled this matter and has no interest in crowding its docket with cases that merely repeat what has already been decided. This is confirmed by an article written by retired Chief Justice Warren Burger that appeared in *Parade* magazine.[60] Lower federal courts and state courts generally have followed the Supreme Court's interpretation.[61]

In the most famous of these cases, the Supreme Court declined to hear an appeal of two lower federal court rulings upholding the constitutionality of a strict gun control law passed in Morton Grove, Illinois, in 1981. The ordinance banned the ownership of working handguns by anyone except peace officers, prison officials, members of the armed forces and National Guard, and security guards, as long as such possession was in accordance with their official duties. The ordinance also exempted licensed gun collectors and owners of antique firearms.[62] Brushing aside arguments of those opposing the law, the court of appeals confirmed that possession of handguns by individuals is not part of the right to keep and bear arms; that this right pertains only to militia service; that the local law was a reasonable exercise of police power; and that the Second Amendment does not apply to the states, "even if opponents to gun control find it illogical."[63]

One recent federal court case produced a finding different from all the others discussed above. A physician named Timothy Joe Emerson was charged with violating a federal law that barred him from possessing firearms because he was under a domestic violence protection order, prompted by his brandishing of a gun in the presence of his estranged wife and child. In a federal district court ruling that surprised observers on all sides of the gun debate, the judge determined that the restraining order against Emerson was unconstitutional as a violation of his Second Amendment right to bear arms. This finding was appealed to the federal Court of Appeals (*U.S. v. Emerson,* 270 F.3d 203, 5th Cir. [2001]), which reversed the lower court verdict on the grounds that the federal law was a proper exercise of federal government power. Yet two of the three federal judges went beyond this ruling to argue at length that the Second Amendment did, in fact, protect an individual right to bear arms aside from militia service (what is referred to as the "individualist" view, discussed below). The third judge in the case agreed that Emerson's conviction was proper but dismissed the part of the majority opinion dealing with the Second Amendment as "dicta," saying further that the majority commentary "is therefore not binding on us or on any other court."

The Textbook Bill of Rights

Added confirmation of the courts' understanding is found in most standard texts on the Bill of Rights. From classic nineteenth-century analyses such as those of Joseph Story and Thomas Cooley,[64] to modern treatments, the verdict is the same. In his classic book on the Bill of Rights, Irving Brant writes: "The Second Amendment, popularly misread, comes to life chiefly on the parade floats of rifle associations and in the propaganda of mail-order houses selling pistols to teenage gangsters."[65] Similar, if less sarcastic, sentiments are found in other standard works. In the words of Robert A. Rutland, the Second Amendment (along with the Third, having to do with the quartering of troops in private homes) has become "obsolete."[66] Moreover, standard legal reference works used by lawyers and judges parallel this perspective.[67]

Constitutional Contortionists

This chapter is devoted to the background, meaning, and interpretation of the Second Amendment. The conclusions to this point are that the amendment reflected a vital concern of the country's founders pertaining to (1) the type of military force that would defend the country from manifold threats within and outside the country, and (2) the desire to protect state power and sovereignty against the federal government; but as in the case of some other elements of the Constitution, such as the Third Amendment, the concerns that gave rise to it evaporated as reality changed—that is, as the country turned away from citizen militias, the Second Amendment was rendered obsolete; and that the courts have consistently recognized this fact and thus have not incorporated the Second Amendment, as they have most of the rest of the Bill of Rights (also not incorporated: the Third Amendment, the grand jury clause of the Fifth Amendment, the Seventh Amendment, and the excessive fines and bail clause of the Eighth Amendment).[68] The consensus of constitutional law scholars is that the incorporation process is at an end (since the last incorporation decision in 1969), with the possible exception of the fines and bail clause.[69] Thus, *even if the Second Amendment did protect an individual right to bear arms outside of service in a militia, it would still not apply to the states because it has not been incorporated, and thus would not be a right citizens could claim in their daily lives. Conversely, even if the Court reversed itself and incorporated the Second Amendment, it would apply only to the old concept of universal militia service—a practice abandoned before the Civil War.*

Indeed, even the National Rifle Association has abandoned the legal challenge to gun laws based on alleged violations of Second Amendment rights.[70] Why, then, all the fuss and the insistent claims to rights pertaining to hunting, personal protection, sporting, or other such uses? There are two answers. First is the sheer repetition of the alleged existence of Second Amendment rights in the public press and the general public debate on gun control. The frenzied nature of this "rights debate," discussed at the beginning of this chapter, is such that it is extraordinarily difficult to conduct a rational discussion in such a white-hot political environment. When this repetition is paired with the complexity of the full story of the amendment—witness the length of this chapter—it is not too surprising that the complex truth gets lost.

The second, if less visible, reason is the persistence of a few lawyers and academics who seek to support other explanations for the Second Amendment in an attempt to resurrect or reinterpret its meaning.[71] Even though these writings represent a relatively new view that is not shared by most in the legal community (as some of the authors admit),[72] they often provide justification for the more public trumpeting of imagined Second Amendment rights. Leaving aside the question of motivations and the inclination of academics to offer unusual or counterintuitive arguments for the sake of intellectual jousting, one can identify a few common critiques of the existing law and its interpretation. These critiques warrant our attention because the arguments they forward attempt to provide an intellectual foundation for oft-heard emotional public appeals.

The "Individualist" Critique

The most common objection stems from what is labeled the "individualist" approach—that is, that the Second Amendment really bestows on every American citizen a right to have guns, aside from or in addition to the militia principle.[73] This argument is usually supported by plucking key phrases from court cases or colonial or federal debate to emphasize the right of all Americans to carry guns. The first problem with this analysis is that it often relies on supporting quotes pulled out of context.[74] As discussed here, the issue of the bearing of arms *as it pertained to the Constitution and the Bill of Rights* always came back to military service and the balance of power between the states and the federal government, as seen in the two most important historical sources: the records of the Constitutional Convention and those of the First Congress when the Bill of Rights was formulated. Second, the definition of the citizen militias at the center of this debate has always been men roughly between the ages of seventeen and forty-five.[75] That is, it has always excluded a majority of the country's adult citizens—men over forty-five, the infirm, and women. Therefore, it is not, and never has been, a right enjoyed by all citizens, unlike such Bill of Rights protections as free speech, religious freedom, or right to counsel.[76]

Some have argued that the reference to "the people" in the Second Amendment has the same meaning as it does in other parts of the Bill of Rights, as in "the right of the people [to] peaceably assemble" in the First Amendment, or the "right of the people to be secure in their persons, houses, papers and effects" in the Fourth Amendment. Because all citizens are considered to have such First and Fourth Amendment protections, why shouldn't the Second Amendment be read as meaning that all citizens have a right to bear arms? In support of this claim, some have pointed to a 1990 Supreme Court case, *U.S. v. Verdugo-Urquidez* (494 U.S. 259) for support.[77]

This claim is false on four grounds. First, as discussed earlier in this chapter, militia service, from colonial times on, always pertained only to those capable and eligible to serve in a militia—that is, healthy young-to-middle-aged men (excluding the infirm, old men, and nearly all women). Second, the courts (especially in the *Presser* case) and federal law have clearly defined and interpreted the Second Amendment as having this specific meaning. Third, no evidence suggests that the authors of the Bill of Rights attempted, or succeeded, in imposing a single, uniform definition of "the people" in the document; the Bill of Rights was the product of many hands and many ideas, a fact reflected in the variety of ideas, interests, and concerns addressed in the first ten amendments. Fourth, and most important, the *Verdugo-Urquidez* case has nothing to do with interpreting the Second Amendment. In fact, the case deals with the Fourth Amendment issue of whether an illegal alien from Mexico was entitled to constitutional protection regarding searches (the court ruled that non–U.S. citizens were not "people" as the term is used in the Fourth Amendment). In the majority decision, Chief Justice Rehnquist discussed what was meant by the phrase "the people," given that the phrase appears not only in several parts of the Bill of Rights, but also in the Constitution's preamble, in order to determine its applicability to a noncitizen. Rehnquist speculated that the phrase "seems to have been a term of art" that probably pertains to people who have developed a connection with the national community. Rehnquist's speculations about whether the meaning of "the people" could be extended to a noncitizen, and his two passing mentions of the Second Amendment in that discussion, shed no light, much less legal meaning, on this amendment.

Selective Analysis

Other critiques tell only part of the Second Amendment story, leaving aside or misconstruing the whole matter of incorporation, for example, or ignoring the actual developments in national defense between colonial times and the present.[78] Obviously, the American system of national defense today is very different from what the founders envisioned. One might therefore argue that the courts or Congress have deviated from the principles on which the country was founded by not ensuring that Americans today be armed, and thus they have somehow betrayed the country's principles. Yet to argue thus is to ignore two centuries of development and the organic nature of the Constitution. After all, the original Constitution countenanced slavery, made no provision for an air force, and could not have foreseen the need to protect citizens from electronic surveillance. Yet we accept that these matters can and should be dealt with within the constitutional framework. Some constitutional structures that have not been altered, such as the Electoral College, operate in a way entirely different from what the founders envisioned.[79] Nevertheless, we accept these developments because they arise from changing needs, with political consensus, and (as necessary) the blessing of the courts. So, too, with the Second Amendment; that is, the fact that the nation's military and defense structure is very different from that of the eighteenth century is by itself no condemnation of the current system. Indeed, a constitutional system incapable of adapting to changing circumstances is probably one that cannot survive the test of time. The purpose of the careful examination of the intentions of the country's founders here is not to argue that we should be forever frozen in the grip of the eighteenth century, but simply to establish a clear understanding of their thinking, and of the law and history that followed. Finally, other critics simply object to the courts' Second Amendment rulings, often expressing unvarnished frustration or dismay.[80]

Self-Defense

Critics also argue that the principle of self-protection or self-defense is (or ought to be) covered by the Second Amendment.[81] In doing so, some of this analysis intermixes the defense needs of early Americans (against Native Americans or predators, for example) with modern personal self-defense against robberies, assaults, rapes, intrusions into people's homes, or other life-threatening circumstances. Yet as the discussion in this chapter shows, the Second Amendment by design and interpretation has to do not with these very real modern-day threats, but with the threats posed by armies and militias.

This does not mean that the law affords no legal protection to individuals who engage in personal self-defense—far from it. American and British common law has recognized and legally sanctioned personal self-defense for hundreds of years, prior to and independent of the Second Amendment. But it arises from the area of criminal law, not constitutional law.[82] A standard, long-accepted definition of self-defense from common law reads:

> A man may repel force by force in the defense of his person, habitation, or property, against one or many who manifestly intend and endeavor, by violence or surprise, to commit a known felony on either. In such a case he is not obliged to retreat, but may pursue his adversary until he find himself out of danger; and if, in a conflict between them, he happen to kill, such killing is justifiable. The right of self-defense in cases of this kind is founded on the law of nature; and is not, nor can be, superseded by any law of society.[83]

The Second Amendment is as superfluous to legal protection for personal defense or defense of the home today as it was more than two centuries ago. Indeed, as defined in the common law tradition, the self-defense principle supersedes even constitutional guidelines.

The "Right of Revolution" and Oppression

An additional challenge to the militia view argues that the Second Amendment does or should incorporate arms for everyone because of an innate "right of revolution," or as a mechanism to keep the country's rulers responsive to the citizens.[84] While these theories pose interesting intellectual questions about the relationship between citizens and the state, they do not translate into meaningful policies for modern America. Most citizens recognize the importance of exercising democratic values by participating in elections, juries, public opinion, and interest groups rather than by pointing guns (whether by threat or deed) at congressional leaders or the White House. Few Americans approve of those few groups in America that actively pursue something resembling a right of revolution—the Ku Klux Klan, the skinheads, the Branch Davidians, Los Angeles rioters, or those responsible for bombing the federal office building in Oklahoma City in April 1995. As the legal scholar Roscoe Pound noted, a "legal right of the citizen to wage war on the government is something that cannot be admitted. . . . In the urban industrial society of today a general right to bear efficient arms so as to be enabled to resist oppression by the government would mean that gangs could exercise an extra-legal rule which would defeat the whole Bill of Rights."[85] In any event, any so-called right of revolution is carried out against the government, which means against that government's constitution as well—including the Bill of Rights and the Second Amendment. In short, one cannot carry out a right of revolution against the government and at the same time claim protections within it. This fact was well understood by the country's founders, for in 1794 the government, through its militias, moved to suppress the Whiskey Rebellion, an uprising that was denounced by Federalists and Anti-Federalists alike. As historian Saul Cornell noted, in the 1790s there was "widespread agreement that the example of the American Revolution did not support the rebels' actions" because Americans at the start of the Revolution "did not enjoy the benefits of representative government," whereas those who fomented the Whiskey Rebellion "were represented under the Constitution."[86]

The Constitution itself makes this point forcefully, as Congress is given the powers "To provide for calling forth the Militia to execute the Laws of the Union, *suppress Insurrections* and repel Invasions (emphasis added)" in Article I, section 8; to suspend habeas corpus "in Cases of Rebellion or Invasion" in section 9; and to protect individual states "against domestic Violence" if requested to do so by a state legislature or governor in Article IV, section 4. Further, the Constitution defines treason in Article III, section 3, this way: "Treason against the United States, shall consist only in levying War against them" (the United States was originally referred to in the plural). In other words, the Constitution specifically and explicitly gives the national government the power to suppress by force anything even vaguely resembling revolution. Such revolt or revolution is by constitutional definition an act of treason against the United States. The militias are thus to be used to suppress, not cause, revolution or insurrection. These powers were further detailed and expanded in the Calling Forth Act of 1792 (1 U.S. Stat. 264), which gives the president broad powers to use state militias to enforce both state and federal laws in instances where the law is ignored or in cases of open insurrection. This act was passed by the Second Congress shortly after the passage of the Bill of Rights.[87] In current law, these powers are further elaborated in the U.S. Code (10 U.S.C. 331–34) sections on insurrection.

Along these lines, others have argued that traditionally oppressed groups, such as women and African Americans, should aggressively claim for themselves a right to bear arms.[88] Blacks in particular have been subject to race-based violence for hundreds of years and were unquestionably denied arms "as a means of racial oppression."[89] Yet the key handicap for blacks and other oppressed groups has not been the denial of Second Amendment rights but the denial of *all* basic Bill of Rights freedoms, not to mention denial of the basic common law principle of self-defense. Further, an article by legal scholar Carl Bogus presents substantial evidence that southern state leaders supported inclusion of the Second Amendment to ensure that they could use their state militias to suppress slave revolts.[90]

Getting It Wrong

The most flawed of these critiques are those that willfully distort the legal and historical record. To pick a particularly flagrant example, a report of the Subcommittee on the Constitution of the Senate Judiciary Committee, published in 1982 under the chairmanship of gun control foe Orrin Hatch (R-Utah), stated that the Supreme Court "has only three times commented upon the meaning of the second amendment";[91] erroneously omitting *Cruikshank* and *Presser* entirely, the discussion mentioned *Dred Scott* v. *Sandford* (1857), *U.S.* v. *Miller*, and *Lewis* v. *U.S. Dred Scott*, a pre–Civil War case that dealt with the question of whether a slave could assert citizenship rights after living in freedom, was cited in the Senate committee report because it "indicated strongly that the right to keep and bear arms was an individual right; the Court noted that, were it to hold free blacks to be entitled to equality of citizenship, they would be entitled to keep and carry arms wherever they went."[92] The foolishness of an argument predicated on a court case that ruled against the rights of blacks at a time when slavery was still legal, and when southerners were terrified by the prospect of slave rebellions, indicates why the justices' concern over blacks carrying guns arose in the first place. Moreover, *Dred Scott* was overruled by the passage of the Thirteenth and Fourteenth amendments. By any standard, it does not stand as law, and it is irrelevant to the interpretation of the Second Amendment. The report also omits the primary finding of *Miller* and misrepresents the *Lewis* case.[93] Yet the report that offered this and other comment as competent analysis has been widely reprinted and quoted by gun control foes. Regardless of one's feelings about gun control, the cause of rational policy debate is only throttled by the proliferation of bad analysis.

Conclusion

The Second Amendment emerged from the great political struggle in the latter part of the eighteenth century between those who wanted a strong national government (the Federalists) and those who believed that the states should retain more power over their own affairs (the Anti-Federalists) in order to protect a system they believed would keep government both more responsive to the people and less likely to usurp individual liberties.[94] The sweeping new powers given to the national government in the modern Constitution included not only the authority to create a standing army, but also the ability to create and regulate militias. The inclusion of the Bill of Rights as a means of limiting national governmental power was the political compromise the Federalists accepted in order to win support for the new Constitution. The inclusion of the Second Amendment embodied the Federalist assurance that state militias would be allowed to continue as a military and political counterbalance to the national army at a time when military takeovers were the norm in world affairs. Yet it soon became apparent that the politically popular but militarily inefficient state militias were of little military value. The country's civilian and military leaders realized that American security needs could not and should not be left to the ineffective and unreliable unorganized militias. And in one of the great triumphs of American democracy, civilian control of the military became a fixture of our system. Thus the fears that gave rise to the Second Amendment never materialized.

This key fact has been reflected in court decisions and congressional enactments. In a handful of key cases, the Supreme Court has ruled that the definition of militia as it arises in the Second Amendment applies not simply to citizens with weapons but only to individuals enrolled in militia service to the government. As the historian Garry Wills noted about the pre-Constitution period, "at no time preceding the passage of the Second Amendment could any man be considered a militia member just by picking up his gun and proclaiming himself one."[95] In any case, this amendment does not apply to the states through the process of incorporation. Congressional enactments are also important, yet often overlooked, as they chronicle the disintegration of the old general militias and the eventual legal recognition of the select or volunteer militias as the National Guard. The modern purposes for which the Second Amendment is often cited—hunting, sporting, personal self-protection, a "right of revolution"—bear no relation to that amendment. This does not mean that these activities are not legal or are otherwise illegitimate (aside from the "right" to attempt to overthrow the American government). On the contrary, as discussed in chapter 1, hunting as an American cultural tradition is older than the Constitution. Self-protection is both longer and more deeply protected in common law than in the Constitution. The so-called right of revolution, however, operates entirely outside the constitutional structure.

The desire to treat the Second Amendment as a constitutional touchstone by gun control opponents is understandable, given the "rights talk" that pervades American political discourse and the enormous political legitimacy that accompanies anything dubbed "constitutional." Such claims are, however, without historical, constitutional, or legal foundation. More problematic, this constant and misplaced invocation of rights only serves to heighten social conflict, cultivate ideological rigidity, and stifle rational policy debate.

To return to the primary policy questions guiding this book, the Second Amendment poses no obstacle to gun control as it is debated in modern America, a conclusion supported by the fact that no gun law has ever been struck down as a violation of the Second Amendment. Consistent with social regulatory policy theory, the courts have indeed provided a key avenue for defining the issue. Reflecting this important fact, gun control opponents dissatisfied with court rulings have repeatedly sought court judgments in recent decades that would support incorporation of the Second Amendment and an interpretation expanding it beyond the realm of a "well-regulated militia." At the federal level, at least, these efforts have been unsuccessful. This fact helps explain the abundant and frenetic activity in the "political" branches of government—Congress and the presidency. Before turning to those arenas, however, we first examine the criminological debate over gun control.

CHAPTER 3

The Criminological Consequences of Guns

Guns don't kill people—people do.

—NRA slogan

Guns don't die—people do.

—Pete Shields

Case 1: On 14 October 1989, three teenage boys were examining a .38-caliber automatic pistol that belonged to the father of one of the boys. Thinking that the gun was unloaded because the ammunition magazine had been removed, one of the boys pulled the trigger, accidentally shooting and killing fourteen-year-old Michael J. Steber of Clay, New York. The boys had not realized that a round was still in the gun's chamber. Two years later, the parents of the dead boy filed a civil suit against the gun's owner (and father of the shooter), Gordon Lane, a former Syracuse police officer and head of the state's chapter of Vietnam Veterans of America, and against the gun manufacturer for failing to include a 75-cent safety feature that would have prevented the gun from firing without the ammunition clip. Lane had several guns in the home and had guided his son's use of them. The father of the dead boy questioned the justification for keeping such weapons in the home. "I'm a Vietnam veteran too," said Mr. Steber, "and I don't have a gun around the house. I don't need it."[1]

Case 2: One evening, Marion Hammer was on her way to her car, located in a parking garage in Tallahassee, Florida, when she noticed a car carrying six drunken men following her. Less than five feet tall and weighing 111 pounds, she feared trouble when some of the men made comments that amounted to a threat of rape. Reaching into her purse, Ms. Hammer produced a Colt .38 Detective's Special. When the car's driver spied the gun, he stopped the car, turned around, and peeled out of the garage. "Had I not had my gun," said the fifty-one-year-old woman, "I might not have lived to talk about it."[2]

Case 3: The school day began like any other at Cleveland Elementary School in Stockton, California. But shortly before noontime, on 17 January 1989, a twenty-four-year-old drifter named Patrick Edward Purdy opened fire on the crowded schoolyard with a Chinese-made AK–47 assault rifle (purchased in Oregon) fitted with a "drum" magazine holding 75 bullets (purchased in Rhode Island). Purdy laid down a line of fire that killed five students and wounded thirty-three others. After firing 105 rounds, Purdy fired one final shot from a Taurus 9-mm semiautomatic pistol, killing himself on the spot. Purdy's motives were never entirely discovered, but investigators did find a history of drug and alcohol abuse, mental instability, brushes with the law, and a fascination with weapons of all kinds.[3]

Case 4: In late 1997 and early 1998, a rash of schoolhouse shootings perpetrated by children and teenagers erupted around the country. On 14 March 1998, eleven-year-old Andrew Golden and thirteen-year-old Mitchell Johnson gathered several weapons from one of the boys' relatives and then stationed themselves on a hill overlooking the Westside Middle School in Jonesboro, Arkansas. One of the boys entered the school and pulled the school's fire alarm, prompting what everyone assumed was a fire drill. When the school had emptied, the two boys opened fire, killing four girls and a teacher. Ten students were injured. The boys were taken into custody along with an assortment of handguns and long guns, but the fatal gunfire came mostly from an M–1 carbine replica and a Remington .30–06 hunting rifle. A partial motive seemed to be that one of the boys had been spurned by a girl at the school.

As IS TRUE with public debate over the Second Amendment, most public debate and much policy discourse on the criminological consequences of guns is fragmentary in its treatment of fact, polemical in its tone, and narrow in its consideration of options. The four cases that begin this chapter typify some of the key criminological consequences of guns. They also exemplify the nature of public discourse on the gun issue, in that tragic incidents such as the Stockton and Jonesboro massacres receive considerable attention and therefore rivet public attention; moreover, the increase in such incidents in the past two decades has fanned reformist flames, supporting the call for stronger gun control, as well as for stiffer penalties for gun-related crimes.

While such incidents may serve the purposes of particular policymakers and interest groups, it is difficult to have confidence that good policy will result from a knee-jerk reaction to an unanticipated disaster. Yet this is a common pattern for the gun control issue, as the outrage-action-reaction cycle described in chapter 1 summarizes. To be sure, disasters have prompted desirable policy change in such areas as coal mine safety, automobile safety, and earthquake preparedness. In these and many other instances, necessary policy changes occurred only after significant human disasters. Yet it is difficult to have much confidence in a policy process that operates primarily through the outrage-action-reaction cycle.

The criminological debate assessed in this chapter is also politically significant for how the gun problem is defined. The "rights talk" surrounding the Second Amendment, discussed in chapter 2, is a political means used by control foes to blunt criminological analysis that supports stronger gun control. "Even if guns are harmful," the argument goes, "I have a right to own and lawfully use them as I see fit." Such an argument parallels others in which questionable behavior that might otherwise be controlled or prohibited is allowed because it falls under the Bill of Rights umbrella. For example, a wide array of hateful, hurtful, and otherwise objectionable speech is nevertheless protected by the courts because of the preeminent importance attached to the First Amendment's free speech protection. As chapter 2 noted, the Second Amendment does not fall into this same category, but its location in the Bill of Rights encourages gun control opponents to use "rights talk" to political advantage.

Arrayed against this view is a growing effort that emphasizes the gun problem as a public health issue. Spearheaded by public health and medical professionals, this effort dates to 1983, when the Centers for Disease Control (CDC) declared firearms violence to be a significant public health threat. That year, the CDC created a unit to gather and encourage research on gun-related violence, which in turn has spawned considerable public health and medical research (much of it discussed in this chapter) underscoring the public health threat posed by guns.[4] President Reagan's surgeon general, C. Everett Koop, and President Clinton's first surgeon general, Joycelyn Elders, both weighed in strongly to push the public health definition of the problem. By tagging guns with the "public health threat" label and comparing them to such public health risks as smoking and automobile accidents, members of the medical community have sought to redefine the gun issue in order to alter public policy outcomes. It is a classic example of what the political scientist Murray Edelman has labeled symbolic politics—that is, shaping language and perception to political advantage: "The words a group employs and on which it relies . . . can often be taken as an index of group norms and conceptual frameworks."[5] The concern expressed by the public health community became sufficiently threatening to gun control opponents that an effort was launched in 1995 by the National Rifle Association to get Congress to stop funding for CDC research on gun issues. (Firearms-related research by the CDC amounted to about $2.3 million a year.) That effort eventually succeeded.[6]

Bearing in mind the role of language and symbols in the criminological debate over guns, the best way to assess the real consequences of guns in American life is to move beyond anecdote and outrage and examine instead the existing scholarship on the criminological consequences of guns. Of necessity, then, this chapter departs from the more purely political analysis of the rest of this book, although an understanding of the criminological debate over guns is essential to understanding the larger public policy debate concerning gun control, as organized by the policy framework set out in chapter 1. But just as chapter 2 examined whether the Constitution imposes any obstacles to gun control, so too must we examine whether the criminological consequences of guns pose obstacles or encouragement to gun control. It may be, for example, that the best available analysis points toward stricter regulation as a feasible means for stemming gun-related violence. Conversely, data and evidence may suggest that regulatory efforts are fruitless or even counterproductive. It may also be that existing analysis cannot offer any clear direction. No matter what the conclusion, it is impossible to understand the gun issue, and therefore its place in the larger policy framework, without consideration of this central issue. While the connections between guns and crime discussed here suggest a panoply of possible policy responses, this chapter focuses primarily on the general criminological picture. Specific policy options are discussed in chapters 5 and 6.

As noted in chapter 1, maintaining public order and safety are primary, even primordial purposes of government. Regardless of one's view of guns, it is clear that firearms are intimately associated with a variety of disruptions of public order in American homes and on American streets. Thus, we begin with the nature of those disruptions.

America and Violence

America has long reigned supreme in levels of violence among the developed nations of the world. A Centers for Disease Control study of gun deaths worldwide in 1994 found that, among the thirty-six richest nations of the world, the United States had by far the highest rate of gun deaths (combining homicide, suicide, and accident), amounting to 14.24 per 100,000 people. Of 88,649 gun deaths reported by these countries, 45 percent occurred in the United States.[7] As table 3.1 shows, the United States has a far higher firearm death rate than other developed nations, and it has a higher ratio of gun homicides and gun suicides.

The gulf between the United States and other nations was dramatized by an incident that occurred on Halloween night in 1992, when a Japanese exchange student was shot and killed at a home near Baton Rouge, Louisiana. The student, sixteen-year-old Yoshihiro Hattori, was looking for a Halloween party in the neighborhood of Rodney Peairs when he mistakenly approached the Peairs door. As the student (costumed as John Travolta from the movie *Saturday Night*

TABLE 3.1   Firearms Mortality Rates in Eleven Countries[a]

Country	Overall Death Rate	Firearm Homicide Rate	Firearm Suicide Rate
United States	13.7	5.9	7.0
France	6.3	0.4	5.1
Norway	4.3	0.3	3.9
Canada	3.9	0.5	3.2
New Zealand	3.1	0.4	2.3
Australia	2.9	0.4	2.3
Israel	2.8	0.7	1.7
Denmark	2.1	0.3	1.7
Scotland	0.6	0.1	0.4
Netherlands	0.5	0.4	—[b]
England/Wales	0.4	0.1	0.3

Source: Lois A. Fingerhut et al., "International Comparative Analysis of Injury Mortality," *Advance Data from Vital and Health Statistics* 303 (7 October 1998): 1–20. These data are from the 1993–95 period.

a. Figures presented are per 100,000 population.
b. Fewer than twenty deaths.

Fever) and a friend approached the door, Mrs. Peairs yelled to her husband to get his gun, apparently believing the two to be assailants. When the students entered the family's carport, Mr. Peairs ordered them to "freeze." When Hattori continued to advance toward the man, Peairs shot the student once with a .44 Magnum revolver. Peairs was tried for manslaughter in 1993 but was acquitted on the grounds that he believed the threat to be legitimate (the student carried a camera in his hand, which Peairs took to be some kind of weapon). It turned out that Hattori spoke little English and probably considered Peairs's actions to be consistent with Halloween traditions.[8]

The man's acquittal sent shock waves throughout Japan, which had followed the trial closely. One Japanese professor, an expert on American studies, said, "We are more civilized. We rely on words." The incident "seemed to confirm the Japanese view of America as a place rife with guns." A major Japanese newspaper said that the town where the student was killed "is like an old-frontier town of the old wild west." To the Japanese, the killing and its justification were almost beyond understanding and seemed to confirm the belief that America was a nation of lawless, gun-toting vigilantes. The parents of the dead student did prevail in a civil action, winning $650,000 in damages in September 1994. The judge observed that "there was absolutely no need for the resort to a dangerous weapon."[9]

In image as well as in fact, guns are closely linked to American patterns of vi-

olence. The homicide rate began to rise dramatically in the 1960s, as did the production and sale of handguns. Two-thirds of homicides and three-fifths of suicides
are committed with guns, as are one-third of robberies and one-fifth of aggravated
assaults. In all, guns are used in more than one million violent crimes each year.[10]

Americans are by no means unmindful of gun and violence problems. Concerns about crime, violence, and law and order have been important political issues for decades. In 1968, Richard Nixon won the presidency on a tough
law-and-order platform that resonated with voters concerned about crime and
lawlessness. With some fluctuations, the issue has continued to be potent from
the national to the local level, with a notable upswing in 1993 and 1994, when
crime and violence were considered the second most important problem facing
the country, exceeded only by the economy and jobs.[11]

In every year since 1972, guns have accounted for more than 30,000 deaths annually. Yet for nearly all those years, more gun deaths are attributable to suicide
than to homicide. In 1991, for example, of the 38,317 reported gun deaths, 18,350
were homicides, but 18,526 were suicides. The remainder, 1,441, were accidental
deaths. In 1994, gun deaths totaled 39,720, including 20,540 suicides and 13,593
homicides. In 1995, there were 18,503 gun suicides, 15,853 gun homicides, 1,225 accidental gun deaths, and 394 deaths from undetermined gun-related causes, totaling 35,957 Americans who died from firearms. In 1998, records show that 30,708
gun deaths occurred, including 17,424 suicides, 11,798 homicides, 866 fatal accidents, and 620 other gun-related deaths. By way of comparison, the FBI reported
167 justifiable gun homicides by civilians in 1998.[12] This ratio of homicides to suicides is especially significant from a policy standpoint because the primary, almost
exclusive, focus of public and governmental attention has been the crime problem.
A primary purpose of this chapter is to provide a unified examination of all three
gun-related problems: homicide, suicide, and accident. The failure to consider all
three, along with the role of guns in self-defense, represents a failure to examine
the full scope of the policy problem at hand.

One way to gauge this loss of life is to compare it to other circumstances when
Americans have died in large numbers. For example, about 42,000 people were
killed in highway accidents in 1997, compared with 32,436 firearms deaths the same
year (although the auto fatality figure has been declining in recent years because of
increased auto safety and a decline in drunk driving).[13] Roughly 400,000 Americans were killed in World War II. About 60,000 were killed in the Vietnam War.

In demographic terms, gun homicides do not affect the population uniformly
but occur disproportionately among youths, males, and African Americans.[14]
These three groups in particular have experienced a rapid rise in gun deaths. Between 1979 and 1991, 24,552 children and adolescents were gun homicide victims,
16,614 committed suicide with guns, and 7,257 were killed in gun accidents. In
1993, 5,751 people under the age of twenty died from guns. This figure includes

3,661 homicides, 1,460 suicides, 526 accidents, and 104 deaths from undetermined causes. These data were compiled by the Children's Defense Fund, drawn from the National Center for Health Statistics. For the fifteen to nineteen age group, the fatality rate from automobile accidents (the leading cause of death) was 44 per 100,000 people in 1979; by 1989, that rate had fallen to 34 per 100,000. But in the same time span, homicide and suicide gun deaths rose among the same age group from 12 per 100,000 to 18. Among black males ages fifteen to nineteen, the gun death rate rose from 37 per 100,000 in 1985 to an alarming 105 in 1990. From 1985 to 1993, the number of homicides of male African Americans ages thirteen to seventeen tripled. In the early 1990s, homicide rates of African American males in their early twenties were more than eight times as high as those for males as a whole. While overall gun deaths declined on a per capita basis in the 1990s, these demographic groups continued to be most susceptible to gun violence. According to a 1999 U.S. Department of Justice report, "firearms play a large role in juvenile violence," reflected in the facts that firearms played a role in more than 80 percent of juvenile violence incidents discussed in the report, and accounted for 83 percent of juvenile homicides in Milwaukee, 85 percent of juvenile homicides in the District of Columbia, and 91 percent of such homicides in Los Angeles.[15] Further, these changes have occurred at a time when the proportion of young people as a percentage of the total population has actually been declining. According to criminal justice expert Scott Decker, the "decreasing age of both offenders and victims is the most profound change in homicide rates since World War II." According to one police figure, the explanation is "population [shifts], gangs and easy accessibility of weapons." A 2000 government report noted that the sharp increase in juvenile homicides from the mid–1980s through the early 1990s, and the subsequent drop in such homicides in the late 1990s, were both "firearm-related" and "linked to gun use."[16]

In addition to gun deaths, a far larger number of people are injured by guns each year, whether by intention or by accident. For every gun death, there are an estimated five to seven gun injuries. Despite the vagueness of this figure, it is generally accepted. (The vagueness of this ratio is attributable to the fact that data on gun-related injuries are not systematically kept on a national scale.[17]) The public policy and public health consequences of gun injuries are substantial: the annual national cost of intentional and unintentional gun injuries was estimated in 1993 to be more than $14 billion per year, with most of those costs covered directly or indirectly by public monies. Direct costs to hospitals were about $1 billion. According to policy analysts Philip J. Cook and Jens Ludwig, the total yearly costs of all gun violence nationwide, taking into account the full range of costs borne by society including health care, security, prevention efforts, familial consequences, and other factors, are a staggering $100 billion.[18]

Some consider these death and injury figures sufficient, in and of themselves, to justify much more stringent gun control laws. Others argue that they simply represent the inevitable by-product of a modern, complex society that is also armed, and for which the justification for having guns outweighs these negative consequences.

Choice of Weapons

Most guns owned in America are long guns—rifles and shotguns. Yet handguns are becoming more prevalent. In the 1950s only about one-fifth of all gun purchases were handguns. But starting in the 1960s, handgun sales began to rise in proportion to other guns. By 1992, almost 50 percent of new gun sales were handguns. From 1981 to 1993, Americans bought a total of 50 million guns, of which 20 million were handguns. In 1994 Americans owned about 192 million firearms; approximately one-third of those, 65 million, were handguns. The reported total number of guns owned in America continued to hover at about 200 million through the end of the decade. At the close of the twentieth century, about 35 percent of households reported having at least one gun (down from about half of all households in the 1960s). Three-quarters of these people owned more than one gun. By the mid–1990s, households with guns reported an average ownership of 4.4 guns, an increase from the 1970s. Gun owners were mostly likely to be male, from the South, and living in rural areas or small towns, and least likely to be women, from large cities, from the far West or Northeast.[19]

As table 3.2 shows, gun ownership is far more prevalent in the U.S. than in almost any other developed nation. The sole exception is Finland, a highly homogeneous and rural nation with a population of five million. Given America's population of more than 280 million, its predominantly urban-suburban nature, and its enormous diversity, it is not surprising that guns pose a uniquely important issue for this country. The particular public policy concern with handguns arises from the fact that they are far more likely to be used to intimidate, injure, and kill than are long guns. Even though handguns account for only about one-third of all guns owned in the country and are generally more difficult to obtain than long guns, they were used in 80 percent of gun homicides in 1993, about 57 percent of all homicides in 1993 (including homicides from other weapons and instruments), and 80 percent of robberies involving firearms. Of the 1.4 million Americans who were victimized by criminals carrying guns and committing crimes such as rape, robbery, and assault in 1993, 1.1 million of those incidents (86 percent) involved handguns.[20] By one estimate, a handgun has a one-third chance of being used in a crime over the life of the weapon.[21] The appeal of handguns for criminal use arises from their smaller size (allowing for easy concealment), convenience, and ease of use. In fact, long guns are actually more deadly because they usually propel a larger-caliber bullet and always propel at a

TABLE 3.2   Firearms Ownership in Fourteen Countries

Country	Percentage of Homes with Firearms
Finland	50
United States	41
Norway	32
Switzerland	27
Canada	26
France	23
New Zealand	20
Belgium	17
Australia	16
Spain	13
Germany	9
United Kingdom	4
Netherlands	2
Japan	1

Source: Wendy Cukier, "Firearms Regulation: Canada in the International Context," *Chronic Diseases in Canada* 19 (1998): table 2. The author drew her data from a variety of sources from 1989 to 1997. Percentages are rounded to nearest whole number. By 1999, only 36 percent of American households reported owning one or more guns.

higher rate of speed. Both factors increase the likelihood of injury.[22] Even so, handguns continue to be the firearm preferred by criminals.

Similarly, handguns are far less useful for hunting and other recreational purposes. Handguns are, however, more convenient for self-protection. Even so, only 20 percent of gun owners and 40 percent of handgun owners cite self-protection as their reason for gun ownership, although self-protection is the most commonly cited reason among those who purchase handguns.[23]

It is clear that guns, especially handguns, have far-reaching consequences for American life. Yet these summary statistics merely outline the scope of the gun issue. What follows is a more detailed consideration of guns' criminological consequences.

Homicide and Malicious Injury

Many weapons can be used to kill, injure, and intimidate. Yet guns are different from weapons such as knives (the second most commonly used weapon) in that guns can be used from a distance; they act quickly and require little effort; and they pose a universally understood threat.[24]

The attractiveness of guns to criminals is confirmed by a study of prisoners conducted in 1982. Although the study suffers from a series of problems that limit its applicability to prisoners in general, much less to the criminal population as a whole, it provides some information where relatively little exists.[25] When asked why they carried guns, the prisoners surveyed cited wanting to avoid hurting the victim as the most important reason (as did those who carried other kinds of weapons). Several other responses emphasized the convenience and ease of gun use, and the gun's deterrent value (a consideration underlying the desire to avoid harm to the victim). The prisoners surveyed also reported a preference for more rather than less expensive handguns, and most of the handguns were purchased rather than stolen.[26]

The unique significance attached to guns is summarized by the "weapon instrumentality effect." This phrase refers to the independent impact of weapon type on crime, a factor dramatically illustrated in cases 3 and 4 at the beginning of this chapter. That is, the death rate and degree of injury associated with crimes involving guns is far higher than it would be if guns were not involved.[27] One study concluded that assaults with guns were five times more likely to result in death than knife assaults. Comparable findings have emerged from other studies.[28] In addition, in the case of robberies, the successful completion of the crime is more probable when guns are used as compared to other weapons.[29] Some evidence also supports the idea that the mere presence of guns sometimes precipitates violence that would not otherwise occur.[30]

A 1998 study of the impact of guns on homicide concluded that the sharp increase in the homicide rate in the 1980s and early 1990s occurred because "the weapons involved in settling young people's disputes have shifted dramatically from fists or knives to handguns, which are much more lethal. The growth in homicides by young people, which accounted for the entire growth in homicides in the post–1985 period, was all due to handguns." The study also noted that the decline in homicides in the 1990s was similarly attributable to reduced handgun availability and use by the young.[31]

Thus, guns in and of themselves wreak more havoc, in terms of violence and death. Were guns less available, fewer deaths and less serious injuries would result. Nevertheless, there is little reason to believe that the overall amount of crime would appreciably diminish. It might cause less serious harm, but it might prompt more nonfatal injuries.[32] This fact takes on greater significance with the realization that about three-fifths of handgun murders are committed against relatives, friends, neighbors, or other acquaintances. About half of handgun killings escalate from arguments that get out of control.[33]

Suicide

As mentioned earlier in this chapter, gun-related deaths from suicide account for more annual fatalities than do those from homicide, a fact that has received little attention in news accounts or from policymakers. Roughly 60 percent of all suicides are committed with guns. Those who use guns for this purpose are most likely to be white males; women are much more likely to rely on poison, although the gun use rate among women is increasing.[34] Guns are by no means the only means for committing suicide, but they are the most lethal. The success rate for gun suicide attempts is about 90 percent, compared with about 80 percent for hanging, 77 percent for carbon monoxide asphyxiation (usually from car exhaust), 70 percent for drowning, and 23 percent for poisoning.[35] Analysts generally agree on the accuracy of these numbers but disagree as to whether the difference between gun suicides and those from other forms is significant. One considers the differences "slight"; another considers them "impressive."[36] Still, considerable evidence supports the proposition that the mere presence of guns increases the number of successful suicides. For example, men attempt suicide only one-third as often as women, yet men are four times more likely to die in the attempt as women, a disparity explainable in large part by men's preference for guns over other methods.[37]

Does the Presence of Guns Matter?

Regardless of the interpretation, it is clear that guns result in a higher death rate than other methods. It may be true, however, that those who choose guns are more serious about ending their lives than those who select other methods.[38] The key policy question is whether the availability of guns in and of itself enhances the likelihood of suicide. That is, if guns were not available, would individuals simply turn to other means (a phenomenon labeled "displacement"[39])? This question takes on added importance when we note that from 1968 to 1985, firearms suicides increased 36 percent, whereas the suicide rate from all other methods remained constant.[40]

A growing number of studies have addressed this question. First, virtually all researchers agree that restricting gun availability does result in fewer gun suicides. This finding is significant from a public health and public policy standpoint because other means of suicide are less lethal; therefore, some lives are or would be spared because of the switch to nongun methods. This finding aside, some have concluded that gun availability bears no significant relationship to the overall suicide rate among the adult population. That is, when guns are less available, the suicide-prone simply turn to other means.[41] Other studies have concluded the contrary—that gun availability has an independent (although not necessarily large) effect on the suicide rate.[42] A large and ambitious study of suicide, a book-length analysis based on fourteen separate studies and the extant literature, concluded that states with stricter gun control laws have a lower suicide rate (although some "displacement" was observed), and specifically that firearms availability as measured by strict gun laws was the most powerful explanatory variable, accounting for about 30 percent of the variation in suicide rates among the states.[43] A subsequent study relying on different methodology concluded that the presence of one or more guns in the home increased the likelihood of suicide by a factor of five.[44] In contrast, a study relying on comparable methodology concluded that restricting access to handguns decreased the suicide rate of the young, but not of adults.[45]

None of these studies can claim to offer final proof for their arguments, and much research in this area is yet to be done. Probably the most reasonable synthesis is offered by policy expert Philip Cook, who concluded that "the argument here is *not* that the availability of lethal means is the *sole* determinant of suicide rates but, rather, that the availability of lethal means influences the extent to which suicidal impulses are translated into complete suicides. Depriving a suicidal person of a lethal and attractive means of self-destruction may well save his [or her] life."[46]

Suicide and the Young

While the question of the impact of guns on adult suicide is still open to debate, the impact of guns on youthful suicide is not. Ample research indicates that the presence of guns has had a profound effect on youthful suicide. This fact takes on particular and alarming significance with the realization that the adolescent suicide rate tripled from the 1950s to the 1980s, whereas that for all ages increased only slightly. As of 1992, suicide was the second-leading cause of death among older teenagers, and the third-leading cause among children as a whole.[47] "Nationwide, the presence of a loaded handgun in the house is the most potent risk factor for successful suicide among children."[48] A study of adolescent suicide in Chicago found, for example, that children of law enforcement officers accounted for an unusually large number of adolescent suicides. This finding is striking because nearly all the law enforcement officers kept guns in the house and were carefully trained about the use, care, and dangers of weapons in the home.[49]

The young are especially susceptible to the suicide impulse, and while they may exhibit symptoms of suicidal depression, they do not approach suicide with the same determination as the elderly, who, by comparison, are more likely to "have a clear and sustained intent" to find an alternate suicide method if guns are not available.[50]

In the comparative study of suicide rates in King County, Washington, and in the Vancouver metropolitan area in Canada (cited earlier), the comparative suicide rate reflected the displacement principle; that is, with guns less available in Canada, those committing suicide turned to other means. The sole exception to this trend was the fifteen to twenty-four age group, where the 1.38 times greater suicide rate among the American group was attributable almost entirely to the presence of handguns. The *Journal of the American Medical Association* reported that the odds of suicide-prone adolescents actually succeeding increase seventy-five times when guns are present in the home. A study published in 2002 examined suicide rates of young African Americans (ages 15 to 24) from 1979 to 1997 and observed a quadrupling of that rate up to 1994, when rates then began to drop off. The study concluded that a contributing factor to this pattern was gun availability among a population where impulse-based action was high.[51]

The impulsive nature of adolescent suicide is reflected in a study of adolescent suicide and alcohol consumption. While it comes as little surprise that the combination of alcohol and guns is associated with a dramatic increase in suicide, researchers found evidence that alcohol was not consumed as a direct prelude to suicide (that is, to "brace" themselves for death), but that being intoxicated when guns were present or readily available increased the likelihood of suicide attempts. This behavior is generally consistent with the fact that alcohol acts as a depressant.[52] In sum, the most plausible conclusion regarding guns and suicide is that the presence of guns probably results in a modest increase in the overall suicide rate and a significant increase in the rate for adolescents.

Accidents

As reported earlier in this chapter, the accidental discharge of weapons accounts for a relatively small percentage of gun deaths—roughly 5 percent. In addition, the accident fatality rate has been declining on a per capita basis since the early 1970s, although accidents account for around 40 percent of all gun injuries.[53] This comes as little surprise, because by definition injuries caused by accident are not prompted by any intent to kill (unlike suicide and, to a lesser extent, homicide). More than half of all gun accidents occur in and around the home; most of the rest are hunting related. Male adolescents are most likely to die in such accidents, and indeed accidental deaths from guns are most common among children and young adults; 60 percent of those killed by accidental shooting are under the age of thirty, and about 33 percent are younger than twenty. These statistics have put greater focus on stemming gun accidents among the young, given their preventability.[54] As is true of some other gun-related data, gun accident data is often ambiguous or imprecise.

One study of accidental shootings by children in California found that three-quarters of the accidents occurred when children played with guns alone or with friends. In about half the incidents, the children were playing with guns stored loaded and unlocked in the house.[55] Unsafe storage of guns in the home increases the likelihood of accident, yet children have demonstrated that they can unlock and load weapons unless they are completely inaccessible. For older adolescents, no number of locks may suffice. In one embarrassing instance in 1994, the twin sixteen-year-old sons of the former Syracuse, New York, police chief Leigh Hunt stole seven handguns from their father and illegally sold them. In order to get to the guns, the boys had to break through a locked door and into a locked cabinet holding the guns. The theft of the guns was discovered only when one was used to commit a crime. This problem of gun storage and access raises still another paradox, because the possibility of using a weapon for self-protection (discussed below) is greatly diminished if too much time or effort is required for the owner to obtain access to the gun.

Accidents are directly attributable to three factors: gun availability or density (the number of guns in a locality), the accessibility of guns (the ease or difficulty in operating a gun), and conduct (how guns are actually handled, including frequency and skill). Accidents are most likely to occur when availability is high, when guns are handled often, and when skill is low, and least likely to occur under the reverse circumstances. In particular, one study of handgun purchases in Detroit over a twenty-six-year period found a "remarkable" and "strong" relationship between handgun purchases and fatal firearm accidents.[56]

Some critics argue that too much is made of gun accidents because the numbers are small, are declining, and involve high-risk populations.[57] Yet the special issue raised by accidents is underscored by (1) the involvement of innocents in unintentional or at worst reckless actions, especially given the disproportionately high accident rate involving minors; (2) the ease of preventability (e.g., use of gun locks or devices to prevent gunfire when clips are removed); and (3) the high nonfatal injury rate. These three features explain the emphasis on policy intervention, especially as advocated by health professionals.

Few would dispute the assertion that anyone who owns or has legitimate access to a gun should be properly skilled in its use. The just-mentioned issue of availability is both more complex and more controversial, for it goes to the question of why citizens own guns.

By far the most common reasons for gun ownership are hunting and related recreational uses, a fact consistent with the prevalence of long guns over handguns. Self-protection is the second most frequently cited reason (mentioned about one-third as often as hunting/recreation), and it is the main reason cited for handgun purchases. In public policy terms, legitimate hunting purposes are not questioned, aside from issues related to safety. The self-protection issue, however, poses a different problem. Specifically, how does the injury and death rate compare with the defensive use of guns?

Self-Defense

Those who acquire or own guns for self-protection are reacting to the perceived and real threats of modern American life. One study of those who own guns for self-protection found key explanations in feelings of vulnerability to crime and police ineffectiveness. In addition, men are more likely to purchase guns for security, as are those who have been victimized by crime or who believe the risk of crime is increasing.[58]

The fear of crime is certainly real, although it is also often unrelated to actual crime rates. From 1979 to the mid–1990s, roughly one million residential burglaries occurred per year while at least one member of the household was at home (this figure represents a minority of all burglaries). About one-third of these intrusions included assault, robbery, or rape. Nevertheless, fear of crime remained high, and even increased, in the late 1990s, even though crime in virtually every category declined during the same period. In the aftermath of the 11 September 2001 terrorist attacks in New York City and Washington, D.C., handgun purchases rose dramatically, even though there was no direct connection between actual threats against individuals who purchased guns and the overall terrorist threat against the U.S.

Clearly, the value of a gun to a potential victim parallels that to the criminal; that is, a victim can use a gun to "equalize" differences in size or strength or simply to deter or thwart the commission of a crime against his or her home or person, assuming that the victim can "get the drop" on an assailant. Anecdotal information, such as case 2 at the beginning of this chapter, illustrates the intuitive plausibility of the self-defense logic. The National Rifle Association reprints many such anecdotes in its magazines *American Rifleman* and *American Hunter* under the heading "The Armed Citizen." Yet anecdotes do not answer the safety versus self-defense paradox.

National statistics reveal that people who use guns to defend themselves are usually able to thwart crimes. Yet such instances are rare—only about 1.2 percent of incidents—for the simple reason that victims are usually not present during home robberies and are rarely armed during attacks away from home. Moreover, even if the victim is armed, the criminal initiates the encounter, making it difficult or impossible for the victim to deploy a gun first.[59] This raises an immediate question: is it rational to escalate the process of arming the population in order to deter or otherwise thwart crime? While the Wright and Rossi study of prisoners reports concern by some over the prospect of confronting an armed victim, two studies based on crime statistics concluded that there was no statistical relationship between the prevalence of guns in an area and the robbery rate, nor any evidence that burglaries were deterred by higher gun ownership rates.[60] Moreover, there is reason to believe that more guns in the home are an enticement rather than a deterrent to theft. In 1994, for example, more than 300,000 guns were reported stolen (at least 60 percent were handguns). Alternately, the prospect of confronting an armed victim simply pushes crime into other areas or invites the escalation of violence.[61] Still, a number of related questions require attention.

Defense Data

In 1991, Criminologist Gary Kleck produced an estimate that yielded what he characterized as "implying 606,000–960,000 defensive uses of all guns" per year. This "implied" figure was subsequently rounded up to a figure of one million and publicized by gun control opponents such as the NRA. Indeed, in the introduction to his own book, Kleck rounds his own data up to "as many as a million times a year"[62] instead of proposing a midpoint of 783,000 for data that is, by his own assessment, speculative. Yet his estimates are at odds with national crime data and suffer from severe methodological problems.[63] According to the National Crime Victimization Survey, about 50,000 defensive gun uses in violent crimes were reported annually between 1979 and 1985. While these data probably represent an underestimation, policy expert Philip Cook examined this issue by obtaining special calculations from the federal Bureau of Justice Statistics. Cook concluded that guns were used for self-defense in roughly 80,000 instances (including robbery, rape, assault, and burglary) per year. Cook's estimate is generally consistent with the simple fact that "most crimes do occur in what might be referred to as nondeterrable situations."[64] More recent studies verify a defensive gun use rate of about 100,000-plus times per year.[65]

In a follow-up study conducted in 1993, Kleck and a coauthor produced an estimate of as many as 2.5 million self-defense uses of guns each year. Kleck argues that his estimates are more accurate because his survey was anonymous and included follow-up questions to determine the accuracy of reported instances of self-defensive uses of guns. He criticizes the lower National Crime Victimization Survey (NCVS) estimates by saying that they are from "a single source of information," the results of which are inconsistent with the several polls he cites. He also argues that people interviewed may be reluctant to tell the truth to the in-person government interviewers, in part because their use of a gun under such circumstances might be illegal.[66]

Yet Kleck cites no evidence to support his allegation that interviewees systematically lied to NCVS interviewers, or that NCVS methods produce results that are less accurate than his own poll. Indeed, it is just as likely that those interviewed in Kleck's survey were more prone to exaggeration because the interviews were conducted anonymously over the telephone and deliberately focused on obtaining anecdotes from people concerning potentially justifiable uses of guns. If the alleged defensive uses cited in Kleck's poll are actual events that were illegal, however, then the justifiability of the acts themselves is suspect. Moreover, the NCVS survey is not "a single source," as though its results came from a single poll, but rather an annual survey of 100,000 people in 50,000 households. The validity of the survey methods used has been examined repeatedly. Highly trained interviewers conduct seven separate, on-site, confidential interviews with respondents over a three-year period. These surveys have been conducted since 1973, producing numerous, voluminous data sets that are widely used and accepted in the realm of criminology. According to public policy specialist Philip Cook, the NCVS approach "reflects the best thinking on how to get reliable answers to sensitive questions about crime."[67] Further, Kleck's figure of 2.5 million defensive gun uses seems dubious because it is almost twice as high as the total number of all gun crimes in 1993, 1.3 million. An additional criticism raised by several researchers pertains to so-called "false positives" in the Kleck survey, a common problem in surveys that attempt to identify a phenomenon based on a small percentage of a larger survey. To illustrate, if a survey reported a phenomenon occurring at a rate of 60 percent, but the actual rate of occurrence was 62 percent, the statistical difference or significance would be small. Yet if only 2 percent report a phenomenon, but only 0.2 percent actually engage in the phenomenon, the 2 percent poll estimate would be inflated by a factor of ten, yielding a gross distortion of reality. As research Tom W. Smith notes, "the rarer the event the greater the over-reports because there are many more true negatives than can be 'accidentally' misclassified as false positives than there are true positives that could by chance be misreported as false negatives."[68] Smith concludes that defensive gun uses most likely number 100,000–400,000 per year.

Defense versus Accident

Guns are useful for self-defense only if individuals have them at the ready or are at home (in the case of burglaries, for example) when a crime is committed. Under such circumstances, guns used for self-defense are "associated with a reduced risk of physical attack and injury."[69] But the small number of instances when guns are actually used for defense (a little more than 1 percent of all incidents) may be attributable to the victim's getting the jump on the assailant, rather than the simple presence of a gun. Even among trained professionals, the presence of a gun for defense is no guarantee of safety or success. Among all police officers killed in the line of duty from 1980 to 1995, about 16 percent were killed with their own weapons or those of their partners.[70] A recent study of police shootings in major cities found that more than half of the bullets fired by police miss their targets because "even the best marksmanship training programs do not prepare officers for the stress that affects accuracy in real-life situations."[71] Obviously, the prospect of unintended and undesired harm from gun use by civilians in potential crime situations, when those civilians generally do not possess the kind of regular training given to police, is far greater.

A few studies have attempted to compare directly the benefits of guns in deterring or thwarting crimes versus the costs of accidents and other gun-related harm. One estimate from the 1970s, based on FBI data, concluded that a gun "kept in the home for self-defense is six times more likely to be used in a deliberate or accidental homicide involving a relative or a friend than against a burglar or unlawful intruder."[72] A study of all gun deaths in King County, Washington, from 1978 to 1983 concluded that for every instance of justifiable homicide, there were 1.3 accidental deaths, 4.6 criminal homicides, and 37 suicides with guns.[73] A subsequent study of homicides in homes in the most populous counties in Tennessee, Washington State, and Ohio concluded that the presence of guns in the home increased the risk of homicide by nearly three times. In three-quarters of the homicides, the victims were killed by family members or acquaintances. Even in instances of forced entry or victim resistance, guns were of little value, the researchers concluded.[74] Similarly, a comparative study of homicide rates and gun use in Seattle, Washington, and Vancouver, British Columbia, found that only about 4 percent of gun homicides from 1980 to 1986 were justifiable or committed in self-defense.[75] A more recent study of home invasion crimes in the Atlanta area concluded that in homes where criminal entry took place but where guns were also present, homeowners rarely deployed the guns. A subsequent study of 239,000 handgun owners in California found that the presence of the guns increased the likelihood of violent death, including homicide, suicide, and accident. A study published in 2002 found that gun availability was associated with a higher rate of gun deaths among children ages five to fourteen. A 2001 study also found that general gun availability was directly related to fluctuations in gun accidents and gun homicides, meaning that when availability increased, gun-related deaths increased; when availability dropped, gun deaths dropped. The researcher concluded that one-third of the decrease in gun homicides since 1993 could be explained by the continuing drop in the percentage of American homes with guns.[76]

Most of these latter studies focus on homicide in the home, omitting instances where injuries do not result in death, where a confrontation without injury occurs, and where the incident takes place outside the home. As B. Bruce-Briggs has argued, the "measure of the effectiveness of self-defense is not in the number of bodies piled up on doorsteps, but in the property that is protected."[77] While property protection and general crime deterrence are undeniably important considerations, all the consequences attendant to the presence of guns need to be considered. But the emphasis on death rates is understandable given the assumption that most would consider deaths to be of greater importance than, say, protection of property.

For the circumstance of gun-related incidents outside the home, the prospect of encouraging citizens to carry guns as a general policy is rejected by most in law enforcement as an invitation to even greater street violence. Even so, arguments for an armed citizenry often accompany instances of public violence.

For example, two years after the assassination of President John F. Kennedy, a lawyer writing in the *American Bar Association Journal* opined that it was "conceivable that an armed witness in Dallas might have been alert enough after the first shot to have prevented the fatal shot."[78] Leaving aside the fact that the highly trained Secret Service agents guarding the president were themselves unable to protect him from the final, fatal shot, no serious expert on safety would argue that the president would be safer if random citizens in a large crowd were allowed to carry handguns or rifles, for the simple reason that the risk of being shot by intention or accident would *increase*, not *decrease*, with an armed crowd. In any case, it is impossible to imagine an individual on the Dallas street on that day being able to identify the source of the shots, aim at, and disable or kill Lee Harvey Oswald in a 6- to 8-second time frame.

Similar comments appeared in the aftermath of a massacre on a New York commuter train that occurred on 7 December 1993, when Colin Ferguson killed six passengers and wounded nineteen others with a semiautomatic pistol he had purchased in California.[79] Undeniably, the massacre could have been avoided or minimized had one of the passengers on the ill-fated train been carrying a gun. Yet because such random attacks are unpredictable and infrequent, some kind of policy first would have to be established regarding passengers carrying guns (leaving aside a different, and arguably more sensible, policy solution of placing armed professional guards on passenger trains). But if, *as a matter of policy*, train authorities allowed or encouraged passengers to carry guns, the likelihood of gun injuries and deaths would certainly escalate. And suppose Ferguson himself (a man without a criminal record), or someone with similar intentions, was the designated passenger gun carrier?

Concealed Carry Laws

As of 1998, thirty-one states had enacted liberal laws allowing qualified citizens to carry concealed weapons. Such "shall carry" laws, most enacted since 1988, require local police to grant carry permits to anyone who applies, unless the individual is a convicted felon (some states have stricter "may carry" laws that require justifiable reasons and expertise for permission to carry guns). Enacted in part because of political pressure exerted in state capitals by the National Rifle Association, such laws are viewed by supporters as a proper extension of rights to law-abiding citizens, as a means of self-protection, and as a method of deterring or thwarting crime. Relatively few citizens have availed themselves of this carry option, yet even a modest rise in lawful carrying may pose an increased safety problem. A study of homicide rates in urban areas in Florida, Mississippi, and Oregon found that homicide rates rose after the enactment of liberalized carry laws. In Florida, about 18 percent of 500 concealed carry licensees used a firearm to commit a crime. In Texas, licensees were arrested for a total of 2,080 crimes between 1996 and 1998, including fifteen murder or attempted murder charges, six kidnapping or false imprisonment charges, twenty-eight arrests for rape or sexual assault, and 103 charges of assault or aggravated assault with a deadly weapon. These crimes occurred at a time when Texas residents had about 184,000 concealed carry handgun permits, representing about 1.4 percent of the state's population of 13 million.[80]

Such evidence has been cited by critics to argue for repeal of concealed carry laws. Conversely, proponents of such laws argue that lawful carrying has not resulted in an increase in crime but instead has had beneficial effects. In this instance, both claims are at least partially correct. Without a doubt, some crimes have been committed by people who have concealed carry permits. Yet as the numbers for Texas suggest, these criminals probably represent a statistically small percentage of licensees, and the number of crimes small in comparison with total crime rates, meaning that any increase in crime among those with permits would be statistically invisible.

Beyond this, local law enforcement efforts have been moving in a contrary direction—that is, police forces have been escalating efforts to force guns off the streets to reduce crime. Police in such cities as New York, Indianapolis, Boston, and Kansas City have directed patrol officers to watch for any infraction that might allow for a stop-and-search of individuals and cars. Their purposes are to seize illegal guns, to discourage gun use in crime, and to keep guns in general off the streets. Kansas City reported a 50 percent drop in gun crimes where the program was carried out; New York City reported a 41 percent drop in handgun murders. In Philadelphia, a loosening of the gun carry law in 1995 is blamed by local law enforcement officials for an upsurge in homicides in the subsequent two years. In 1994, before passage of the new law, 1,500 gun carry permits were issued; by 1996 that number had risen to 11,500. The number of crime-linked guns purchased locally also rose significantly during this period of time. In general, police disapprove of liberal gun carry laws, even though such laws are supposed to be limited to law-abiding citizens.[81]

More Guns, Less Crime?

Militating against these arguments are those of economist John R. Lott. In a highly publicized and controversial study first published in 1998, Lott summarized his argument in the book's title: *More Guns, Less Crime*.[82] Using models drawn from economics (referred to as "econometric" models), Lott argues that states that have adopted "shall issue" concealed carry laws (meaning that individuals seeking to carry guns need only apply for permission to do so) have seen reductions in violent crimes, without any increase in gun accidents. In fact, he estimates that a 1 percent increase in gun ownership causes a 3 percent decrease in murder, as well as declines in rapes, robberies, and aggravated assaults. Lott graphed some of his data, which seemed to show sharply rising crime rates, followed by steep drops in crime rates after the passage of concealed carry laws in selected states. These conclusions derive from Lott's statistical analysis of county data from all 3,054 counties in the U.S. from 1977 to 1992. Such a massive data base, accompanied by such precise numerical predictions, would seem to imply a high degree of accuracy and objectivity. Yet critics have assailed both.

Students of statistics understand well that precise numbers are no guarantee of accuracy, because the numbers produced by any statistical model are only as good as the assumptions of the model itself. The looming problem with Lott's analysis is that many factors account for fluctuations in crime rates, including poverty, drug use, gang activities, numbers and practices of police, and unemployment. Further, the reasons for crime rate fluctuations in states with concealed carry laws are likely to be different than those in states without such laws. Lott argues that his models are able to quantify all of these factors and control for the numerous differences among the states, allowing him to isolate the impact of concealed carry laws. Yet the first problem with Lott's claim is that his models never establish a causal relationship between concealed carry laws and declining crime rates.

This problem was illustrated when two researchers, Dan A. Black and Daniel S. Nagin, analyzed Lott's data and concluded that there was "no statistically significant evidence that RTC [right to carry] laws have an impact on any of the crime rates." Among their criticisms, they note that Lott's model over- or underestimates crime rates in states that adopted concealed carry laws; that his model erroneously assumes "uniform impact" of concealed carry laws across states that enacted them; that when the single case of Florida (a state where crime rates are highly volatile) is removed from the total analysis, all of the beneficial consequences Lott attributes to the enactment of concealed carry laws disappear. In sum, Black and Nagin conclude that Lott's model is "inappropriate" for his stated purposes, and that his findings "cannot be used responsibly to formulate public policy." Even Gary Kleck, whose arguments are discussed above, doubts the veracity of Lott's claims. After discussing the speculative nature of Lott's findings, Kleck concludes: "More likely, the declines in crime coinciding with relaxation of carry laws were largely attributable to other factors not controlled."[83]

An additional reexamination of Lott's data raised similar questions. Economists Hashem Dezhbakhsh and Paul H. Rubin objected to two bedrock assumptions in Lott's analysis: (1) that "behavioral parameters" are fixed, meaning that social, demographic, and other traits, including arrest rates in the counties, do not change over time; and (2) that the effects of concealed carry laws on crime patterns are assumed to be exactly the same in every county. Dezhbakhsh and Rubin say that these assumptions are "unwarranted," and therefore undercut Lott's conclusions, because (1) the purpose of the model is to observe how, or whether, enactment of concealed carry laws alters the behavior of citizens and criminals; and (2) the effects of such laws will surely vary from county to county because of population, age, education level, income level, poverty rate, racial composition, male-female ratio, and the like. Recalibrating Lott's model to allow for these changes, including the separation of places that enacted concealed carry laws from those that did not, Dezhbakhsh and Rubin find that concealed carry laws produce, at best, mixed results—modest drops in certain crimes in a few places, increases in more crimes in more places, and no significant effect in most places and most crimes. An important lesson learned from these studies is that minor changes from one model to another produce results that are statistically small but may produce major changes in public policy recommendations, a trend that raises doubts about using such models to formulate policy.[84]

Problems arising from Lott's statistical weighting techniques are revealed in his chapter "Gun Ownership, Gun Laws, and Gun Crime." Therein, Lott uses an unusual source of data to examine the nature and extent of gun ownership in America. Rather than relying on conventional public opinion polls that regularly ask questions about gun ownership, he instead uses 1988 and 1996 election day exit polls, which in those years included a question about gun ownership. Lott's use of exit polling is puzzling because the main purpose of such polling is to give the news media data on the likely outcome of federal and state elections. Exit polling occurs when questioners stop voters leaving polling places around the country to ask them how they voted, and a few other questions. Needless to say, such polls are not only brief, but relatively haphazard, as many people refuse to talk to pollsters as they hurry from the voting booth. A larger problem with using this data for purposes other than predicting election outcomes is that only about half of eligible adults have actually voted in recent national elections, making such polls a poor choice to examine the entire American public, for the obvious reason that half of the adult public is excluded from the sample. In 1988, nationwide voter turnout was about 53 percent; in 1996, it was about 48 percent.

Lott claimed to statistically control for the fact that his data excluded half of the country's adult population by "weighting" the responses given to the interviewers so that the sample would statistically resemble the total adult population. But weighting procedures fail to give him an accurate picture of the general public, so his subsequent analysis is unreliable. This fact is evident in his results: according to Lott's reconfiguration of this exit poll data, gun possession *rose* significantly in America, from 26 percent in 1988 to 39 percent in 1996. Yet several other polls designed to measure the opinions of the entire national adult population allow for independent verification. These other results show that Lott's statistical manipulations have, in this case, generated a false conclusion. To cite two of the nation's most reliable and respected polls, Gallup reported gun ownership rates of 47 percent in 1989 (the data was not available for 1988) and 38 percent in 1996. The National Opinion Research Center reported national gun ownership rates of 40 percent in 1988 and 40 percent in 1996 (in the intervening years, the rate fluctuated 6 percent). Kleck's compilation of survey data from a variety of polling organizations (including CBS/*New York Times*, *Los Angeles Times*, Harris, and the Center for Social and Urban Research) posing the same question reveals a general downward trend with percentages in roughly the same range. None of these polls reveals the upward trend Lott alleges, nor do any report a possession number as low as 26 percent (Lott's figure for 1988) at any point between 1959 and the end of the 1990s. Further, it is well understood (as these and other data show) that gun ownership in the United States gradually declined from the 1960s, when about half of all homes had at least one gun, to the end of the 1990s, when a little more than one-third of homes reported having a firearm. This downward trend is generally accepted;[85] there is no reason to believe that gun ownership rose 13 percent from 1988 to 1996, either as a temporary spike or as part of an upward trend, as Lott asserts. Lott does not explain why he declined to use other, more reliable data to examine gun ownership in America. We can conclude, however, that the kind of statistical analysis that undergirds his book here yields a conclusion that is demonstrably false.

Another critic noted that Lott's data set of all counties in the country was inappropriate to his task, in part because counties vary so widely in population and in social, demographic, and other characteristics. Further, only a very small percentage of counties account for most major crime, including murder, which receives special emphasis in criminal justice analysis, and most of these high-crime urban areas are found in states that do not have concealed carry laws. According to sociologist Ted Goertzel, Lott "had no variation in his key causal variable—'shall issue' laws—in the places where most murders occurred"; therefore, "Lott's massive data set was simply unsuitable for his task," even though Lott claimed he had controlled for population size. Yet statistical controls cannot conceal the fact that Lott "simply had no data for the major cities where the homicide problem was most acute." Goertzel concludes:

> What actually happened was that there was an explosion of crack-related homicides in major eastern cities in the 1980s and early 1990s. Lott's whole argument came down to a claim that the largely rural and western "shall issue" states were spared the crack-related homicide epidemic because of their "shall issue" laws. This would never have been taken seriously if it had not been obscured by a maze of equations.

Using a different data set to examine the impact of concealed carry laws, researcher Mark Duggan found no evidence to support Lott's claims, arguing instead that "More Guns" mean "more Crime."[86]

These criticisms emphasize the considerable difficulty in isolating the impact of the passage of a single law among states of the union that are otherwise very different from each other. Yet Lott's own analysis reveals still other problems. In his book, he gives little credence, and even less attention to, the many studies (some of which are cited in this chapter) that examine the social and criminological costs of guns, and that offer conclusions at odds with his own. Lott mentions only two such studies, which he dismisses because of what he considers their limited scope. He also fails to consider the social costs of gun availability relating to suicide, a subject that receives only the briefest mention in his book. Even though more Americans die annually from gun suicide than gun homicide, he sweeps aside the suicide question as statistically insignificant "if a person becomes depressed while away from home." That is, his analysis assumes that concealed carry guns exist and pose a suicide risk only when they are being carried on the street, ignoring their presence in the home, possible use or misuse by the owner or others when the gun is not being carried on the street, theft risks, and the like. Such assumptions are symptomatic of analysis that is disconnected from actual human behavior.[87]

When one considers the very small percentage of people who actually obtain carry licenses—in North Carolina, for example, only 0.3 percent of the state's population acquired a concealed carry permit within a year after enactment of such a law there[88]—the smaller-still percentage of people who actually carry guns with any regularity (even police officers often do not carry their service weapons with them when off duty), and the little attention most citizens pay to state politics, simple common sense suggests that the likelihood that such laws could produce any measurable decrease in crime is extremely small. Further, on a per capita basis, most concealed gun carrying occurs in low-crime rural areas, whereas most crime occurs in urban areas, enforcing the disconnect between the enactment of concealed carry laws and any possible drop in crime. Guns have been used, at least on some occasions, for successful defensive or other crime-thwarting purposes. But Lott's study fails to alter the continuing debate over the relative costs and benefits of gun possession and carrying.

Gun Thefts

One other consideration in this already complex equation is the theft of legally owned guns. Gun control opponents are quick to point out that stricter gun laws would result in less gun availability for law-abiding citizens but that criminals would continue to get guns anyway, because most obtain them by illegal means. The problem with this logic (leaving aside for the moment the self-defense side of the equation) is that it begs the question of where the guns used by criminals come from. Most stolen guns, and guns used to commit crimes, begin as weapons produced and sold legally.

Two studies of prison inmates who reported having guns found that most of their guns were obtained by retail purchase or other private transactions (including in trade and as gifts). About one-quarter to one-third of guns were reportedly obtained by theft. Most estimates of guns used in crimes conclude that about 20 percent of these weapons are stolen.[89] Obviously, not all weapons obtained illegally are used in crimes.

Guns tied to crime may come from four possible sources: licensed dealers, private transfers, theft, and the black market (those who traffick in illegal guns). A study of the national flow of handguns examined these four routes to judge the relative importance of each. It concluded that roughly 1.5 to 2.3 million handguns were transferred annually by licensed dealers, with around 50,000 of these falling into the wrong hands; about 500,000 handguns were transferred yearly in private transfers, with an unknown percentage falling into the wrong hands; and about 170,000 handguns were stolen each year. The black market was essentially a blend of the private transfer and theft routes. All these routes were seen as viable means of gun transfers to criminals.[90] If one route was constricted or interrupted, those seeking guns would presumably pursue another route. According to another estimate, about 500,000 handguns are stolen from private residences and legitimate owners every year.[91]

Gun Availability

More to the point, the general prevalence of guns (especially handguns)—that is, the density of gun ownership in an area—is directly related to criminal gun access. One study noted that the percentage of burglaries that include gun thefts rises with the proportion of households where guns are owned. Another study found that, holding other factors constant, burglary rates rise with the rate of gun ownership.[92] A third study found gun density to be directly related to the homicide rate. Moreover, overall gun density in a locality is a matter of major concern to local law enforcement agencies.[93]

It is well understood that guns, especially handguns, are valued prizes for criminals because of their street and crime value. Thus a general reduction in gun (especially handgun) availability is directly related to gun availability for criminals and criminal use, although firearms may pass through many hands between the point of legal purchase and illegal use. Stated another way, any effort to impose meaningful gun/handgun control has to address the flow of firearms from all sources, not just thefts. Several studies have found a close connection between the availability of guns and the homicide rate, as discussed earlier in this chapter.[94] One analyst observed a 5 percent drop in gun robbery and a 4 percent drop in robbery murder with a 10 percent drop in local gun ownership—although there was no discernible drop in the overall rate of robbery.[95]

In addition, the enormity of the existing pool of handguns in the United States does not necessarily mean that efforts at regulation are futile. A study of the flow and use of handguns concluded that new handguns are proportionately more likely to be involved in crimes than older guns, suggesting that the regulation of new handgun manufacture and sale would have a proportionately greater impact on gun-related crime. As law professor Franklin Zimring notes, "Older handguns include a large number that are packed away in attics or kept in homes for self-protection. Such weapons show up in crimes or confiscations only if used by their owners or transferred by sale or theft to other individuals."[96] Guns used in crimes are likely to be disposed of or to be confiscated by police. Law enforcement authorities have speculated that even though there are more than 200 million guns in America, "far fewer—perhaps 100,000 or so—firearms are used to commit crimes." In addition, according to a study published in 1998, as many as half of handguns used in crimes have been obtained within the previous three years.[97]

The Feeling of Safety

Various surveys have reported that many citizens believe they are safer, or feel safer, by possessing guns. A 1990 survey of gun owners found that 42 percent reported feeling safer, 2 percent less safe, and 56 percent said it made no difference. From this type of data, criminologist James D. Wright and colleagues assert that this feeling, whether correct or not, is in itself a benefit of weapons ownership because such people will "lead happier lives because they feel safer and more secure."[98]

In contrast, a 1994 survey came to a different conclusion. Of the population as a whole, 71 percent reported that they would feel less safe if more people in their communities acquired guns, compared to 19 percent feeling more safe. Among non–gun owners, 85 percent reported feeling less safe, compared to 8 percent feeling more safe. Among gun owners, the split was even, with 41 percent feeling less safe and 40 percent feeling more safe. A study published in 2001 found similar results: 59 percent of respondents in a 1996 national survey would feel "less safe" if more people in their local communities carried guns; and 88 to 94 percent interviewed in 1999 said that citizens should not be allowed to carry guns into various public places.[99]

While such feelings are not without significance, the evident problem is that such feelings by themselves count for little when fundamental issues of public safety, welfare, or morals are at stake. Some motorists continue to feel safer driving without seat belts; some smokers do not feel that the smoking habit diminishes their quality of life or that of those around them; consumers of pornographic materials believe such materials to be benign in their effects; racial segregationists believed that they as well as African Americans were better off when the races were kept apart. Yet in these and many other instances, government has concluded that the feelings of some citizens should be set aside and various regulations imposed as a matter of public policy. So, too, with guns, assuming that the weight of data and argument is sufficiently persuasive.

Alternative Means of Defense

Most discussion of the role of guns in self-defense neglects the consideration of alternatives. Guns aside, home defense may be effectively implemented through the use of locks, alarm systems, safes, improved lighting and landscaping, window bars, dogs, the activation of neighborhood watch groups, and the like. Attacks and assaults away from the home can be minimized or fended off by modifications in behavior and the use of alternative means of defense, such as mace or pepper spray, and general improvement of street safety (e.g., more police on the beat, better street lighting). The point is not that guns should never be used for defense, but that any consideration of personal defense and deterrence should not be limited to guns.

Guns and School Violence

In the late 1990s, the country's attention was riveted by a series of schoolyard shootings committed by school-age boys in small cities, towns, and rural areas, including Jonesboro, Arkansas; Springfield, Oregon; Pearl, Mississippi; Bethel, Alaska; Edinboro, Pennsylvania; Johnston, Rhode Island; Pomona, California; Fayetteville, Tennessee; and West Paducah, Kentucky. This seeming crescendo of schoolyard mayhem reached its peak on 20 April 1999, when two teenage boys shattered the relative security and placidity of their public school, Columbine High, located in Littleton, Colorado, when they brought four guns to school and began shooting. When they were done, twelve students and one teacher had been killed in the space of less than fifteen minutes. Twenty-three others were wounded. As police closed in on eighteen-year-old Eric Harris and seventeen-year-old Dylan Klebold, the two turned the guns on themselves.

The guns had been purchased on the teens' behalf in 1998 by Klebold's eighteen-year-old senior prom date and friend, Robyn Anderson, who purchased two shotguns and a 9-mm Hi-Point carbine for them at the Tanner Gun Show in nearby Denver. They supplied the money; she supplied the identification. At the time of Anderson's purchases, neither boy was old enough to buy the guns (Harris was still seventeen at the time). The fourth gun, a TEC-DC9 semiautomatic pistol, was provided to them later by a friend, twenty-two-year-old Mark Edward Manes, who bought the gun at a different gun show, and then resold it to the boys for $500. All four of the gun show purchases were conducted by private sellers exempted from background check requirements—the so-called "gun show loophole" that allows sales at gun shows by unlicensed dealers to be conducted without checks or waiting periods. When Anderson purchased the guns on behalf of the boys, she was acting as a "straw buyer," a practice outlawed in some states, but not in Colorado. Repeated efforts to close the gun show loophole had been defeated in the Colorado State legislature, although the political momentum generated by the Columbine shooting led to a statewide referendum on the measure, which won approval by a wide margin in November 2000 (Oregon also adopted by referendum a measure to close the gun show loophole in the 2000 election).[100]

The extensive national attention given to these shootings undoubtedly fed public concerns about crime. Indeed, polls revealed that the fear of crime rose throughout the 1990s, including fear of school-related crime. Yet this rise has occurred at the same time that crime in virtually every category has been declining, both in schools and in society. Student attitudes about school safety follow a similar, contradictory pattern. In 1989, according to the Annual Report of School Safety for 1998, produced by the U.S. Departments of Education and Justice, 6 percent of students ages twelve to nineteen reported fear of attack or harm at school. By 1995, this figure had risen to 9 percent. Yet actual school crime rates reflect the opposite trend. In fact, American public schools are relatively safe places, as compared with local communities and even homes. By itself, this is a remarkable fact given that American public schools enrolled almost 46 million students during the 1996–97 school year, and that teens and young adults compose the most crime-prone segment of the population.

More specifically, school shooting deaths (which account for three-fourths of all violent deaths in schools) are both rare and declining. According to the National School Safety Center, 45 school shooting deaths occurred in the 1992–93 school year, 41 in 1993–94, 16 in 1994–95, 29 in 1995–96, 15 in 1996–97, 36 in 1997–98, 25 in 1998–99 (the year of the Littleton shootings), 16 in 1999–2000, and 18 in 2000–2001. The heightened attention given to schoolyard shootings has no doubt fanned fears about school safety, coupled with their occurrence in low-crime rural areas and the rise in attention-grabbing multiple-victim shootings, from two in 1992–93 to six in 1997–98.

Generalized downward crime trends apply to other school crime patterns as well. According to the government's Annual Report on School Safety, in 1996, children ages twelve to eighteen were subjected to serious violent crime at a rate of 26 crimes for every 1,000 students away from school, totaling about 671,000 incidents nationwide. That same year, the same age group was victimized by violent crime within schools at a rate of 10 per 1,000 students (about 255,000 incidents, or 38 percent of the out-of-school crime rate). In addition, overall crime rates have been declining in the 1990s, both within and outside of schools. From 1993 to 1996, the overall crime rate in schools for this age group dropped from 164 incidents per 1,000 students to 128 per 1,000. From 1995 to 1999, the number of students reporting that they had been victimized by crime in school dropped to 8 percent from 10 percent. Outside of schools, the rate dropped comparably. These trends are more significant given the fact that nationwide crime rates such as homicide are proportionately highest among eighteen- to twenty-four-year-olds, followed by fourteen- to seventeen-year-olds.[101] School violence continues to be a serious national concern; nevertheless, it is also important to note that violence occurs in schools at lower rates than in society at large, and has followed a downward trend in the 1990s.

Aside from children's safety, an added concern is violence against schoolteachers. From 1992 to 1996, an average of 30 teachers per 1,000 were victims of violent crimes at school, amounting to about 123,000 per year. Concern also has arisen over the persistence of student gun-carrying. Although the percentage of students who report carrying guns to school has been declining in grades nine through twelve, about 9 percent of students reported carrying a gun onto school property in 1997 within the previous 30 days, according to the Annual Report on School Safety (down from 12 percent in 1993). A scattered few would like to see armed teachers and administrators, but for the most part, virtually no one argues that guns belong at a school, except perhaps in the hands of properly trained security guards or police. The obvious problems with the introduction of guns into schools include the risk of gun theft, accident, suicide, and the tacit encouragement of even more guns in schools.

Several observations emerge from these events. Schoolyard shootings have occurred in urban areas in the past, but those incidents received less attention than the spate of shootings discussed here because the latter have occurred in suburban or rural areas, where crime rates are generally lower, and arguably because urban shootings are more likely to affect ethnic populations, a pattern that supports preexisting racial stereotypes. The schoolyard shootings examined here were committed by young white males. These boys all exhibited warning signs of depression, suicidal tendencies, or alienation, and they were often picked on by others. And, most pertinent to the subject of this book, they all had ready access to guns. It would be unrealistic to suggest that no harm would have been done had these boys not been able to arm themselves easily, but the degree of death and injury would undoubtedly have been reduced if they had had less firepower. Typical is the case of fifteen-year-old Kip Kinkel, who fired fifty-one shots in his school cafeteria in Springfield, Oregon—a state with higher gun ownership rates than the national average—with a .22-caliber Ruger semiautomatic rifle, killing two and injuring twenty-two others. Kinkel was subdued only when he stopped to reload. Kinkel's weapon increased the "lethality" of the attack when compared to, say, an attack with a knife, or even compared to guns that hold fewer rounds of ammunition or to single-loading, bolt-action models. In the case of the Columbine shootings, the two boys also brought about fifty explosive devices with them, but all of the deaths and injuries came from gunshots, emphasizing both the ease and lethality of gun use.

While adults commit similar crimes, such school incidents heighten public concern because they involve the young, both as innocent victims and as impulsive perpetrators. Society controls or restricts children's access to many products, from alcohol to automobiles, precisely because of the inherent dangers attendant on their use and the resulting need for adult judgment. (Most of the child assailants, including Kinkel, were trained in the proper handling of firearms.) By their nature, children are more likely to respond on impulse and less likely to understand the consequences of their actions, facts of great importance in understanding the link between young people and suicide, as discussed earlier. As argued in this chapter, tighter control of guns would not eliminate violence, but it would render many criminal acts less lethal and also increase the degree of difficulty in committing crimes—observations borne out in the schoolyard attacks.[102]

Conclusion

What does this survey of the criminological consequences of guns lead us to conclude about the regulation of guns in the United States? Without question, guns are inextricably linked to violence in America. The available evidence does not, however, answer the causal question of whether guns cause violence or whether the violence-prone simply turn to guns. The most likely answer to this riddle is probably a combination of both conclusions. If guns disappeared tomorrow, violence would surely continue. But it would probably be less devastating, especially for such at-risk groups as the young and African Americans.

Beyond this, we can reasonably come to the following conclusions:

1. Handguns are a disproportionate component of gun harm. Even though long guns are more abundant and usually easier to obtain, handguns are the weapons of choice for criminals.[103] Handguns are useful for self-defense, but the opportunity for a victim actually to deploy a handgun is so small as a percentage of the more than one million annual gun crimes (much less of all crimes) that it cannot be considered an adequate counterbalance to the handgun crime prob-

lem. In addition, a long gun is a viable substitute for the handgun for purposes of home defense. While some have suggested that an across-the-board restriction of handguns would at best only push criminals to greater long-gun use, the existing ratio of handgun to long-gun use in crime, the greater difficulty in obtaining handguns, and handguns' greater concealability, undercut this argument.

2. Homicide attempts would continue regardless of gun regulations. But the "weapon instrumentality effect" alone makes clear that significantly fewer would die and that injuries would be less severe—although the total nonfatal injury rate might rise absent guns because of the greater difficulty of controlling a situation with weapons other than guns. In addition, there is reason to conclude that guns facilitate some homicides that would not occur were guns absent.

3. The suicide rate among the adult population would probably undergo a modest reduction without guns because some would not seek other methods, and guns are more lethal than other suicide methods. The suicide rate of young people, however, would certainly undergo a significant drop. Indeed, specialists interested in reducing suicide from all means have focused increasing attention on restricting access to lethal agents, including guns, carbon monoxide (notably, eliminating this toxic gas from automobile exhaust, as was done in Britain in the 1960s and 1970s), and drugs. Gun control in this area is thus consistent with what is known about suicide prevention.

4. A reduction in gun availability would probably have some impact on the accident rate, but the numbers are small enough (and have been declining for some years) that any degree of change would likely be modest. More effective here would be regulations to require added safety features and improved training.

5. The most reliable estimate suggests about 100,000-plus defensive uses of guns each year. Even if that number is doubled or tripled, it does not come close to matching or counterbalancing criminal gun uses, much less the more than 30,000 gun deaths logged each year and the tens of thousands of gun injuries reported each year. Remembering that roughly 35 percent of all American homes already have at least one gun, there is little reason to expect any dramatic rise in successful defensive uses if the rest of the population suddenly decided to obtain guns. One could, however, expect an appreciable rise in homicides, suicides, accidents, and injuries from guns.

6. Greater gun availability in an area is associated with greater gun availability for criminals. Far from serving as a deterrent to crime, guns in the home are especially tempting targets for theft, particularly because

most burglaries occur when no one is home. On an individual level, a gun in the hand of a victim can thwart or stop a crime. On an aggregate level, however, more guns mean more gun problems, even though many citizens believe that guns make them safer.

7. It makes no sense to consider self-defense, deterrence, or related issues of gun ownership without considering the numerous other means by which citizens may protect themselves and their homes, both individually and collectively. Even though citizens often feel alone in the fight against crime, allies are to be found in neighbors, local governments, and law enforcement. To isolate defense and safety issues from this larger context is to fail to understand the dimensions of the problem to which guns are related.

8. School violence continues to be a national concern, even though schools are statistically safer for children than are their local communities, or even their homes. School crimes, including school shootings, have been declining since the early 1990s, although this is not to suggest complacency on the part of families, teachers, and others involved with schools.

Considering the role of guns in homicide, suicide, accident, and self-defense as reviewed in this chapter, the regulation of guns is a rational policy step, not because it represents a panacea or because the research all points in the same direction, but because the weight of evidence favors societal benefits significantly over the likely costs. Admittedly, this conclusion begs the question of the kind, degree, and practicality of regulation. These are of course vital questions, but they cannot be addressed before we examine the contemporary politics of the gun control issue.

Political Fury: Gun Politics

> If Congress sent one message to America's gun owners in 1993 it was . . . "YOU ARE THE ENEMY." Indeed, hearing Congress rant and rave about gun control in recent weeks was enough to make any freedom-loving American sick.
>
> **—From a letter to NRA members,**
> **produced by Institute for Legislative Action, NRA, 1993**

> WE MUST GET THESE KILLING MACHINES OFF OUR STREETS!
> **—From a flyer depicting six semiautomatic weapons,**
> **sent to members of Handgun Control, Inc., 1993**

WHITE-HOT RHETORIC is no stranger to American political discourse. Yet one would be hard pressed to find an issue that provokes more anger and vitriol across years and even decades than the gun debate. The National Rifle Association's (NRA) Institute for Legislative Action (ILA) summary of Congress's legislative activities for 1993, printed above, and Handgun Control, Inc.'s ([HCI] now known as the Brady Campaign to Prevent Gun Violence) communication to its members are typical of the tone and style of the messages these groups transmit to their members, as well as much of the political discourse on gun control.[1]

Admittedly, these strident appeals are not unusual in the world of targeted mailings; in fact, the standard wisdom on effective direct mail is that it be both emotional and personal.[2] Needless to say, the NRA and the Brady Campaign are likely to pull out all the stops when it comes to mobilizing their members. Yet the point is that this kind of rhetoric spills beyond the groups themselves and into the national gun debate, as is true of other examples of social regulatory policy. To state the matter in its simplest terms, rational policymaking recedes from view when the political combatants spend most of their time screaming political obscenities at each other.

As I argue in chapter 1, these traits are symptomatic of social regulatory policies, where the primary focus is on social relationships rather than economic transactions. The political traits of social regulatory policy, which are the focus of this chapter, include the following:

1. The prevalence of single-issue groups. The significance of these groups, which have proliferated in recent decades, is that they maintain a narrow and intense focus on a specific issue of morality or set of related concerns. This narrow focus, combined with intense feelings associated with a value issue such as gun control, cultivates absolutism within the group, which in turn polarizes the larger public debate. Because the policy battleground revolves around activities viewed in moral terms, those engaged in the political struggle are highly motivated to defend what they believe are fundamental and very personal values. One consequence of this pattern is that it enhances the internal cohesiveness of the organization because the existence of external "enemies" sustains and cultivates the "we-feeling" (sense of unity and solidarity) of the group. This in turn can make the group a zealous participant in the political process.[3] Conversely, Raymond Tatalovich and Byron Daynes note that single-issue groups bring "a disruptive influence to normal political discourse and undermine political stability and consensus building."[4] The evidence of this intense struggle is readily visible for such issues as abortion, school prayer, and civil rights. It is no less true for gun control.

2. Grassroots activism. Social regulatory politics is not confined to an "inside the beltway" struggle in Washington, D.C. It emerges in states, cities, towns, and villages across the country. Unlike issues on which national political figures may provide leadership for the rest of the country, pressure from the political grassroots can have a profound impact on how national political leaders respond to these issues.

3. Public opinion. Public opinion can be mobilized behind change, but such mobilization is likely to be sporadic. Most citizens hold opinions on social regulatory issues but do not share the same intense feelings of interested groups. Thus, pivotal events, such as an assassination or a mass murder, or longer-term issue shifts, such as the rising fear of crime, play a vital role in public issue consciousness. More important, the outcome of a political controversy may vary according to the ability of key groups to mobilize and sway popular sentiment in the aftermath of a pivotal event.

4. Political parties. The political parties often seek to exploit differences over social regulatory issues. Republicans are likely to use such issues to appeal to core conservative constituencies, while Democrats seek to appeal to traditional liberal

constituents. The significance of this trait lies in the fact that American political parties are noted primarily for their tendency to seek the political center and to minimize rather than maximize their differences on most issues.

As I argue in chapters 2 and 3, the present state of American gun policy cannot be explained by constitutional prohibitions or by any straightforward conclusion from the criminological evidence. Unquestionably, gun policy continues to be defined by its politics.

Single-Issue Gun Groups: The NRA

A handful of groups have played the primary role in defining and shaping gun politics. While the list of groups that focus on the gun issue includes several participants, this chapter concerns itself with those that have had important political effects: the National Rifle Association and the Brady Campaign.[5]

Looming like the fierce three-headed watchdog from Greek mythology, Cerberus, the NRA has dominated and defined gun politics for most of the twentieth century. By one assessment, the NRA is "the prototypic single-issue interest group in America."[6]

NRA Background

The NRA was formed in 1871 by Colonel William C. Church, editor of the *Army and Navy Journal,* and by Captain George W. Wingate, an officer in the New York National Guard. Its original stated purpose, reflecting concern over the Union Army's relatively poor marksmanship skills during the Civil War, was "improvement of its members in marksmanship."[7] The group languished in its early years, prompting New York State to withdraw its subsidy of NRA shooting matches in 1880 (from which the NRA had benefited since its founding). In 1900, the moribund group served as the vehicle for a revival in marksmanship (prompted partly by the Spanish-American War of 1898) when Albert Jones, an officer in the New Jersey National Guard, promoted its involvement. With the assistance of gun enthusiast Theodore Roosevelt, Congress was prompted to create the National Board for the Promotion of Rifle Practice as part of the Militia Act of 1903. At its first meeting in 1905, this board authorized the sale of government surplus weapons and ammunition to rifle clubs, which proved to be a critical boost for the organization. Two years later, the NRA moved its headquarters to Washington, D.C. In 1921, the still small NRA (it had about 3,500 members) took on new life thanks to the efforts of C.B. Lister, the organization's promotions manager, who affiliated the NRA with 2,000 local sporting clubs. By 1934, membership had grown tenfold, making the organization the largest and best-organized association of firearms users in the nation. By the start of World War II, membership was 50,000.[8]

While the NRA played a role in limited political efforts to alter national gun policy in the 1920s and 1930s, its primary focus continued to be marksmanship and related sporting activities. NRA leaders did, however, play an active role in shaping what became the National Firearms Act of 1934, the first major national law to regulate guns (see chapter 5). At the end of World War II, the influx of returning soldiers provided a significant membership boost. Within three years of the end of the war, membership had tripled, although most of these new members had a greater interest in hunting. The NRA quickly adapted to this new priority. In the mid–1950s, with a membership of 300,000 and 140 paid employees, the organization moved from its old Washington location to an eight-story building in downtown Washington, which it occupied until the end of 1993, when it moved to a new location in Fairfax, Virginia.[9]

When Congress turned its attention to gun control in the 1960s, so too did the NRA. From that point on, the NRA devoted increasing time and resources to its political agenda. These shifting organizational priorities are confirmed in a content analysis of the NRA publication the *American Rifleman*, in which the proportion of space given over to target shooting declined from about 40 percent before World War II to about 20 percent after the war. Similarly, the percentage of space devoted to legislation rose from less than 4 percent before 1965 to around 10 percent after that time.[10]

By the mid–1970s, membership reached one million. It hit 2 million by the early 1980s, peaked at more than 3 million in the mid–1980s, declined to about 2.5 million around 1990, then climbed to about 3.5 million by 1995 but dipped again to 2.7 million by 1997. By 2001, membership again rose, this time to a peak of slightly more than 4 million. In 1992, the organization's annual budget was about $90 million, most of which came from membership dues. By 1995, its total budget had risen to about $150 million, but it had also run up a debt of about $60 million. By 2000, its budget was $168 million, and much of its debt had been retired. Its office maintains a staff of more than 300 employees, including 65 devoted specifically to lobbying efforts.[11] The NRA's political significance is best understood through an analysis of its links to the government and industry, and its targeted political operations.

Government Subsidies

Ironically, the NRA probably owes its existence to its long-term, intimate association with governmental subsidies and other forms of support, illustrating how government actions can prompt the formation and cultivation of interest groups. According to interest-group specialist Jack Walker, the NRA "was launched in close consultation with the Department of the Army."[12] The irony of this fact stems from its contemporary fierce government-is-the-enemy rhetoric. Only a year after its founding, State Assemblyman David W. Judd, an NRA ally, pushed through the New York State Legislature a $25,000 appropriation to purchase a 100-acre site on Long Island for NRA use as a rifle range.

The NRA's rebirth in the early 1900s was made possible by the National Board for the Promotion of Rifle Practice. As mentioned, the board's first action was to authorize the sale of surplus weapons and ammunition, at cost, to gun clubs sponsored by the NRA. In 1909, the NRA amended its bylaws to include five additional governing board members selected by the secretaries of war and navy, along with the heads of the state National Guards. In 1910, the army decided to give away the surplus rifles and ammunition, but again only to NRA members and their recognized groups. Needless to say, these giveaways provided a powerful incentive for gun enthusiasts to join the organization.[13]

Two years later, Congress began to fund NRA marksmanship contests and allowed the army to provide soldiers to assist in running the annual events, all at government expense.[14] In the 1912 Army Appropriations bill, $25,000 was allocated to fund the NRA matches. The National Defense Act of 1916 appropriated $300,000 for civilian marksmanship training, opened army rifle ranges to civilians, and allowed military instructors to teach shooting skills to civilians. It also created the Office of the Director of Civilian Marksmanship under the Rifle Practice Board to supervise civilian marksmanship activities. By the 1960s, the office was spending $5 million a year; yet some complained when, during the Vietnam War, the office was using 3,000 troops at Camp Perry, Ohio, for the NRA-sponsored events. The primary rationale for the program—to provide a pool of trained shooters for possible military induction—was never borne out, as a survey in 1965 revealed that only about 3 percent of military inductees had participated in the program before joining the military, and less than half of those who participated in the contests were of military draft age. A 1990 study by the General Accounting Office reported that only 200 civilian graduates of the marksmanship program entered the military each year, meaning that the program was spending $23,000 per recruit—hardly an efficient use of government dollars.[15] More to the point, sharp-shooting skills were no longer decisive or even important in a wartime situation, as they had been at the turn of the century.

Weapons sales continued to escalate. From 1959 to 1964, the army sold 500,000 guns to civilians. At the end of the 1960s, the Rifle Practice Board was providing 60 million rounds of ammunition free and was selling M–1 rifles for $17.50. The sale of guns was sharply curtailed at the end of the 1960s, however, at least in part because of concern that weapons were falling into the hands of such fringe groups as the Ku Klux Klan and the Minutemen. In another ironic twist, 400 members of the Detroit Police Department had to join the NRA in 1967 in order to obtain surplus army carbines for riot control.[16]

A 1979 lawsuit filed by the National Coalition to Ban Handguns (NCBH) challenged the NRA's exclusive agreement with the Department of Defense. A federal court agreed, striking down the NRA membership requirement. Those eligible to obtain surplus guns would still have to belong to a government marksmanship club, however, and many continued their NRA affiliation.[17]

Despite periodic exposes and public criticism, the Division of Civilian Marksmanship continues to operate more than 2,000 clubs with about 200,000 members. The clubs are also affiliated with the NRA. About 40 million rounds of ammunition are made available free each year, at a cost of about $1 million. The civilian participants continue to have free access to military shooting ranges, and Camp Perry continues as the site of the annual NRA competition, at government cost of about $2.5 million. In all, the program costs about $5 million annually. An effort to kill the program was brought to the floor of the House of Representatives in October 1993, but it failed. While this program today represents a small component of the NRA agenda, it was instrumental in the organization's early development and continues to represent a unique benefit for the NRA that critics consider to be unjustifiable pork barrel, providing for nothing more than "a subsidy of a hobby."[18]

The NRA also continues to benefit from special concessions from other governmental agencies. Both the Bureau of Land Management and the National Forest Service granted the NRA permission to build target ranges on federal land in 1990. The opportunity to use the hundreds of millions of acres of federal land (found in most states) controlled by these agencies allows the NRA to avoid zoning and other problems in securing shooting sites; it also provides an additional recruitment tool for the organization. The NRA has also pressed to repeal the century-long ban on hunting in national parks. Opposition to this effort swelled in 1994 as environmentalists and others worried about the effects of such hunting on other park users, as well as on park wildlife.[19]

Finally, the NRA benefits in another way from the government. Although it is a political organization, the NRA has set up several related organizational entities to which citizens may make tax-exempt contributions. These include the Firearms Civil Rights Legal Defense Fund, the International Shooter Development Fund, the NRAF Junior Programs Fund, the National Firearms Museum Fund, the NRAF Range Development Fund, the NRA Special Contribution Fund, and the NRA Foundation, a nonprofit corporation. The NRA's Firearms Civil Rights Legal Defense Fund has been particularly active in funneling money to support legal challenges to gun control laws. In 1994 it contributed more than $500,000 to this purpose. In 1996 it contributed $20,000 to the legal defense of Bernhard Goetz, who shot four men in a New York City subway in 1984 after they allegedly threatened to rob him. Goetz lost the civil suit. The NRA also offers various estate planning and will services, hoping to encourage gifts and donations to it from "life insurance, securities or real estate gifts and charitable remainder trusts."[20]

The Gun Industry

The NRA has also had a long and intimate relationship with gun makers and sellers. Policy analyst Josh Sugarmann has gone so far as to conclude that the NRA "has evolved into the unofficial trade association for the firearms industry."[21] The link between the two is, first, pragmatic, in that general gun advocacy on the part of the NRA helps generate and sustain a market for the firearms industry's products. Similarly, gun sales benefit gun users, who compose the core NRA constituency. Second, the link is ideological, because both manufacturers and the NRA embrace and extol the gun culture (described in chapter 1) for emotive, symbolic, and patriotic reasons. Two specific interests have animated the NRA-industry link: the desire to maintain or boost firearms and ammunition sales at a time when the percentage of gun users in America has been declining, and the desire to avoid any gun regulations that might impinge on sales. The first goal is facilitated through the extensive weapons advertising found in NRA publications; the second constitutes the core of the NRA's political agenda.

As early as the start of the twentieth century, a "revolving door" commonly existed between personnel in the NRA and the weapons industry. Indeed, from 1927 to 1935, the NRA actually sold firearms supplies to its membership through the NRA Service Company. The practice was halted, however, when the discounted pricing and overhead expenses pushed the organization into the red.

In the 1950s and 1960s, the then-$1.5 billion arms industry accelerated its political and advertising efforts to boost sagging gun sales and fight proposed government regulations.[22] Yet the industry was able to curtail its direct foray into politics by the early 1970s because at the same time the NRA assumed a more aggressive political role. The acceleration of campaign finance reform in the 1970s also made this desirable for the gun industry. Symptomatic of the embarrassment the industry sought to avoid was the revelation in 1973 that the Olin Mathieson Corporation, owner of the Winchester-Western Division (the nation's second-largest gun producer), had made the fourth-largest single contribution to Richard Nixon's 1972 reelection campaign.[23] The *New York Times* noted: "Many firearms manufacturers have chosen to remain in the background of the raging debate over tighter restrictions on the sale and possession of guns, preferring to leave their public talking to the National Rifle Association."[24]

Aside from the NRA's conventional political activities, it helps boost the firearms industry through invariably favorable reviews of various weapons in its publications. In addition to NRA publications, more than a dozen other magazines are devoted to promotion of guns and gun products. The NRA provides extensive advertising space in its publications, which also accounts for a significant percentage of NRA revenues. In 1990, for example, about $7.5 million in revenues (about 8 percent of the organization's total budget) was generated from industry ads.[25] Moreover, manufacturers insert NRA membership applications in their packaging, while the NRA provides discount gun purchase offers as well as advertising and publicity for a wide array of accessories—camping equipment, clothing, and the like. In recent years, the NRA has provided a commission to gun dealers for every person they sign up as an NRA member. In addition, the NRA and gun companies cooperate in tandem to generate "new kinds of target sports" in order to draw in more people as gun users, and to create markets for new gun designs, as a way to prod what the gun industry considered sluggish sales in the 1980s and 1990s.[26]

More important, the NRA has in recent decades assumed the political point on gun issues in the political arena, turning the spotlight away from industry. Not until 1989 did the gun industry hire a Washington lobbyist, and then only because of the concern that the NRA was losing some of its political clout. The gun industry was pushed further into the public spotlight in the late 1990s when more than thirty lawsuits were filed against gun manufacturers by cities and counties around the country, charging them with manufacturing unsafe products and with marketing their products irresponsibly. These legal efforts were spurred by successful litigation against the tobacco industry during the 1990s. Gun liability suits received a major boost in 1999 when, for the first time, a Brooklyn jury found nine gun manufacturers legally liable in a shooting incident because of the industry's marketing and distribution practices that allegedly encouraged gun trafficking from states with weak gun laws to those with stricter laws, such as New York. The half-million-dollar verdict against the gun manufacturers was overturned on appeal in 2001, but numerous other suits around the country posed a considerable financial threat to the gun industry. Unlike the tobacco industry, whose deep pockets could afford financial payouts (in 1997, the tobacco companies generated almost $50 billion in sales), the ailing gun industry could ill afford to lose many such suits, as its total 1997 sales were only about $1.4 billion. For example, the city of Chicago filed a $433 million suit against gun manufacturers, which alone could have a devastating effect on the industry if the effort were to succeed. In response, the NRA has pushed legislation in many states to bar localities from filing such suits, having seen enactment of such "preemption" legislation in at least twenty-four states by early 2002.[27]

Of particular interest to the firearms industry has been the avoidance of gun regulation by the Consumer Product Safety Commission, from which gun and ammunition regulation was specifically exempted in the 1972 act creating the agency, and the continued ease in obtaining federal firearms licenses, which allowed individuals to become weapons dealers for a modest fee. In the early 1990s, only about 20 percent of licensed dealers operated a storefront; the rest were "kitchen table," noncommercial dealers who accounted for about one-quarter of all weapons sales. Monitoring and regulating such sales has been notoriously poor, prompting an increase in the licensing fee from $30 to $200 for a three-year license in 1994. The industry has also benefited from NRA resistance to regulation of new, more destructive, compact, or undetectable weapons.[28]

The Institute for Legislative Action (ILA)

In the late 1960s and early 1970s, the NRA focused political efforts for the first time at specific legislative races, claiming credit for defeating two gun control proponents in the Senate, Joseph Clark (D-Pa.) in 1968 and Joseph Tydings (D-Md.) in 1970.[29] Buoyed by these victories and persuaded to make politics a higher priority, the NRA reconstituted and concentrated its lobbying activities in 1975 with the creation of its ILA. Focusing primarily on legislative efforts in the states and in the nation's capital, the ILA has become the primary power center in the NRA. Commenting on the ILA's effectiveness, the *Washington Post* admitted that "few lobbies have so mastered the marble halls and concrete canyons of Washington."[30] In recent years, the ILA has consumed 25 percent or more of the NRA's total budget. In 1988, the ILA spent $20.2 million on political activities. By 1992, its spending had risen to $28.9 million.[31]

Beyond its lobbying activities, the ILA has become the primary means through which the NRA mobilizes political support among NRA membership and sympathizers. In 1991, for example, the NRA spent about $10 million on "legislative alert," fund raising, and other mass mailings. The tone of the politically charged mailings has been labeled by journalist Osha Gray Davidson the "Armageddon Appeal." As a former NRA head said, "You keep any special interest group alive by nurturing the crisis atmosphere. 'Keep sending those cards and letters in. Keep sending money.'"[32] After the 1984 Bernhard Goetz subway shooting incident, the NRA ran afoul of the law when it printed on the outside of one of its mailings, "If you fail to respond to this letter you could face a jail term." The New York State Attorney General's office charged the NRA with fraud. After resisting investigative efforts by New York to examine its other mailings for two years, the NRA finally complied. The matter was resolved when the NRA promised to avoid such tactics in the future.[33] A study of NRA advertising conducted by the Congressional Research Service found numerous inaccuracies in the way NRA literature described gun bills before Congress.[34]

Even though the NRA is by no means the largest lobbying group in the country, its belief in membership mobilization for political purposes is most clearly reflected in its spending on internal communications designed not only to buttress support for the NRA agenda but to rally support for political candidates sympathetic to the NRA perspective. In almost every year since the end of the 1970s, the NRA has spent more money on internal communications than any other comparable group. During the 1991–92 election cycle, for example, the NRA spent $8.4 million on political mail and other related internal political spending aimed at members and others. This level of spending represented a 90 percent increase over its spending for the same purpose four years earlier. Unlike donations to candidate fund-raising committees, there are no federal spending limits on such internal communications.[35]

The NRA's Political Action Committee

The ILA also manages the NRA's political action committee (PAC), called the Political Victory Fund. Formed in 1976, its specific purpose is to channel campaign contributions to sympathetic officeholders and seekers. In 1988, it channeled $1.5 million into George Bush's presidential campaign (it refused to endorse Bush in 1992 because of his support for restrictions on assault weapons imports). In all, it spent $4.6 million during the 1987–88 election cycle, making it the fifth-biggest PAC spender during that period.[36] During the 1991–92 election cycle, the PAC contributed more than $1.7 million directly to U.S. Senate and House candidates, ranking it the ninth-biggest PAC spender. In addition, it spent $958,000 on its own against or in favor of selected candidates (unlike contributions made directly to candidates, such independent spending is not limited by federal law). In 1994, the PAC spent more than any other—$5.3 million in campaign contributions, independent expenditures, and other campaign activities. In 1995 and 1996, it raised and spent more than $6.6 million. In the 1999–2000 cycle, the NRA PAC raised spent more than $20 million on federal and state elections.

As is true of most PACs, the Political Victory Fund gives most of its money to incumbents. It also favors Republicans over Democrats. From 1978 to 2000, the NRA gave about 84 percent of its money to Republicans. This ratio shifted even more dramatically in the 2000 elections, when it gave 94 percent of its money to Republicans. This shift reflected the NRA's conscious decision to throw its lot in with the Republican Party, which it viewed as far more friendly to its agenda.[37]

The political priority has come at a cost. Fewer NRA resources have been devoted to traditional hunting, shooting, and other programs. In 1980, 19 percent of the NRA budget went to hunter safety programs, police training courses, and the like. By 1988, only 11 percent of the budget was devoted to such programs. The dramatic upsurge in political spending ran the NRA deeply into the red in the early 1990s. In 1991, it posted a $9 million debt. In 1992, the debt was $34 million, out of a total budget of about $84 million, and its liquid assets dropped from $91 million to $68 million. Its 1993 debt was $32.7 million; in 1996, it reported a debt of $43 million and laid off up to 70 of its 400 employees. Clouding the financial picture further have been charges of mismanagement. In particular, Executive Vice President Wayne LaPierre was accused of awarding a no-bid contract to a direct-mail firm to which he had close contacts. Further, some in the NRA believe that membership recruitment has been mishandled, as the organization was spending more to recruit new members ($87 per new member) than it was receiving in dues from them ($35 per member).[38]

These suspicions were fanned when internal NRA documents were leaked to the press in 1995. They revealed that the recent, intensive recruitment efforts were a money-losing proposition for the organization both because of cost and because only about one-quarter of these members renewed their memberships.

About 70 percent of the total deficit accumulated by the NRA between 1991 and 1994 was caused by ILA spending, which in 1994 lavished $28.3 million on its various political activities. (The NRA financed the budget gap by selling off more than half of the stocks, Treasury bonds, and corporate bonds that constituted the organization's nest egg. The NRA also borrowed $32 million to cover the costs of its new headquarters in Virginia.) In the 1994 elections, when the NRA's PAC was the biggest-spending PAC in the country, its bookkeeping practices were being characterized as "sloppy" by insiders. At the time, the chair of the NRA's finance committee wrote that the "disintegration of the assets of the N.R.A. under current spending policies have eroded our future viability."[39] The private credit-rating agency Dun & Bradstreet gave the NRA its lowest possible rating on its credit risk scale in a report delivered 30 June 1995.[40] A few months before the release of the credit report, the Internal Revenue Service informed the NRA that it would be audited. In the late 1990s, however, the NRA's financial picture improved as it trimmed costs, increased membership (more than half of the NRA's revenues come from membership dues), and accelerated fund-raising activities.

In the midst of these changes, the NRA expanded its political efforts to the international stage. Joining with gun manufacturers and gun groups from eleven countries in 1997, it sought to fight international efforts at gun control, including the enactment of tougher gun laws in such countries as Britain, Australia, Canada, and New Zealand. Further, the NRA obtained advocacy (akin to lobbyist) status at the United Nations in 1997, and in 1998, it unsuccessfully opposed a UN resolution to curb illicit international firearms trade. The NRA's stated goal is to pressure the UN to sidestep any involvement in gun control matters.[41]

Explaining the NRA's Effectiveness

As mentioned previously, the NRA probably owes its existence to government support and largesse. Its long-term, intimate link to the gun industry—the NRA's political silent partner—was also important in its development and is a continuing source of political and financial support. Yet these two elements contribute little to an understanding of the NRA's contemporary political effectiveness.

Member Incentives

Standard wisdom on the influence of interest groups identifies a handful of key factors that explain a group's effectiveness. They include money, membership, reputation, and some combination of information, expertise, and skills. These factors are not all equal in importance, although the NRA excels in all these areas. Compared to similar groups, the NRA is considered to have a large, intense membership; a fat budget; and skilled, experienced leaders.[42]

Popular analysis in the press often points to the NRA's political spending through its PAC as a key explanation for its influence. Commenting on an NRA-supported bill successfully forced out of the House Judiciary Committee in 1986 by discharge petition (gun control proponents sought to keep the bill, the Firearms Owners Protection Act, in committee), the *Washington Post* noted that 84 percent of the members of the House who signed the petition had also received NRA PAC money within the previous two years. The paper editorialized that the NRA "has done a bang-up job of buying support in Congress."[43]

The common assertion that PAC spending buys votes in Congress is one that is mostly unsupported by analysis.[44] In fact, contributions to members of Congress most often serve as a reward for supporting the position of the PAC, rather than as a way of swaying or switching votes, although money is more likely to be important when the issue is narrower and of lower visibility. Some of the heaviest PAC spenders in Washington, such as the American Medical Association and the National Association of Realtors, are often big losers on Capitol Hill. The main consequences of PAC spending are reinforcement of existing loyalties and the acquisition of interest-group access to the legislator. These are important considerations in the interest-group process, to be sure, but PAC spending by the NRA's PAC, or that of any other, can rarely be tied directly to the purchase and subsequent casting of votes by legislators.[45]

The key to the NRA's effectiveness that distinguishes it from other interest groups lies in its highly motivated mass membership and the organization's ability to bring pressure from that membership to bear at key moments and places. Central to this effectiveness is the fact that gun control opponents are more likely to engage in political action—letter writing, contributing money, attending meetings, and the like—than gun control proponents. As *Congressional Quarterly* observed, the NRA's strength rests with "a body of gun lovers linked by a common activity that continues even when the legislative front is quiet." And the *New York Times* observed: "The real power of the rifle association stems from the fervor of its members, their apparent devotion to a single, overriding issue, and their determination to judge politicians on a 'for-us-or-against-us' basis."[46]

The question of member motivation is central to understanding and gauging the effectiveness of interest groups. Political scientist James Q. Wilson identified four kinds of member incentives: material, specific solidary, collective solidary, and purposive. Material incentives are tangible rewards, including money, services, or gifts. Specific solidary include intangible rewards such as honors, the bestowal of rank or office, and the granting of special respect or deference. Collective solidary are also intangible, but can be acquired only through a group experience, such as the enjoyment, comradeship, and esteem one might feel by belonging to a group. Purposive incentives are those that might be most nearly considered ideological—those based on the support of a cause or ideal. The satisfaction of membership comes from belief in and advancement of a cause, not from receiving immediate concrete benefits.[47]

In the case of NRA members, one can observe each of these incentives. People who join the NRA receive several concrete benefits for their $35 dues, including a magazine subscription (the *American Rifleman,* the *American Hunter,* or *America's First Freedom,* its newest publication), a cap bearing the NRA logo, travel and auto discounts, a Visa card (for which members must apply), $1,000 in firearms insurance and $10,000 in personal accident insurance (although the terms of these policies are very narrow), information on and access to hunter tours and sporting events, as well as other information and expertise on gun-related activities. While certainly a draw to some, these modest incentives alone are hardly adequate to explain the zealotry of NRA membership.

Specific and collective solidary incentives can also be found in the organization. The NRA offers various awards, offices, and other forms of recognition to individual members who show particular devotion to the organization's political goals and to those who demonstrate marksmanship and hunting skills. Collective incentives include participation in the NRA's various marksmanship competitions and other meetings that bring together those who share a common interest in guns.

The final type of incentive, purposive, is certainly the most significant. Much of the analysis in this chapter illustrates the primacy of purposive motivations, in that the high and intense degree of NRA member involvement connects most directly to the NRA's ideological agenda. As Wilson noted, members animated by purposive incentives "care passionately about goals," which for the NRA focus preeminently on avoidance and repeal of gun controls.[48] The acceleration of the NRA's political agenda, dating to the 1960s, is both a cause and a reflection of member concerns—concerns that the NRA fans in its numerous strident communications with its members. The NRA's use of mass mailings is especially important as a communications link between the national organization and the grassroots, and as a mobilizing tool to energize and direct member animus. The political consequence of these mailings is revealed by the fact that the NRA's mailing lists are organized by congressional district.[49]

As political scientist Jeffrey Berry notes, the key to effective mass mail is to provoke anger or fear or both. For the NRA in 1993 and 1994, this included regular demonization and vilification of Bill and Hillary Clinton, Attorney General Janet Reno, the Bureau of Alcohol, Tobacco, and Firearms (ATF), and Handgun Control head Sarah Brady. These efforts are enhanced when they are "tied to highly visible current events."[50] During the 1993–94 period, the salient current events included passage of the Brady bill and the assault weapons ban. In the aftermath of the 11 September 2001 terrorist attacks, the NRA rallied members, arguing that pro–gun control groups were trying to exploit people's fears of terrorism to increase gun regulations.

In short, the gun culture unites and motivates gun enthusiasts. No parallel force provides similar unity and motivation to gun control proponents, although groups such as the Brady Campaign have sought to replicate the NRA's organizing successes. The NRA membership has maintained its singular devotion for decades. Elected officials who support the NRA's position are motivated by a combination of grassroots pressure from constituents, the desire to avoid potentially nasty confrontations with NRA supporters (what has been labeled the "hassle factor"), and ideological sympathy.

Access

Closely related to this is the question of access. Almost unique among interest groups, the NRA has counted among it members several presidents, including Theodore Roosevelt, John F. Kennedy, Dwight Eisenhower, Richard Nixon, Ronald Reagan, George H.W. Bush, and George W. Bush. Key congressional leaders, including former House Speaker Tom Foley (D-Wash.) and former House Commerce Committee chair John Dingell (D-Mich.), have been members. Dingell also served on the NRA board.

The significance of the political access represented by these memberships is evidenced by the case of the Consumer Product Safety Commission (CPSC). The CPSC was created in 1972 to test and regulate the production and marketing of thousands of products to determine if they pose a health or safety risk to consumers. Gun control opponents played no role in the legislation's initial consideration in committee; no one from the NRA, for example, testified about the bill in committee. Yet during the adoption struggle, Rep. Dingell inserted a provision that specifically exempted guns and ammunition. While the matter received some debate in the final stages of the bill's consideration, it prompted relatively little scrutiny or outcry outside Congress.[51]

Twenty-two years later, the CBS news program 60 *Minutes* ran a feature on the still-existing exemption, highlighting several popular guns that had caused injuries and death because of defective parts or workmanship. For example, the popular Remington Model 700 bolt-action rifle was shown to discharge without pulling the trigger (the gun would sometimes fire, for example, by the act of unlocking the safety). More than 1,000 such instances had been reported to Remington, suggesting a far larger number of incidents not documented. An internal company memo revealed that Remington had been aware of the problem as far back as 1979. The popular Chinese-made SKS semiautomatic rifle was shown to fire in a fully automatic fashion without even pulling the trigger, because of defective parts.

When asked why his bill to incorporate guns under the CPSC had failed to advance in Congress, Senator Howard Metzenbaum (D-Ohio), a gun control proponent, said, "The NRA's position is consistent. They're opposed to any legislation that has the word 'gun' anywhere in it." When asked what would happen if the NRA dropped its opposition to the bill, Metzenbaum replied, "We would pass the bill overnight." Key to keeping the bill bottled up had been the fact that John Dingell had blocked consideration in the House. An NRA representative argued that the NRA continued to oppose the bill because it was simply a back-door method to regulate or ban guns entirely, even though legislative language could be written to avoid such a problem. By one estimate, regulation of defective or flawed guns and use of inexpensive technology could prevent 500 accidental gun deaths and numerous gun injuries every year.[52]

Access has provided the NRA with the ability selectively to apply pressure effectively, particularly when relatively few others in the political process are paying attention or when the focal point of the pressure has been relatively narrow. Consider these illustrative examples:

1. In 1965, Congress considered a bill to regulate mail-order gun sales, spurred in part by the fact that President John F. Kennedy's killer, Lee Harvey Oswald, had purchased his rifle through a mail-order ad in an NRA publication, the *American Rifleman*. The NRA alerted its membership, exhorting them to write to Washington against the bill. In the month preceding the NRA alert, the White House received fifty letters, split evenly for and against the bill. Within two weeks of the NRA alert, the White House received 12,000 letters, nearly all against the bill. The two key congressional committees considering the bill also received a sudden flood of angry mail—3,400 letters within two weeks. Senators expressed astonishment at the volume and angry tone of the letters. According to Gale McGee (D-Wyo.), "I can recall no issue, either international or domestic, in my tenure in the Senate that has aroused the people of Wyoming as this one."[53] Gun mail-order regulation was averted until 1968, when public fury at the assassinations of the Reverend Martin Luther King Jr. and Senator Robert Kennedy spurred the passage of the Gun Control Act of 1968. The pattern set by the NRA in the 1960s has subsequently become its political signature.

2. During the summer of 1982, the otherwise placid Long Island community of Brookhaven erupted in political controversy. The issue that rocked the New York township was an attempt by the Brookhaven Town Board to outlaw the possession of handgun bullets capable of piercing a bulletproof vest. The armor-piercing bullets, also known as KTW bullets, had been developed the previous decade to provide police with a means for piercing automobile engine

blocks in order to provide literal stopping power.[54] Yet the police found the bullets to be unusable precisely because their ability to penetrate dense objects meant that the bullets' flight could not be controlled. Worse, such bullets could pierce the body armor worn by police. The president of the International Association of Chiefs of Police stated flatly that KTW bullets had "no legitimate use . . . either in or out of law enforcement."[55]

The Brookhaven Town Board's attempt to ban the bullets, an effort supported by local police organizations, was defeated when hundreds of angry local residents turned out at a town meeting to denounce the proposal. The outpouring was prompted by NRA "alert" telegrams sent to local members. Speaking against the ordinance, NRA lobbyist James Baker commented, "You can't moderate behavior by controlling objects."[56] A toothless version of the ordinance was eventually passed.

The armor-piercing bullet controversy spread to Washington, where the NRA's fear of any form of gun control prompted the organization to fight enactment of a federal law for nearly four years. Seeking to avoid antagonizing police organizations that supported the bill (and whose support the NRA sought for the Firearms Owners Protection Act, being considered at the same time), the NRA finally yielded in 1986, and a revised bill banning the import, manufacture, and sale of KTW bullets was signed into law in August that year.[57]

3. Freshman Representative Peter P. Smith (R-Vt.) felt NRA wrath in 1989 when he cosponsored a bill to ban semiautomatic weapons. This action prompted particular ire because Smith had signed a petition in 1988 saying he would oppose gun controls. NRA members in his district demanded his resignation, and the NRA spent $18,000 in the campaign to defeat him in 1990. "Impeach Peter Smith, Traitor" posters sprang up in his district. Flyers pairing his picture with that of Adolf Hitler were circulated. "I've never been through anything like this. It was astounding," he noted.[58] Speaking about his subsequent unsuccessful reelection bid, Smith said, "my mother was almost driven off the road. People were shooting my lawn signs at night. That is the level of emotion the NRA was able to stir up."[59] Smith was defeated by socialist Bernard Sanders, who had also expressed support for an assault weapons ban. Yet the NRA was less concerned with Sanders's position than with punishing Smith. After election to the House, however, Sanders voted against a waiting period for handgun purchases in 1991, and again in 1993 when the measure passed.

4. Michigan Congressman Bart Stupak, considered one of the most conservative Democrats in the House of Representatives, had a long history of NRA support. The former Michigan state trooper, whose district included the state's rural and conservative "upper peninsula," had received almost $50,000 in campaign contributions from the NRA in his four previous election bids. The NRA's support seemed well justified, as Stupak always voted with the NRA's position

on gun issues; Stupak's voting trend was logical because hunting and sporting are important activities in that district, where more than 60 percent of households own guns. In the 2000 race, however, the NRA turned against Stupak. It was instrumental in recruiting his Republican opponent, Chuck Yob, to whom it funneled $5,000, and the NRA advertised for Stupak's defeat. His sin? Stupak voted in 1999 in favor of a House bill that would have imposed a three-day waiting period for background checks for firearms sales at gun shows. The measure failed to win enactment. In a closely watched campaign, Stupak won reelection with 58 percent of the vote, only slightly less than his 59 percent margin of victory in 1998."I'm a hunter and I have been since I was a kid," said Stupak. "I've never voted to take away a single gun. Never."[60]

The Politics of Purity

Coupled with the fervor of its membership is a related key organizational trait: the increasingly polemical, ideological, and zealous nature of the organization's leadership, a tendency that further underscores the purposive motivations of the NRA's adherents. Long known for its zealotry, the NRA accelerated its insistence on absolute issue purity in the aftermath of a furious internal power struggle that came to a head in 1977.

Although it had opposed gun controls for decades, the NRA leadership had maintained the organization's primary focus on sporting, hunting, and other recreational gun uses. To the dismay of NRA "hardliners," Executive Vice President Franklin Orth had given at least partially favorable testimony before Congress on the 1968 gun control bill. The hard-liners tried but failed to remove Orth. Meanwhile, the "old-guard moderates" in control of the organization sought to turn the organization away from politics and back toward hunting and conservation.

Symptomatic of this effort were plans promoted by the old guard to create a national shooting center in New Mexico and move the NRA's headquarters to Colorado Springs. Meanwhile, the NRA's recently formed ILA, headed by hard-liner Harlon Carter, complained bitterly at the devotion of organizational resources to these nonpolitical efforts. The response of the old guard was to fire seventy-four employees, most of whom were hard-liners. The simmering dispute surfaced at the NRA's 1977 convention in Cincinnati. Rallying a faction called the Federation of the NRA, Carter won organizational changes giving the convention members greater control over decision making. He and his allies then used those rules to depose the old guard at the convention in what was dubbed the Cincinnati Revolt. From this point forward, the ILA became the primary power center of the NRA, and as Osha Gray Davidson noted, "the NRA became more than a rifle club. It became the Gun Lobby."[61]

Since that time, the hard-liners have pushed the organization toward total, unwavering opposition to all forms of gun regulation.[62] This emphasis on 100 percent purity has helped the organization mobilize and activate its faithful; but it has also alienated former and potential allies.

One of the most highly publicized consequences of this unyielding approach has been the alienation of most national police organizations. The split between these former allies can be traced to the NRA's opposition to any regulation of armor-piercing (so-called cop-killer) bullets, a stand that infuriated many in law enforcement, because the bullets had no sporting or hunting purposes—unless the quarry was a police officer wearing a bullet-proof vest. Police organizations began to side with HCI's lobbying efforts, spearheaded by Sarah Brady, to impose a waiting period for handgun purchases.

The final straw for police organizations came when the NRA began to single out for attack particular police chiefs who supported gun controls. In 1988, for example, the NRA ran advertisements in national publications claiming that Joseph McNamara, the police chief of San Jose, favored legalizing drugs. The charges were false. McNamara had spoken publicly in favor of banning armor-piercing bullets and assault weapons and in favor of a waiting period. He had also publicly derided the NRA as being anti–law enforcement. In addition, the NRA worked, with some success, to keep police chiefs who had spoken out in favor of gun control from being hired in other cities.[63] The NRA also worked to have Nashville police chief Joe Casey fired for his gun views. As a consequence, nearly every established police organization has broken with the NRA, siding with the gun control efforts of HCI and others.[64]

NRA attacks have targeted established political figures as well. Most notably, President (and former NRA life member) George H.W. Bush was the focus of an unsuccessful effort of expulsion from the NRA as the result of his 1989 decision to ban the import of semiautomatic rifles. Bush's decision came in large part because of the recommendation of drug czar William Bennett, who was threatened with political retaliation from the NRA for his gun stand. According to a spokesperson for the Bush administration, Bennett said he was told through an intermediary that "if he has thoughts of a political future, he can forget them if he doesn't respect the power of the NRA."[65]

Even though Bush's 1992 opponent Bill Clinton supported gun control more strongly, the NRA refused to endorse Bush (as it had in 1988) or contribute any money to his campaign. In 1996 the NRA turned its back on Republican presidential nominee Robert Dole because of his refusal to support repeal of the 1994 assault weapons ban, even though the incumbent, Clinton, had become the NRA's arch foe.

The NRA's narrow rigidity has also sparked increasing frustration from conservative groups that have sought alliance with the organization on other issues. For example, the NRA refused to cooperate with conservative groups that supported the 1987 nomination of Robert Bork to the Supreme Court, apparently because Bork's judicial record did not include a sufficiently sympathetic view of the Second Amendment. The NRA's opposition to armor-piercing bullet regulation, a waiting period for gun purchases, and its alienation from police groups have all come under fire from conservatives with whom the NRA might otherwise seek common ground. The benefits of compromise have been discarded for continued issue purity.[66]

This trend is seen in recent leadership shifts within the NRA. In 1994, longtime gun activist Tanya Metaksa was named head of the powerful NRA-ILA. Metaksa had worked for the ILA in the late 1970s but was fired by then–NRA President Harlon Carter "for being too aggressive."[67] Viewed as an ultrahardliner, she has been joined by another NRA activist, Neal Knox. Knox headed the ILA under Carter but was also pushed out because he was considered too hardline. According to journalist Jack Anderson, Knox was "so intransigent that he made too many enemies on Capitol Hill, and the NRA was forced to fire him."[68]

Yet Knox returned to the NRA in 1991 as an influential member of its governing board and then became the NRA's second vice president. The extremist proclivities of Metaksa and Knox seemed to be counterbalanced by the election of Thomas Washington as NRA president in 1994. Washington was a conservationist and outdoorsman who more closely reflected the older hunting-sporting traditions of the earlier NRA. Yet when Washington died unexpectedly of a heart attack at the end of 1995, his successor was another political firebrand, Marion Hammer, who had served for several years as the NRA's lobbyist in Florida and was an early associate of Metaksa. While some have assumed that the elevation of two women might at least soften the male-dominated NRA's image (only 12 percent of NRA members are women), such an assumption is not consistent with their political records. By one account, "Metaksa and Hammer are NRA hard-liners who believe that even the slightest compromise with gun control advocates paves the way for government to disarm citizens."[69] The NRA's increasingly extremist turn has also been reflected in repeated reports of ideological feuding within the organization and exodus of moderates from the organization. Richard Riley, who served as NRA president from 1990 to 1992, commented similarly that the NRA had become too extremist. "There could be a lot of members who resign because the NRA has been embarrassed by some of the people running it now."[70]

In an effort to find a more effective political approach, the NRA has launched a new political assault by accusing gun control supporters of being soft on crime, urging the construction of more prisons and tougher sentencing, and avoiding any direct claims about gun control. Among its first targets was Representative Charles Schumer (D-N.Y.), who sponsored a major crime bill in 1994 and was a leading proponent of gun control. The NRA took out a full-page ad in *USA Today* that accused Schumer of being "The Criminal's Best Friend in Congress." Although the NRA is quick to project a tough crime-fighting image, it lobbied successfully in 1996 to kill key provisions in a counterterrorism bill that was introduced in response to the 1995 bombing of a federal office building in Oklahoma City. Among the provisions opposed by the NRA and successfully deleted from the bill were measures to make it easier to deport illegal aliens charged with terrorism, enhanced government powers to crack down on fund raising by foreign terrorist groups, studies of armor-piercing ammunition and explosives, and measures that would have made it easier for the government to prosecute those who provide weapons that are used in crimes. A watered-down version of the bill was signed into law in April 1996.[71] Despite the shift in focus, the NRA's objective remained the same—to combat gun control advocates.

The NRA's continuing efforts to undercut its foes have also generated new controversies. The NRA's longstanding hostility toward the Bureau of Alcohol, Tobacco, and Firearms (the agency charged with carrying out most gun laws; see chapter 5) prompted the NRA to release to the press in 1995 a videotape that allegedly depicted ATF and other federal agents at an annual "Good Ol' Boys Roundup" in rural Tennessee getting drunk, uttering racial slurs about African Americans, and hanging signs extolling "white power." The revelations sparked fierce controversy and a government investigation. About a month after the revelations, however, the NRA (which had passed the information to the media) admitted that the man who reported the alleged racist behavior and who made the videotape, Richard Hayward, had in fact been barred from the Roundups for attempting to distribute white power and other racist literature. Reports also revealed that Hayward had been closely associated with former Ku Klux Klan leader David Duke and with racist organizations. When questions were raised regarding the authenticity of the videotape, the Justice Department attempted to obtain the original tape to see if it had been tampered with. Hayward instead turned the tape over to a paramilitary group in Alabama with which he had been associated. The group ignored a government subpoena, promising a "Waco Two" if federal agents attempted to retrieve the tape.[72]

The NRA also came under fire in 1995 when it was revealed that some NRA staff had falsely represented themselves to potential government witnesses as congressional investigators attached to the Government Reform and Oversight Committee of the House of Representatives during that committee's investigation of the 1993 government assault on the Branch Davidian compound near Waco, Texas (the ATF suffered fierce criticism for its handling of the standoff and eventual armed assault, which resulted in seventy deaths). The chair of the committee, Rep. Bill Zeliff (R-N.H.), denied that the NRA was given any special privileges or access. Even so, NRA staff members were involved in an investigative committee staff trip to Texas, were allowed to sit in the section of the congressional hearing room normally reserved for congressional staffers, and otherwise worked closely with Republican committee leaders. Rep. Charles Schumer denounced the close relationship between Republican leaders and NRA staffers, saying, "We now see an emerging pattern of very deep N.R.A. involvement in the planning of these hearings. It raises a very serious question about whether these hearings are being conducted in an impartial manner or even in accord with House ethics." House Judiciary Committee Chair Henry Hyde (R-Ill.), whose committee was also involved in the Waco hearings, also expressed "outrage" at the NRA's role.[73]

In still another controversial move, the NRA pressured Congress in 1995 and 1996 to cut off all government funding for research on studies investigating the medical consequences of firearms injuries and deaths. These studies have been funded through the National Center for Injury Prevention and Control, a part of the Centers for Disease Control, since the George H.W. Bush administration. Out of an annual budget of about $43 million devoted to the study of deaths from such causes as poisoning, drowning, fires, and industrial accidents, about $2.3 million is allocated annually to the medical consequences of guns. NRA representatives have derided the studies as unscientific and biased; yet the studies stemming from this research have appeared in reputable medical journals and other publications, and the NRA was criticized for trying to silence research that it found inconsistent with its political objectives. The effort to end funding passed in the House in the spring of 1995, but the funding was subsequently restored. The NRA vowed to continue the fight. In 1996 it challenged a similar, $2.6 million appropriation and ultimately succeeded in pushing funding cuts.[74]

The NRA's most serious gaffe arose from a fundraising letter sent out shortly before the bombing of a federal office building in Oklahoma City on 19 April 1995. In the six-page letter, signed by NRA Executive Vice President Wayne LaPierre, federal government agents were compared to Nazis, in that they were said to wear "Nazi bucket helmets and black storm trooper uniforms" and to "harass, intimidate, even murder law-abiding citizens." In the wake of enhanced national sensitivity to the extremist antigovernment rhetoric of those believed to be responsible for the bombing and other acts of domestic terrorism, many expressed outrage at the letter. In particular, former President George H.W. Bush publicly resigned his life membership in the organization, noting that a Secret Service agent killed in the bombing, ATF agents killed in the line of duty, and the heads of these and other federal law enforcement agencies were not fascists. He called the NRA letter a "vicious slander on good people."[75]

In response, NRA President Washington published a full-page written response in several prominent newspapers, defending LaPierre's incendiary letter. Shortly thereafter, however, LaPierre apologized for the letter and expressed regret for offending federal law enforcement officials. Yet the apology did little to dampen criticism of the NRA's apparent sympathies for extremist groups. This criticism intensified when it was revealed that Tanya Metaksa had met with members of the Michigan Militia in a hotel lobby in Michigan a few months before the Oklahoma City blast (although no one suggested that the NRA knew of or discussed any plans to blow up the building or engage in other violent acts). Bemoaning the NRA's tarnished image, former NRA President Riley said, "now we're cast with the Nazis, the skinheads, and the Ku Klux Klan."[76]

Internal power struggles between NRA factions took a Hollywood twist in 1997 when hardliner and then–First Vice President Neal Knox was defeated in his reelection bid by actor and gun activist Charlton Heston. Heston's nomination was propelled by Knox nemesis LaPierre, who had been targeted by Knox for defeat. Heston's election served several purposes. LaPierre was able to exploit Heston's celebrity status to beat back efforts by the more extremist elements within the organization, headed by Knox, to consolidate control. (Heston was elected by an NRA board vote of 38–34; a less-well-known contender would likely have lost to Knox.) Heston's presence also provided a badly needed public relations boost to the organization, and indeed Heston has been a leading spokesperson for the NRA and its causes, lending his name to various paid advertisements, letters to national publications, and the like, extolling NRA positions. As a consequence, those positions have likely received more attention than they would have otherwise. Most notably, Heston has spearheaded a new campaign extolling gun rights as the most important of all civil liberties. Knox, however, continued to criticize Heston as insufficiently strong on the gun issue, and the extended intraorganizational struggles fanned criticisms that the NRA had become too politicized and too extremist, even for its traditional hunter-sportsperson base of support. At its June 1998 convention, the NRA elected Heston to serve as its president, a further defeat for the Knox faction. Heston was reelected in 1999, 2000, 2001, and 2002, eclipsing the organization's two-term limit. In 1999, Knox protégé Metaksa was pushed out of power. The NRA's continuing single-issue zealotry was summarized by former NRA President Warren Cassidy: "You'd get a far better understanding if you just approach us as if [we are] one of the world's great religions."[77]

The Brady Campaign to Prevent Gun Violence

The NRA's primary opponent is the Brady Campaign to Prevent Gun Violence, which was known as Handgun Control, Inc., before 2001. Founded in 1974 by Republican businessman Pete Shields (whose twenty-three-year-old son had been murdered that year) and others, the organization began in partnership with the National Coalition to Ban Handguns (NCBH), formed at about the same time. The groups soon parted ways. The NCBH, renamed the Coalition to Stop Gun Violence (CSGV) in 1990, has generally pursued a tougher stand on gun regulation than the Brady Campaign, and it has been overshadowed by the Brady Campaign's greater size and visibility, especially since Sarah Brady became a prominent figure.[78]

The former HCI had few resources and limited impact until the 1980 murder of John Lennon helped spark interest and fund-raising activities. By 1981, membership had surpassed 100,000.[79] The organization contributed money to congressional campaigns for the first time in 1980, when it gave $75,000; in comparison, the NRA spent $1.5 million for campaigns that year. By the 1991–92 election cycle, HCI had spent $280,000. In the 1995–96 election cycle, HCI spent $315,000, but that figure was dwarfed by the NRA's spending, $6.6 million in those years. In the 2000 election cycle, the Brady Campaign spent at least ten times as much on campaigns as it had in 1996, amounting to more than $4 million; yet its spending was still dwarfed by that of the NRA. Even so, pro–gun control candidates generally fared well in the 2000 elections (see below).[80]

The Brady Campaign has sought to duplicate the tactical and organizational methodologies of the NRA, in particular by building a grassroots base of members willing to write letters, make phone calls, vote, and contribute money to support the gun control agenda. It, too, has sought to demonize the opposition, but it has not matched the NRA in volume or intensity. By 1990 membership reached 250,000; in 1998, it reported membership exceeding 400,000 and a mailing list of more than one million.[81] Its annual budget tops $7 million.

The Brady Campaign's main focus has been national and state lobbying efforts, spearheaded in recent years by Sarah Brady. Daughter of an FBI agent and a Republican activist, Brady achieved notoriety when her husband, Reagan press secretary James Brady, was seriously injured in a 1981 assassination attempt against the president. Four years later, Sarah Brady joined the board of HCI in reaction to a bill then before Congress that would have gutted much of the 1968 Gun Control Act. Two years later, she helped initiate and subsequently led the charge to enact a waiting period for handgun purchases, a law that came to be known as the Brady law (see discussion in chapter 5). Both she and her husband became staunch advocates for this reform, which Congress finally enacted in 1993. Brady has headed the Brady Campaign since 1989.[82]

Aside from maintaining a PAC, the Brady Campaign is affiliated with the Brady Center to Prevent Gun Violence (before 2001, the Center to Prevent Handgun Violence), a nonprofit educational and legal-action organization founded in 1983. Brady also chairs this group. The Brady Campaign can certainly claim some credit for the enactment of gun control measures in Congress and in many states in the late 1980s and 1990s, even though its size and resources are only about one-tenth of those of the NRA. For a brief time, however, this group's efforts were eclipsed by the first genuine modern mass movement on behalf of stronger gun laws.

The Million Mom March

In the aftermath of the 1999 Columbine school shooting (see chapter 3) and other highly publicized acts of gun violence, a grassroots movement of women in support of stronger gun laws sprang up and organized the first mass rally in modern times on the gun issue, and one of the largest mass rallies ever held in Washington, D.C. The idea originated with New Jersey mother Donna Dees-Thomases. Outraged by a 1999 shooting at a Jewish community center in California, Dees-Thomases, who also worked part-time as a publicist, recruited like-minded women who eventually established fifty state-based organizations to coordinate a march on Washington styled after the Million Man March held there several years earlier.

The organization, labeled the Million Mom March (MMM), converged on the nation's capital on Mother's Day in May 2000. It identified six policy goals: uniform "cooling off" periods and background checks for gun purchases; the licensing of handgun owners and registration of all handguns; mandatory safety locks for all handguns; one-handgun-per-month purchase limits; strict enforcement of existing gun laws; and enlisting help from corporate America. On march day, turnout exceeded all expectations, as the day-long event attracted about 700,000 people. Rally speakers included women whose lives had been affected by gun violence, public officials, and celebrities. Smaller rallies were held simultaneously in at least twenty cities around the country. The rally received extensive attention, and it seemed to mark a turning point in the political dynamic of the gun issue. Much of the impetus for the event, and its resonance among women, arose from the fact that women support gun control in significantly greater numbers than men. During the 2000 elections, for example, polls showed that the "gender gap" between men and women on the gun issue was greater than on any other issue. After the march, the organization reorganized itself as the Million Mom March Foundation, hoping to sustain its momentum and political impact in the way that Mothers Against Drunk Driving (MADD) eventually influenced drinking age laws in the 1980s. MMM activities won support from the U.S. Conference of Mayors, the League of Women Voters, the National Parent Teachers Association, and other groups in favor of gun control.

A counterdemonstration group formed during this period, the Second Amendment Sisters (SAS), sought to rally women in support of gun ownership at what it called the Armed Informed Mothers March. Closely paralleling the NRA's stand on gun issues, SAS argued that stronger gun laws would infringe on a woman's ability to defend herself. The NRA also launched a concurrent advertising campaign to counter the MMM's arguments. The SAS counterdemonstration, held at the opposite end of the Washington Mall, attracted about 1,000 protesters.

The MMM's dramatic initial event mushroomed for a time. Within a few months, more than 240 MMM chapters opened in forty-six states. Yet its grassroots base was unable to sustain its momentum and mass involvement. Identifiable membership shrunk, offices were closed, thirty of thirty-five employees were laid off, and in 2001, the MMM organization was folded into the Brady Campaign. On the first anniversary of its landmark march, it was unable to rally more than a relative handful of participants.[83] The MMM's political and organizational arc again underscored limitations on the ability of gun control groups to establish and maintain the kind of political loyalty that has sustained the NRA for decades, despite the fact that public opinion stands closer to the MMM than to the NRA. Before considering public opinion, however, it is necessary to understand why the interest-group battle has been so asymmetrical; that is, why has the NRA enjoyed a near-monopoly over gun politics until recent years?

The Political Balance and the Invincibility Myth

It is evident, first, that the NRA faced no serious counterbalancing single-issue group until the rise of HCI in the 1980s, a time when other groups (such as police organizations) also brought counterpressure to bear. This fact has helped maintain a mythology of political invincibility concerning the NRA. Like any interest group, the NRA trumpets any successes, even if they are not attributable to NRA influence, and minimizes its reverses. For example, it worked with great vigor against 1988 Democratic presidential nominee and gun control proponent Michael Dukakis, considering his loss to George Bush a great victory that was attributable in substantial measure to NRA efforts. Yet the NRA's actual effect on the outcome was marginal.[84]

The spurious nature of the invincibility myth is even clearer in congressional elections. From 1983 to 1988, eleven Senate incumbents endorsed by the NRA lost their seats. During the same period, no pro–gun control Senate incumbents were defeated, despite NRA opposition. When the NRA's total Senate endorsement-opposition scorecard during this five-year time period is tallied, NRA-backed candidates lost in twenty-one instances and won in only five. In 1990, the only incumbent senator to lose a seat was NRA-backed Rudy Boschwitz (R-Minn.). And no House member targeted for defeat by the NRA lost his or her seat in 1986 or 1988.

NRA efforts helped forge the Republican takeovers of the Senate and House in 1994, but that dramatic change was fueled by factors overshadowing the gun issue. In 1996, despite a concerted effort to defeat those who supported the Brady bill and the assault weapons ban, the NRA suffered significant losses, failing to unseat any of the top ten members of Congress it had targeted. Of the twenty-three incumbent members of Congress who lost in 1996, nineteen had voted in favor of repealing the 1994 assault weapons ban. Staunch NRA supporters, including Reps. Harold Volkmer (D-Mo.), Steve Stockman (R-Tex.), Andrea Seastrand (R-Cal.), and Bill Baker (R-Cal.), were defeated. And a Republican, Carolyn McCarthy, switched parties to run against Long Island Republican Dan Frisa (N.Y.) because he had voted to repeal the assault weapons ban. McCarthy, whose husband was killed and her son wounded in a 1993 shooting spree on a Long Island commuter train, defeated Frisa on a gun control platform.

During the 2000 elections, the NRA worked furiously for Republican presidential candidate George W. Bush. It did not officially endorse him at first, though—not because of ideological objections, but because it felt that a loud endorsement might undercut the Bush campaign theme of "compassionate conservatism," Bush's effort to appear less archly conservative and more open to compromise. The NRA's only slip in strategy occurred when a comment appeared in the press quoting an NRA official as saying that a Bush win would mean that the NRA could set up shop in the Oval Office. The NRA's all-out support for Bush was amplified in part because Democratic presidential nominee Al Gore campaigned expressly on a strong gun control agenda, including support for handgun licensing.

In Bush's razor-thin victory over Democratic nominee and gun control supporter Al Gore (Gore actually received 540,000 more popular votes nationwide than Bush, but Bush received 271 electoral votes to Gore's 267), the NRA took credit, pointing in particular to his wins in Arkansas, Tennessee, and West Virginia. Yet Bush failed to win the large and key battleground states of Pennsylvania (the state with the second-largest NRA membership, next to Texas), Michigan, Wisconsin, Iowa, and New Mexico. Moreover, NRA-backed candidates lost in key U.S. Senate races, five of whom were sitting incumbents, in Michigan (incumbent Spencer Abraham lost to Debbie Stabenow), Washington State (incumbent Slade Gordon lost to Maria Cantwell), Minnesota (incumbent Rod Grams lost to Mark Dayton), Missouri (incumbent John Ashcroft lost to Jean Carnahan), and Florida (Bill McCollum lost to Bill Nelson). In addition, statewide referenda to close the gun show loophole in Colorado and Oregon passed by wide margins, despite expensive NRA-backed campaigns to defeat the measures. The NRA fared little better in House of Representatives races. For example, in one of the most expensive House races in the country, NRA-backed incumbent Republican James Rogan lost to Adam Schiff. Even so, the 2000 election persuaded at least some Democrats that the gun issue was a loser for them.[85]

This pattern does not mean that the NRA is without political influence—far from it. Rather, it reflects the simple American political reality that single issues rarely decide electoral outcomes. This observation does not, however, mitigate the fear, felt especially by potentially vulnerable members of Congress, that NRA influence can sway key votes in Congress or swing an election. The NRA's continuing fearsome reputation was reflected in *Fortune Magazine*'s pronouncement on 28 May 2001 that the NRA had become the most powerful lobby group in Washington, D.C., taking the top spot from the powerful American Association of Retired Persons (AARP). The perception of NRA strength and its "hassle factor" can in and of themselves be inhibiting forces. The NRA has been highly conscious of the potency of projecting an image of strength and an unlimited willingness to harass opponents. A confidential memo written in 1993 revealed how the NRA views its strategy: "We may not win a particular election, but our methods have an extremely efficient 'political cost exchange ratio' making it exceedingly expensive, difficult and unpleasant for the target [the NRA's political opponent] to remain in office. Victory springs from imparting excruciating political pain in unrelenting political attacks on a single politician as an example to others."[86]

In contrast, gun control proponents have indeed operated in the political arena for decades—but not as single-issue groups. Both HCI and the NCBH sprang from a coalition of thirty national religious, educational, and social organizations, helped significantly by a grant from the United Methodist Church. Groups as diverse as Common Cause, the American Jewish Committee, the AFL-CIO, the National Women's Political Caucus, and the American Baptist Convention have devoted effort and resources on behalf of stronger gun control. Yet all these groups have multi-issue concerns that dilute their effectiveness and visibility on the gun issue. The NRA, meanwhile, has benefited from and cultivated a single-issue mass constituency for decades. Faced with a coherent single-issue opposition starting in the 1980S, the NRA has used that opposition to consolidate and accelerate its single-issue mission.

The interplay of these groups does not occur in a vacuum. Gun groups, as well as members of Congress and other governmental leaders, are mindful of shifts and swings in public sentiment, which help to explain the changing nature of the gun debate in recent years.

Public Opinion

The initial and most important fact about public opinion on gun control has been its remarkable consistency in support of greater governmental control of guns. As one opinion analyst has noted: "The vast majority of Americans have favored some kind of action for the control of civilian firearms at least as long as modern polling has been in existence."[87] This finding emerged with the advent of modern polling, when a 1938 Gallup poll[88] showed that 79 percent of respondents favored "firearms control." From then through the 1970s, no less than two-thirds of Americans favored stronger controls.[89] As table 4.1 reveals, the size of the majority favoring stronger gun controls has varied, hitting a low point in the early 1980s (at the height of anti–gun control President Ronald Reagan's popularity, and a high

TABLE 4.1

QUESTION: *In general, do you feel that the laws covering the sale of firearms should be made more strict, less strict, or kept as they are now?*

	More strict	Less strict	Same	No opinion
2000	61%	7%	30%	2%
1999	65	5	28	2
1996	61	9	26	4
1995	63	13	23	1
1993	70	4	24	2
1991	68	5	25	2
1990	78	2	17	3
1986	60	8	30	2
1983	59	4	31	6
1981	65	3	30	2
1980	59	6	29	6
1975	69	3	24	4

Source: Leslie McAneny, "Americans Tell Congress: Pass Brady Bill, Other Tough Gun Laws," *Gallup Poll Monthly*, March 1993, 2. Updates from Gallup Organization.

point for the NRA's political influence). Nevertheless, the trend has been consistent in its lopsided support for stricter laws. This broad trend does not reveal how Americans respond to particular varieties of controls and proposed controls, where results do indeed fluctuate, but it is remarkable not only for its consistency and sharp inclination but also for its reversal of the pattern that public opinion usually supports existing government policy.[90] That is, one infrequently finds such strong and durable opinion supporting a policy option or options not already enacted.

Specific Policy Options

Beyond this general trend, pollsters have posed a variety of more specific questions gauging public reaction to particular regulations. The trend on these questions is predictable: public support generally fluctuates with the degree of government control being proposed.

Consistent and substantial majorities of Americans have favored universal handgun registration. According to a succession of Gallup polls (updates obtained from the Gallup website), the percentage supporting registration was 66 percent in 1982, 70 percent in 1985, 81 percent in 1990, 81 percent in 1993, and 76 percent in 2000. Similarly, in a 1988 survey, 84 percent favored laws requiring anyone carrying a gun outside the home to be licensed to do so. A 1988 Gallup survey found 67 percent of Americans favored registration of all firearms.[91] A series of Roper polls have found that, since the early 1970s, an average of 72 percent of Americans have favored a law requiring "a person to obtain a police permit" before buying a gun.[92]

Even larger majorities have consistently supported the idea of a waiting period between the time a person applies to buy a handgun and the time it is actually sold. Gallup polls reported 91 percent support in 1988, 95 percent in 1990, 93 percent in 1991, 88 percent in 1993 (the year Congress enacted a national five-day waiting period, known as the Brady law), and 93 percent in 2000. *New York Times*/CBS News polls in 1992 and 1993 reported 86 and 85 percent support. A Gallup poll taken immediately after passage of the Brady law revealed 87 percent support. A 2000 Gallup poll also found that 79 percent favored requiring all guns to be sold with trigger locks.[93]

The use of so-called assault weapons in some highly publicized killings focused special attention on attempts to regulate or ban such weapons. While some critics have assailed polls mentioning these weapons, arguing that they are misrepresented to the public by pollsters in ways that elicit an artificially high degree of support for stronger controls, mainstream pollsters generally take care to define the question properly. For example, a 1992 *New York Times*/CBS News poll asked, "Would you favor or oppose a ban on assault weapons—that is, semiautomatic military-style rifles that can hold up to 30 bullets?" Seventy-nine percent responded yes, with only 19 percent opposed. A 1993 Gallup poll asked, "Would you favor or oppose a law banning the manufacture, sale, and possession of semiautomatic assault guns, such as the AK–47?" In response, 66 percent said they would favor such an action, with 30 percent against. These percentages are notable not only for the clear preference they represent but because the question poses the prospect of a ban on such weapons, not merely their regulation. Even gun owners support the ban. In a 1995 survey, 69 percent of gun owners favored keeping the assault weapons ban in place, with only 24 percent supporting removal of the ban.[94]

Surveys have also asked about support for an outright ban on sale and possession of handguns, even though this proposal did not receive serious consideration at the national level until the early 1990s (although a handful of towns around the country enacted such a ban in the 1980s). A succession of Gallup surveys have found progressively rising support for a handgun ban (making exceptions for police and "other authorized persons"), starting at 31 percent in 1980 (with 65 percent opposed), rising to 42 percent support (54 percent opposed) in early 1993.[95] The majority position shifted on this question for the first time in 1993 when a Harris poll reported that 52 percent favored a handgun possession ban (except for court-allowed permission), with 43 percent opposed. As the survey results from questions on gun registration, waiting periods, assault weapons, and even a ban on handguns make clear, Americans' decisive support for stronger gun control is not the product of misunderstanding or a failure to comprehend what the gun debate is all about. Americans may not possess the knowledge of a gun specialist, but the policy options under public discussion are straightforward and clear, as are public preferences, which in fact reveal a high degree of sophistication.[96]

Demographics

Not surprisingly, gun ownership and opposition to gun controls are closely related. Those most likely to oppose gun controls are male (about 75 percent of gun owners are men, as are 87 percent of hunters), reside in small towns and rural areas, are registered as Republicans, are white, and live in the South.[97] The important factors that tie these demographic traits together include the male "rite of passage" connection between guns and maturity (a value rarely found in the socialization of females), the rural setting where guns and hunting activities are more common, and "southernness." The particular importance of southernness was examined in a separate study that concluded that the southern subculture was one where the sporting use of guns was emphasized, as was the "attribute of being more defensive"; that is, there was greater suspicion of outsiders, and a stronger belief in the need to rely on personal self-sufficiency. Another study found that gun ownership was highly correlated with individuals who had little belief or confidence in the American national government.[98]

Gun Beliefs and Crime

The generalized support for gun control is typically tied to the fear of crime. Notably, poll results often fluctuate in response to widely publicized acts of violence. Yet the underlying support for gun control does not rest solely on the crime issue. That is, unlike support for tougher sentencing and the death penalty, citizens seem to believe that greater gun control is no panacea for the crime problem, although citizens do see a connection between violence and guns. In a 1983 Gallup poll, for example, only 17 percent said that tougher handgun laws would reduce crime a great deal, 24 percent said quite a lot, 31 percent said not very much, and 25 percent said not at all. In the same poll, those who supported greater restrictions cited "guns too easy to obtain" (48 percent) as their main reason; only 34 percent cited "too much crime/violence" as the main reason. Similarly, a 1994 poll found that only 34 percent believed that gun control laws would reduce violent crime, with 62 percent believing that they would not.[99] Thus, support for stronger gun laws rests partly with concern over crime, but more with the general sense that guns pose an inherent risk to society that ought to be more tightly regulated.

Perhaps even more impressive than the consistently high degree of support for gun control is the fact that it extends even to gun owners. For example, 59 percent of all Americans surveyed in 1983 said that they favored stricter laws regulating handguns. Of that sample, 47 percent of gun owners registered approval for such laws. A 1988 Gallup survey found that 91 percent of Americans supported a seven-day waiting period for a handgun purchase; 90 percent of gun owners supported the measure.[100] In 1993, the difference in support for stronger gun laws between the population as a whole and gun owners was 13 percent (70 percent support by the general population and 57 percent support among gun owners). Thus, gun owners provide a surprising degree of support for the gun control agenda—"surprising" given the stridency and inflexibility of the groups that claim to represent gun users in Washington, D.C.

A final public opinion question brings us back to the NRA. In a national survey conducted in 2000 by the Survey Research Center at Ohio State University, respondents were asked to rate various interest groups from most to least liked. The NRA ranked as the third most well-liked group, yet it also ranked as the third most disliked. What these apparently contradictory findings reveal is that the NRA continues to arouse intense feelings of respect among its adherents, and contempt among its opponents.

The Opinion-Policy Gap

The disjunction between broad popular support for firmer gun laws and the failure to enact most such laws might be interpreted as a failure of democracy. Yet the connection between public opinion and public policy is far more complex than is suggested by such a conclusion. In the absence of a national system of governance by nationwide referendum, it is all but inevitable that such disjunctions will exist. The explanation rests, first, with the difficulty of translating social regulatory policy preferences into policy enactments. Like trying to build a house in the middle of a hurricane, the effort to construct or alter social regulatory policy is notoriously difficult because of the passion and intensity surrounding such issues. This fact takes on added significance when we note that, other things being equal, the enactment of policy is always more difficult than blocking the enactment of policy. Thus the weight of political inertia rests with gun control opponents. Clearly, public opinion swings in recent years have helped win passage of the ban on armor-piercing bullets, the Brady law, and the assault weapons ban (see discussion in chapter 5). Yet the outrage-action-reaction cycle described in chapter 1 means that public outrage is limited in intensity and duration, especially because the gun issue is but one of many that compete for attention on the national issue agenda. Once the outrage has subsided, gun control opponents retain a political edge that generally works against a direct translation of public preferences into policy enactments.

The second and related reason for the opinion-policy gap is the consequence of pressure-group politics. It is well understood that Congress responds to pressures from organized interest groups, especially when broader public tides subside. As former Senator J. William Fulbright (D-Ark.) once observed, the legislator does not serve "constituents as a community, but the best-organized, best-funded, and most politically active interest groups within the constituency." Political scientist Graham Wootton calls this "special-interest democracy."[101]

Political Parties and Guns

As in the case of other social regulatory policy issues such as abortion and women's rights, the national political parties have consistently disagreed with each other on gun control, although the degree and emphasis of rhetoric used has varied according to the nature of the gun debate at the time and the political posturing of the party nominees. This fact takes on added significance with the recognition that America's two major parties have a long-standing reputation for seeking to minimize their differences and for addressing issues in broad, abstract terms, rather than through unambiguous advocacy of specific policies. A study of party platforms by political scientist Gerald M. Pomper found that less than 10 percent of the promises found in platforms involved conflicting positions between the Democrats and Republicans.[102] Not surprisingly, platforms have been ridiculed for their "mindless rhetoric." The 1972 Democratic platform went so far as to admit that "the people are skeptical of platforms filled with political platitudes."[103]

As measured by national party platforms, the Republicans have expressed long-standing support for gun ownership free of government regulation (except for gun use by criminals), and the Democrats have exhibited a similar consistency in favor of gun regulations. The gun issue first surfaced in party platforms in 1968,[104] reflecting the emergence of the issue at the national level in the late 1960s. Both parties usually have addressed the issue in their platforms under the category of crime and criminal justice.

The Republicans

The 1968 Republican Party platform (of nominee Richard Nixon) urged "control [of] indiscriminate availability of firearms" but also "safeguarding the right of responsible citizens to collect, own and use firearms . . . retaining primary responsibility at the state level." The 1972 platform, supporting Nixon's renomination, again endorsed citizen rights to "collect, own and use firearms," but also included "self-defense" as a purpose and emphasized efforts "to prevent criminal access to all weapons," especially cheap handguns, while relying mainly on state enforcement. The 1976 platform took a turn to the right; it simply stated: "We support the right of citizens to keep and bear arms." The platform also stated its opposition to federal registration of firearms and advocated harsher sentences for crimes committed with guns. If the previous GOP platforms contained at least a nod to gun regulation, the 1976 document, produced by the convention that nominated Gerald Ford, conformed closely to NRA policy.

In 1980, the Republican platform wording was duplicated from 1976, with an added phrase urging removal of "those provisions of the Gun Control Act of 1968 that do not significantly impact on crime but serve rather to restrain the law-abiding citizen in his legitimate use of firearms." This sentence foreshadowed the original purpose behind the Firearms Owners Protection Act of 1986. Reflecting the conservative views of party nominee Ronald Reagan, this platform language represented the zenith of NRA-style views in the party.

The 1984 convention that renominated Reagan adopted a platform that dropped any reference to the Gun Control Act or to the lifting of gun regulations and said instead that citizens ought not to be blamed for "exercising their constitutional rights," presumably a reference to the Second Amendment. The 1988 platform of the convention that nominated George H.W. Bush also indicated the party's support for "the constitutional right to keep and bear arms" and called for "stiff, mandatory penalties" for those who used guns in the commission of crimes. This wording was kept in the 1992 platform (despite the NRA's refusal to endorse Bush) along with additional wording tying gun ownership to national defense, and criticizing efforts at "blaming firearm manufacturers for street crime." The 1996 platform again invoked the Second Amendment but added wording about the need for training programs for safe firearms use. It also supported presidential candidate Robert Dole's call for instant background check, a proposal floated by the NRA the previous decade (even though the NRA refused to back Dole because of his opposition to repeal of the assault weapons ban). The platform also called for mandatory penalties for gun crimes. The 2000 platform for nominee George W. Bush paralleled that of 1996, invoking the Second Amendment and citing the importance of self-defense, and also promised vigorous enforcement of existing gun laws. It further stated express opposition to gun licensing and registration.

The Democrats

In its mention of gun control, the 1968 Democratic Party platform urged "the passage and enforcement of effective federal, state and local gun control legislation." Paralleling the nomination of liberal Senator George McGovern (D-S.D.), a specific proposal appeared in the 1972 platform that, after calling for "laws to control the improper use of hand guns," recommended a ban on "Saturday night specials" (i.e., cheap handguns). The 1976 platform again called for strengthening existing handgun controls as well as banning Saturday night specials. But reflecting nominee Jimmy Carter's more conservative views, the platform also urged tougher sentencing for crimes committed with guns and, in a concession to gun owners, affirmed "the right of sportsmen to possess guns for purely hunting and target-shooting purposes." The 1980 platform advocated the same position and reaffirmed support for sporting uses of guns, reflecting the caution of incumbent President Carter.

The 1984 Democratic platform, reflecting the more liberal views of nominee Walter Mondale, dropped any reference to the sporting use of guns. The platform again called for tough restraints on small, cheap handguns. Despite Michael Dukakis's initial support for strong gun control, the 1988 platform backpedaled on previous tough language. Its only specific gun regulation proposal was a call for the enforcement of the ban on "cop-killer" bullets enacted two years earlier, a proposal notable for being both uncontroversial and inconsequential. It also made a vague reference to the procuring of weapons as an impediment to the jobs performed by police, teachers, and parents. This language probably reflected the belief in the Dukakis camp that it needed to backpedal on the candidate's gun control views in order to remain competitive with George H.W. Bush.

The 1992 platform assumed a much stronger and more specific stand on gun control. After asserting that it was "time to shut down the weapons bazaars," it endorsed a waiting period for handgun purchases and a ban on "the most deadly assault weapons." It also called for swift punishment of those who commit crimes with guns, shutting down the gun black market, and stiff penalties for those who sell guns to children. Reflecting nominee Bill Clinton's support for new gun laws but also respect for hunters (Clinton himself is a hunter), the platform stated that "we do not support efforts to restrict weapons used for legitimate hunting and sporting purposes." Clinton's 1996 platform trumpeted the policy enactments sought in the 1992 platform, including the Brady law and the assault weapons ban. It connected crime reduction with restricted availability of certain weapons, but it also repeated the commitment to protect legitimate hunting and sporting gun uses. The 2000 platform extolled candidate Al Gore's record of standing up to the "gun lobby," citing past successes of the Clinton-Gore administration, including the Brady law and the assault weapons ban, reductions in juvenile gun crimes, and also promises of a continued tough approach to crime and especially gun crime. The platform also called for mandatory gun locks, a photo license ID system, full background checks, and more federal gun prosecutors and prosecutions.

Presidential politics in an election year drives party platforms. The variations in emphasis and tone observed in the party platforms since 1968 reflect the ideological leanings of the party nominees, as well as some assessment of the public mood. In 1992, for example, a waiting period for handgun purchases and regulations on assault rifles were prominent policy options that had gained much support in Washington and in many state capitals around the country since the late 1980s. Most important, in the past four decades the political parties have split on the gun issue rather than seek to ignore the issue or mimic the views of the opposition party.

Conclusion

The NRA provides the prototypical example of single-issue interest politics at work. The lengthy and detailed attention it receives in this chapter reflects both the NRA's political importance and the extent to which it typifies the political maelstrom accompanying social regulatory policy. A zealous, highly motivated, and readily mobilizable grassroots base, animated mostly by purposive incentives, has been the NRA's key political force, whether applied in Washington, D.C., or in the town of Brookhaven, New York; the organization's long-standing ties to key public officials have provided key entry points where its political vector has been most effectively inserted. Its influence is maximized when the public's attention is focused elsewhere. Yet in its continuing political battles, NRA leaders have consistently employed a Chicken Little ("the sky is falling") rhetorical style, with constant prophesies of imminent doom. As a consequence, the NRA has often sacrificed both a sense of perspective and the truth, leading to a general erosion of its credibility outside its own core constituency. Unquestionably, this is a tradeoff that most NRA leaders are willing to accept. Whether it is a "right" decision in purely political terms or not, it does place the NRA outside the mainstream interest-group tradition in American politics and even at the outer edge of group dynamics found in other examples of social regulatory policy.

Because NRA positions are largely at odds with public sentiment, its effectiveness has been reduced, even stymied at times, when national attention becomes aroused and focused on selected gun issues. Yet the window of opportunity for gun control proponents has typically been brief because of the limited duration of the public's focus on gun issues. This pattern began to change with the rise in the 1980s of an effective single-issue counterforce: HCI and its allies. Public support for stronger gun laws rests partly in concerns related to crime, but more strongly in the public's sense that guns pose an inherent danger that ought properly to be subject to greater control by the state. The primary proposals of gun control supporters that constitute the gun policy agenda have found consistently wide support among the public.

The political parties have responded to the gun issue as well. While their stands in particular years have been alternately modest and symbolic, on the one hand, and aggressively specific, on the other hand, they have identifiably split with consistency since 1968, as we would expect for social regulatory policy: the Republicans have opposed new gun laws, and the Democrats have supported new laws. In this instance, at least, the parties have offered voters an identifiable choice on the gun control issue. These party differences have not had a greater effect on the national debate because single-issue appeals are rarely decisive in national politics and because the influence of the national parties has decreased in recent years.

In the next chapter, we observe the convergence of these political forces at several key policy moments. As the social regulatory policy framework predicts, a primary convergence point is the legislative arena.

CHAPTER 5

Institutions, Policymaking, and Guns

REPRESENTATIVE McCORMACK: You have contacted such as you could and wired the members of the [National Rife] Association?

GENERAL RECKORD: In each state, or practically every state, we have a state rifle association, and we advised a number of those people that the hearing would be held today. . . .

McCORMACK: Did you ask them to wire here?

RECKORD: I do not recall the exact language of the telegram; I would say yes, probably we did. . . .

McCORMACK: Did you wire the people telling them what the recommendations were going to be to the Committee?

RECKORD: No, except that the legislation was bad.

McCORMACK: And they blindly followed it?

RECKORD: I would not say blindly.

—Exchange between Representative John W. McCormack (D-Mass.) and General M.A. Reckord, executive vice president of the NRA, concerning the flood of mail members of Congress had received in response to an NRA message that erroneously claimed that pending legislation would lead to federal fingerprinting and photographing of all gun purchasers (1934)

THE INTEREST-GROUP PRESSURES discussed in chapter 4 converge primarily on Congress. As the sparring from 1934 between Representative McCormack and General Reckord suggests, the political texture of gun issues in Congress has maintained an astonishing degree of similarity in the past seven decades. The NRA was actually far more amenable to gun regulations in the 1930s, however, than in the past three decades; for example, it helped draft a handgun waiting period law for the District of Columbia in the 1930s. Yet the policy line since that time reflects, one might argue, a regression (either desirable or undesirable, depending on one's point of view). In the 1930s, national gun registration was openly advanced as an achievable national policy. In the 1990s, gun control supporters would have hailed as a great, even landmark, victory the passage of a modest, even marginal, policy change—enactment of a five-day waiting period for handgun purchases.

In this chapter we examine the political and policy roles of Congress, the president, and the key federal agency involved with gun regulation. As hypothesized in chapter 1, we would expect Congress to play an important and highly visible role in social regulatory policy, serving as a primary focal point for national policy conflict. In comparison, the president plays a relatively marginal role in social regulatory policy—marginal, that is, in comparison to the president's involvement with other kinds of policy. This does not mean that presidents are either indifferent to or impotent in the social regulatory area, but that other forces play a larger role and that key political conflict unfolds in the halls of Congress.

In addition, federal agencies involved with social regulatory policy find their work under close and critical scrutiny from the outside. As a consequence, such agencies typically are buffeted by political forces emanating from Congress, the president, and interest groups. The significance of this assertion is that it differs from the general evaluation of the federal bureaucracy as a domineering force in American politics, relatively unimpeded by outside political forces, that suffers from too much, rather than too little, power.[1] The primary federal agency involved with gun matters, the Bureau of Alcohol, Tobacco, and Firearms (ATF), is categorized as a regulatory agency, which supports the idea that its decisions and activities are subject to considerable political counterforce.

Early Legislative Efforts

The first congressional action pertaining to guns was the enactment of a 10 percent federal excise tax, passed as part of the War Revenue Act in 1919.[2] It was more significant as a revenue-raising measure than as a tool of regulation, and it survived the 1920s despite several efforts to reduce the tax.

In 1927, responding to popular fears of handgun use by criminals, Congress passed a bill to prohibit the sale of handguns to private individuals through the mail. This measure passed when other gun control efforts failed because it was justified by its supporters as a measure that supported, rather than eroded, state sovereignty. That is, proponents argued that such a federally imposed ban would prevent the Post Office from unintentionally aiding in breaking the laws of states with tougher gun regulations. The significance of this argument lay in the prevailing reluctance to extend federal power over the states in the period preceding Franklin Roosevelt's New Deal. The Post Office was an enthusiastic supporter of the bill, but it found little support from President Coolidge or others in the executive branch. Thus, more ambitious efforts at handgun regulation, such as a bill to regulate the interstate commerce of handguns, never survived committee consideration. The mail ban on handguns enacted in 1927 was little more than symbolic, however, because no regulations were imposed on sending handguns via private express companies, and individuals were free to cross state lines to make gun purchases.

By the early 1930s, gangsterism had become a national problem, fed by the depression, Prohibition, and a new generation of powerful weapons. Responding to this new wave of crime, and spurred by growing impatience with past federal inaction, the Roosevelt administration won passage of new crime legislation. As part of this effort, the Justice Department pushed strongly for more comprehensive gun control, including registration of machine guns, submachine guns,[3] handguns, silencers, cane guns, sawed-off shotguns, and the like.

Yet the original bill was substantially weakened in committee. Most important, handguns were removed from the bill, at the urging of the National Rifle Association and other gun groups. Ironically, the Roosevelt administration's emphasis on the gangster threat (the notorious gangster John Dillinger was hunted and gunned down in the summer of 1934) as a justification for the bill helped opponents to pare it down so that what emerged focused solely on gangster-type weapons. The National Firearms Act of 1934 (48 Stat. 1236) was the last gun bill actively touted by Roosevelt, although his Justice Department continued to press for national handgun registration. This year also marked the establishment of the NRA's Legislative Division.

A year later, the Justice Department went to work on a new bill, which eventually became the Federal Firearms Act of 1938 (52 Stat. 1250). Once again, however, gun regulation opponents prevailed. The 1938 law gave the Treasury Department control over a national licensing system incorporating gun dealers, manufacturers, and importers. But the key power to prosecute those who bore responsibility for putting guns in the hands of criminals was effectively neutralized when language was added in committee making successful federal prosecution dependent on being able to prove that the gun provider sold guns to criminals knowingly, a standard the Justice Department knew it could rarely if ever meet. (Indeed, those selling weapons were not required to verify the eligibility of those making gun purchases.) Recognizing this, the Justice Department withdrew from further involvement with the bill in Congress, discouraged at the outcome and fearing (correctly) that its association with the bill would undercut future efforts to enact tougher laws, including national firearms registration.[4]

The Justice Department's withdrawal resulted in consolidation of the NRA's control over the bill, as the gun group moved "from coauthor to chief architect of the 1938 act." By the time of its enactment, the bill "had become the gun lobby's protégé."[5] Even so, the NRA continued to tout its fervent opposition to gun regulations.

Symptomatic of the impotency of this legislation is the fact that from the 1930s to the 1960s, fewer than 100 arrests per year occurred under any provision of the act. In addition, the low license fee for dealers ($1 in the 1938 act; the fee was increased to $10 in 1968) encouraged private citizens to acquire dealer licenses to circumvent the law.

These early gun control efforts share several traits in common. First, the primary basis for support for such legislation came from the general public and from elements of the executive branch. Second, these forces by themselves were relatively ineffective and unsuccessful in battling the well-organized and motivated forces opposing such controls as the measures moved through Congress. Even in this early stage, the antiregulation movement was spearheaded by the NRA. Third, the fates of these bills were all resolved in congressional committees. Unlike gun bills to come, no grand floor fights broke out over any of these bills in either the House or the Senate, again a reflection of the relative political weakness of gun control proponents. The bills that passed did so with little or no debate, nor public attention. Fourth, the opposition to these bills was fed less by material or business concerns than by the deep-seated, personal feelings of opponents that these bills would impinge on the values identified here as the gun culture.[6] Thus, except for the absence of nasty floor fights, the political dynamics of these early bills clearly reflected those associated in this book with gun control as a social regulatory policy.

The Gun Control Act of 1968

The effort to revise and strengthen federal gun laws that concluded in 1968 had begun in 1963, when the Senate Judiciary Committee held hearings on a bill to ban mail-order handgun sales to minors. After the assassination of President Kennedy in November, the bill was expanded to include a ban on mail-order purchases of shotguns and rifles, but the bill never left committee, owing to pressure applied by the NRA and its allies.[7] President Lyndon Johnson proposed more sweeping gun control legislation in 1965 and in each subsequent year.

The difficulty Johnson faced in achieving enactment of a new gun control measure is underscored by comparing Johnson's failure to win passage of a gun bill until 1968 with his stunning legislative successes throughout his five years in office. No president in modern times has achieved passage of such a large volume of major legislation, and few presidents have had a higher percentage of bills enacted into law, despite the high volume.[8] Johnson's legislative skills and mastery of the intricacies of Capitol Hill politics, acquired during his years as

Senate majority leader, were legendary. Why, then, did Johnson fail to win enactment of this one bill until 1968, the last year of his presidency and a time when his political influence was at its lowest?[9]

The answer lies in the nature of regulatory policy. Recalling the discussion of the four types of policy discussed in chapter 1 (distributive, regulatory, redistributive, and constituent), previous analysis has shown that regulatory policy is both the most controversial and the one over which presidents have been able to exercise the least influence. This pattern was found to hold true not only for Johnson but for all presidents studied.[10] This does not mean that successful enactment of regulatory policies is impossible, but that the odds of enactment—much less enactment in the form presented—are longest for this type. And when one then factors in the unique characteristics of social regulatory policy in general, and gun control in particular, the political "degree of difficulty" for Johnson or any president turns out to be very high.

Prelude

The first important gun control legislation passed by Congress since 1938 was found in Title IV of the Omnibus Crime Control and Safe Streets Act of 1968 (82 Stat. 234). This provision banned the shipment of pistols and revolvers to individuals across state lines and forbade the purchase of handguns in stores in a state where the buyer did not reside. President Johnson found much of this omnibus bill to be highly objectionable, as it was very different from what his administration had proposed, and he nearly vetoed it. The gun control section was but a small element of what his administration had been pushing for, but it was not the primary source of his dismay over the bill.[11] The fact that this gun control provision was lodged in a crime bill accurately reflected the connection between popular anxiety over crime and the push for stronger gun control. Yet the final boost for this bill came from the assassination of Senator Robert F. Kennedy, with the House voting for the bill on 6 June, a day after the shooting of Kennedy (the Senate had passed the bill the previous month) and two months after the assassination of Martin Luther King Jr.

More Gun Control?

Immediately after passage of the omnibus bill, Senator Thomas Dodd (D-Conn.), chair of the Judiciary Subcommittee on Juvenile Delinquency, introduced an administration-backed gun bill in the Senate that had as its centerpiece the registration of all firearms and licensing of gun owners. The measure was introduced in the House by Rep. Emanuel Celler (D-N.Y.), chair of the Judiciary

Committee. The bill that emerged at the end of the legislative gauntlet was still a gun control bill, but it failed to include these two central provisions.

President Johnson urged Congress "in the name of sanity . . . in the name of safety and in the name of an aroused nation to give America the gun-control law it needs."[12] After weakening Johnson's bill, the House Judiciary Committee initially voted 16–16 on the bill, thus failing to report it out of committee. An agreement was reached to reconsider the legislation, however, and it was finally reported out on 21 June. The House Rules Committee approved a rule for the bill on 9 July, after holding the legislation for nearly three weeks. Rules Committee chair William Colmer (D-Miss.), a gun control opponent, released the bill only after extracting a promise from Celler that he would oppose any efforts to add registration and licensing provisions to the bill on the floor of the House.

The House passed H.R. 17735 on 24 July after four days of vigorous floor consideration characterized by numerous attempts to amend the bill. Efforts were made to strengthen registration and licensing provisions, increase penalties, deregulate ammunition sales, provide exceptions for collectors, and curtail importation of foreign military weapons. Overall, forty-five attempts were made to amend this legislation on the House floor (eighteen accepted, twenty-seven rejected, with wins and losses for both sides), including four roll-call votes plus one more on final passage.

In the more sympathetic Senate, the gun bill found greater support, and more debate centered on whether to strengthen the law or not. Subcommittee hearings began on 26 June, and testimony was received from a wide variety of witnesses, including NRA President Harold W. Glassen, who said that the legislation was part of an effort to "foist upon an unsuspecting and aroused public a law that would, through its operation, sound the death knell for the shooting sport and eventually disarm the American public."

The Senate subcommittee approved the measure unanimously and forwarded it to the full committee, where the bill encountered stiff opposition. The bill was delayed and weakened by gun control opponents, including Judiciary Committee chair James Eastland (D-Miss.). Efforts to push the bill through were hampered by the absence at various times of gun control supporters, including Senator Edward Kennedy (D-Mass.), who was still mourning the loss of his brother.

Finally, the bill was sent by committee to the Senate floor, where it was debated for five days. The opening salvo came from Senator Dodd, who accused the NRA of "blackmail, intimidation and unscrupulous propaganda." Debate centered on attempts to nationalize gun registration, strengthen criminal penalties, and create special exemptions for gun collectors and sportsmen. In all, seventeen formal motions were made to amend the bill on the floor (nine accepted, eight rejected, again with wins and losses for both sides). Eleven recorded votes were taken. After the bill's passage on 18 September, a conference committee ironed out differences with the House, and Johnson signed the bill on 22 October.

As enacted, the Gun Control Act of 1968 (82 Stat. 1226) banned the interstate shipment of firearms (handguns and long guns) and ammunition to private individuals; prohibited the sale of guns to minors, drug addicts, mental incompetents, and convicted felons; strengthened licensing and record-keeping requirements for gun dealers and collectors; extended federal regulation and taxation to "destructive devices" such as land mines, bombs, hand grenades, and the like; increased penalties for those who used guns in the commission of a crime covered by federal law; and banned the importation of foreign-made surplus firearms, except for those appropriate for sporting purposes. These measures represented a significant advance in law over previous federal gun regulation efforts. Yet they were also modest and did not include the blanket registration and licensing proposals Johnson had sought—that is, the core of Johnson's gun agenda.

Political Assessment

The signs of a fierce and difficult political struggle for even this modest bill were everywhere. A useful way to think about political conflict in Congress for this or any bill is to envision each house of Congress as having two "arenas," or areas where important actions on bills are taken: in committee and on the floor. It is a truism of Congress that most important work on bills occurs in committees.[13] Sometimes, however, legislation that is either exceptionally important or very controversial continues to be the focus of deliberation, debate, and amendment on the floor of either or both houses. Thus an important indicator of controversy and political struggle is the extent of debate and amendment on the floor.[14] A second important indicator is the bypassing of standard congressional procedures, such as normal committee consideration, or use of such unusual procedures as the discharge petition in the House or the filibuster in the Senate.

In the case of the Gun Control Act, the legislative history reveals contentiousness both in committee and in floor consideration (it is rare to find no conflict in committee and great conflict during floor consideration). Committees in both chambers made substantial changes to the bill, for the most part contrary to the president's wishes (this is particularly significant in the House Judiciary Committee, where the chair strongly supported Johnson's bill).

The many amendment efforts on the floors of both chambers further reflected controversy, as did the continued failure of the president and his allies in Congress to retain the core gun control provisions they sought. In more quantifiable terms, the number of recorded votes taken on the bill can be compared to those of the 165 most important bills considered by both houses of Congress from 1954 to 1974. By that tally, only 6 bills (out of 165) had more roll-call votes in the House than the Gun Control Act, and only 27 bills had more roll-call votes in the Senate (again out of 165).[15] One may therefore conclude that the gun act was one of the most controversial and contentious bills that was considered by Congress during this twenty-year period.

Given clear evidence of President Johnson's limited influence over the bill, why did it pass? First, as discussed in chapter 4, the public had long favored stronger gun controls. A second and necessary condition was the fact that, like the omnibus act, latent public support was aroused and motivated by the rising fear of crime and was galvanized by the political shock waves caused by recent assassinations.[16] Third, support from the administration was still a factor and a contributing influence. And fourth, gun control supporters gave in on key elements of Johnson's original proposal to win the necessary support to enact some kind of gun regulation bill.

Consequences

The actual consequences of the 1968 act were several. First, the number of gun dealers increased, even though dealer regulations were tightened and gun dealer license fees were increased to $10. Second, the importation of shotguns increased, while that of rifles decreased. Third, even though handguns have little to no hunting purpose, handguns that did not fit the definition of Saturday night special (defined by the ATF as those with a barrel length of three inches or less, that fired a .32 caliber or smaller bullet, and that sold for less than $50) continued to be imported. Even so, total handgun imports dropped, but domestic handgun production increased. Finally, taking advantage of the fact that the law regulated gun imports, but not the import of gun parts, handgun parts imports increased dramatically.[17]

Thus the Gun Control Act was the most sweeping federal gun regulation enacted up to that time. Yet its scope was very modest. As a consequence, its impact was minimal. Despite this fact, gun control opponents immediately set to work to erode the act, if not overturn it entirely. One year later, for example, Congress repealed a provision of the act requiring sellers of shotgun and rifle ammunition to register purchasers.[18] The effort to neutralize the 1968 act climaxed with the Firearms Owners Protection Act.

The Firearms Owners Protection Act of 1986

The passage of this next important gun bill can be traced in large measure to the efforts of two gun control opponents: Senator James McClure (R-Idaho) and Rep. Harold Volkmer (D-Mo.). In fact, the bill passed in 1986 came to be known as the McClure-Volkmer bill.

As early as 1978, Representative Volkmer proposed legislation to repeal much of the 1968 act. Senator McClure's efforts began in the early 1980s. These parallel efforts picked up important momentum from the election of gun control foe Ronald Reagan and the attendant more conservative mood of the country, and from the fact that the Republicans won control of the Senate after the 1980 elections (they lost their majority in the 1986 elections). Intensive and serious pressure picked up in the two years preceding the bill's enactment, as did the protracted lobbying effort of the NRA, joined by the Gun Owners of America and the Citizens Committee for the Right to Keep and Bear Arms.

Earlier versions of the McClure-Volkmer bill had been approved by the Senate Judiciary Committee in 1982 and 1984, but full floor consideration was not obtained until 1985 when, at the urging of bill sponsors, Senate Majority Leader Robert Dole (R-Kans.) authorized the unusual move of bypassing the Judiciary Committee and placing the bill directly on the Senate calendar. Once on the floor, the bill was subjected to a barrage of amendments designed to strengthen gun controls; none of these amendments, however, was accepted. Senator Edward Kennedy proposed that the ban on the interstate sale of handguns be retained. Senator Charles McC. Mathias (R-Md.) moved to eliminate a provision requiring that gun dealers be given prior notice before routine inspections by federal investigators. Senator Daniel K. Inouye (D-Hawaii) proposed a fourteen-day waiting period between purchase and delivery of handguns, a provision supported by many law enforcement groups.

But the bill's chief Senate sponsors, McClure and Orrin Hatch (R-Utah), argued that the proposed restrictions would have no effect on crime fighting but represented unjustified limitations on sportsmen, hunters, and dealers. The one significant restriction adopted by the Senate was a ban on the importation of Saturday night special gun parts.

Bill opponents, led by Kennedy and Howard Metzenbaum (D-Ohio), threatened a filibuster in June if some of the bill's provisions were not softened. Supporters yielded, and after intense negotiations, the bill, S. 49, was passed on 9 July 1985. In all, four roll-call votes were taken.

The final vote for passage of the bill was 79–15, with the strongest support coming from senators from western and southern states. The relatively speedy passage of the bill was attributed to the pressure of the NRA and its allies and to the fact that the Republican-controlled Senate had a sympathetic Judiciary Committee chair (Strom Thurmond, R-S.C.) and majority leader (Robert Dole).[19]

Deliberations in the Democratic-controlled House posed a far greater problem for McClure-Volkmer supporters. Judiciary Committee chair Peter Rodino (D-N.J.), a staunch gun control proponent, had announced early in 1985 that the bill arrived "D.O.A.—Dead on Arrival." Bill opponents were still confident that Rodino would succeed as he had in the past in keeping the bill bottled up in committee. Yet Rodino was unable to fulfill his prediction. By the fall of 1985, bill supporters had begun a discharge petition that, if signed by a majority of the House membership (218), would force the bill out of committee and onto the floor. The drastic and unusual nature of the House discharge petition is revealed by the fact that, from 1937 to 1986, discharge petitions had succeeded in only twenty instances. Of those, only two such bills were actually enacted into law.[20]

Despite the initial opposition of Rodino and Rep. William J. Hughes (D-N.J.), chair of the Judiciary Subcommittee on Crime, they both realized that unless they formulated a substitute compromise bill, the full committee would be forced to report McClure-Volkmer. The committee thus held a markup session on a compromise bill and reported it to the floor by unanimous vote. This remarkable turn of events occurred in March 1986 as the result of a successful discharge petition. By reporting the Rodino-Hughes bill to the floor first (on 11 March) before the actual filing of the discharge petition on behalf of McClure-Volkmer (on 13 March), gun control supporters hoped to salvage some parliamentary flexibility that would allow priority consideration of the Rodino-Hughes bill. This maneuver failed because Volkmer was able to offer his version of the bill as a substitute for that of the Judiciary Committee in a vote on the floor.

On 9 April, Representative Hughes offered a package of law enforcement amendments to McClure-Volkmer, including a ban on interstate sale and transport of handguns and stricter record-keeping regulations. The package was rejected by a wide margin (176–248). During the vote, police officers stood in full uniform at "parade rest" at the entrance to the House floor as a sign of their opposition to McClure-Volkmer. After several other votes on motions to strengthen certain gun control provisions (all were defeated), the House adjourned and then reconvened the next day. This time, on the third try, the House approved (233–184) a ban on interstate handgun sales after proponents stressed the difference between sale and transport. A final amendment to bar all future possession and sale of machine guns by private citizens also passed. The bill was approved by a lopsided 292–130 vote on 10 April. President Reagan signed the measure into law on 19 May 1986 (P.L. 99–308). In all, seven roll-call votes were taken in the House.

As passed into law, McClure-Volkmer amended the 1968 act by allowing for the interstate sale of rifles and shotguns as long as the sale is legal in the states of the buyer and seller. The act also eliminated record-keeping requirements for ammunition dealers, made it easier for individuals selling guns to do so without a license unless they did so "regularly," allowed gun dealers to do business at gun shows, and prohibited the ATF from issuing regulations requiring centralized records of gun dealers. In addition, the act limited to one per year the number of unannounced inspections of gun dealers by the ATF and prohibited the establishment of any system of comprehensive firearms registration. Finally, the act barred future possession or transfer of machine guns and retained existing re-strictions (except for transport) on handguns.

In a final move to tighten up elements of the bill that was also a concession to law enforcement groups that had opposed McClure-Volkmer, the Senate passed a separate bill on 6 May that tightened licensing, recordkeeping, and interstate transport requirements. That bill easily passed the House on 24 June and was signed into law on 8 July 1986 (PL 99–360; 100 Stat. 449).

Political Assessment

The politics of McClure-Volkmer was distinctive in several important respects. First, despite President Reagan's widely known sympathy for the NRA and its causes—marked particularly by his continued opposition to gun controls during his presidency even after the assassination attempt against him in 1981[21]—his administration played a small role. Officially, the administration supported the bill, but the Justice Department offered no testimony at committee hearings, and internal ATF memos released to the press revealed doubts about some of the decontrol provisions. Public comments by Attorney General Edwin Meese were similarly equivocal.

Second, the bill's passage represented the zenith of the NRA's influence on Capitol Hill. The *New York Times* noted, for example, that during House debate, "it was a measure of the power of the gun lobby that no member of Congress, in the day-long debate, spoke in favor of keeping all the existing controls. Rather, the question was the extent to which they should be eased."[22] Passage of the House bill prompted the comment that the NRA "won almost everything it had sought in a lobbying and advertising campaign that cost about $1.6 million."[23] By contrast, the police coalition spent about $15,000, and Handgun Control, Inc.'s spending was similarly modest. Even so, HCI and its allies acquired a first taste of success in the vote to retain the ban on interstate pistol sales and in the halt to the sale and manufacture of new machine guns (Sarah Brady reported being "thrilled" with this particular part of the bill).[24]

Third, wrangling over the bill solidified the split between the NRA and police organizations. Beyond this, the McClure-Volkmer battle served as an important testing ground for the relatively inexperienced police groups. As one member of Congress observed, "The police misunderstood the force of lobbying. Lobbying is not standing in long lines at the door. Lobbying is good information early; it is a presence when minds are being made up."[25]

Fourth, the bill represented the political coming of age of HCI, as well as the establishment of Sarah Brady as primary spokesperson on behalf of gun control. Clearly, the battle over this bill was key to politicizing Brady on the gun issue.

Fifth, interest-group activity was intense and decisive. As a Senate aide who worked for a gun control supporter commented, "I have never gotten so many vituperative calls on any issue that we've ever dealt with as the gun issue. Violent, violent calls. People calling up threatening me, threatening the senator. Death threats."[26] On the political balance scales, the NRA dominated in a way it would not be able to replicate in the future. Yet gun control supporters could also claim some victories.

Sixth, rhetoric aside, the highly controversial nature of the bill was reflected in the procedures followed in both houses. Even though the measure met less opposition in the Senate, the move to bypass the Judiciary Committee was highly unusual; the filibuster threat was a clear symptom of high controversy, as were the numerous efforts to amend on the floor. In comparison with the 1968 gun act and averages of roll-call votes for important regulatory bills, the four Senate roll calls represent a below-average number. Still, other signs of controversy support the social regulatory policy analysis. In the House, the trends are even more marked. The use of a discharge petition, the extensive debate, and the many efforts to amend all follow the social regulatory policy pattern. And the seven roll-call votes exceed the average reported earlier for regulatory bills in the House. The passage of a special clarifying bill after passage of McClure-Volkmer was another unusual action.

Seventh, an analysis of congressional voting patterns reveals that key factors influencing their votes included region (with strongest support for McClure-Volkmer coming from southern and western representatives), constituency (those from rural districts more likely to support the NRA's positions), and attendant ideological disposition toward the gun issue. The NRA's grassroots efforts were politically influential, as was its overall spending. Yet HCI's lobbying efforts conjoined with the police organizations also had some effect on the final outcome.[27]

The Tide Turns: The Assault Weapons Ban

From 1972 (when the Senate passed a ban on cheap handguns) to 1988, no measure to increase gun controls reached the floor of either house of Congress. In the late 1980s and early 1990s, however, gun control opponents pressed their case for stronger national controls with progressively greater effectiveness and skill, often mimicking the lobbying and organizational tactics that had worked for the NRA. Simultaneously, the lurking national fear of crime, coupled with several sensational mass murders, pushed public opinion more firmly and strongly in favor of new gun regulations.

In the forefront of this effort was the move to regulate or ban various styles of semiautomatic assault weapons. The key event spurring control supporters was a senseless January 1989 schoolyard massacre in Stockton, California, when five children were killed and twenty-nine others were wounded in a shooting spree by drifter Patrick Purdy using a Chinese AK–47 assault rifle (see chapter 3). Within weeks, thirty states and many localities were considering bans on these weapons.[28] Indeed, 1989 witnessed an explosion of interest in such weapons. Two years later, the worst such massacre in American history occurred in Killeen, Texas, when George J. Hennard killed twenty-two people and himself, and wounded twenty-three others, in a cafeteria.[29]

Regulation of such weapons posed a practical problem, because the definition of a semiautomatic weapon is one that fires a round with each pull of the trigger, which would include wooden-stocked hunting rifles. Assault-style semiautomatic weapons are distinguished from others in that they are configured specifically for military use. They typically have large clips holding twenty to thirty bullets, are more compact in design, have barrels less than twenty inches in length, take intermediate-sized cartridges, include extensive use of stampings and plastics, and are lighter in weight (six to ten pounds). In addition, they often have pistol grips or thumbhole stocks, flash suppressors, folding or telescoping stocks, grenade launchers, and bayonet fittings.[30] These are partly designed to facilitate "spray fire."

Responding to advice from within his administration and from the First Lady, George H.W. Bush reversed his opposition to assault weapons regulation within the space of a month, announcing a temporary ban on the import of certain assault rifles by executive order in March 1989.[31] The temporary ban was subsequently expanded to include a larger number of weapons, and then made permanent, earning Bush the ire of the NRA. President Bill Clinton expanded the scope of the import ban in 1993, also by executive order, to include assault-style handguns, such as the Uzi. In 1998, Clinton announced a permanent import ban on fifty-eight additional assault weapons.[32]

In Congress, several bills aimed at curbing or banning assault weapons were introduced in 1989, but those bills languished in committee until 1990, when the Senate narrowly approved a provision to ban the production, sale, and possession of nine semiautomatic assault-type weapons. The provision was added to an omnibus crime bill. The House Judiciary Committee had approved a similar measure, but it never left committee. In conference committee, the assault weapons ban was removed from the bill that was enacted into law.

In 1991, the Senate again included an assault weapons ban in a larger crime bill. A similar provision was included in the House version of the bill, but it was stripped out in a highly emotional floor vote that occurred one day after the massacre in Killeen, Texas.

In November 1993, the Senate passed a ban on the manufacture of nineteen assault weapons, but it also included a provision allowing gun dealers to sell guns that had already been produced. The measure, added to a crime bill, also exempted more than 650 types of hunting weapons. That same month, the Senate also passed a measure making it a federal crime to sell handguns to minors.[33]

In the spring of 1994, the House took up the assault weapons ban. From the start, ban supporters shared little optimism that the House would approve the measure. In April, President Clinton weighed in strongly for the ban, enlisting the help of several cabinet secretaries, most notably treasury secretary and gun owner Lloyd Bentsen. Ban supporters received unexpected help from Rep. Henry Hyde (R-Ill.), a staunch conservative who had opposed gun measures in the past. Thanks in part to Hyde's support, the measure was approved by the Judiciary Committee on 28 April, despite the opposition of committee chair Jack Brooks (D-Tex.).[34]

As the House floor vote approached, bill supporters all but admitted defeat, noting that they were probably fifteen votes shy. Democratic leaders were split on the bill, as House Speaker Tom Foley (D-Wash.) opposed the measure, while Majority Leader Richard Gephardt (D-Mo.) favored it. Yet in a stunning finale, the assault weapons ban managed to pass by a two-vote margin, 216–214 on 5 May. The drama was heightened when Rep. Andrew Jacobs Jr. (D-Ind.), at the urging of several colleagues, switched his vote from against to for in the final seconds of the roll-call vote.

As is true of other congressional votes on gun control, more Democrats supported the measure than Republicans, yet party was not the key dividing factor: 177 Democrats were joined by 38 Republicans plus one independent in favor of the bill, with 137 Republicans and 77 Democrats opposed. The bill's strongest opposition came from southern and western representatives. As with other gun bill votes, the politics was intense. A staffer for one freshman Republican representative who supported the bill commented, "You don't know the threats we received."[35]

Because the assault weapons ban was part of a larger crime bill that had passed in different versions in the two houses, a conference committee was called to iron out the differences. Typically, a bill that survives the legislative gauntlet up to the point of conference committee is all but assured final passage. Such was not the case for the assault weapons ban.

Bill supporters initially predicted that the conference committee would complete its work by the end of May. Yet it did not report a bill back to the House and Senate until the end of July, during which time Representative Brooks, a member of the House-Senate conference, attempted repeatedly to kill the assault weapons ban. Brooks's efforts failed, but he did succeed in inserting provisions that exempted pawnbrokers from the Brady law (see below) and that barred all antihunting protests from taking place on federal lands. Meanwhile, Republican leaders launched a full-scale assault on the $33 billion crime bill, calling it a wasteful piece of legislation laden with pork-barrel spending. These criticisms took on added legitimacy when it was revealed that Representative Brooks had succeeded in slipping into the bill a $10 million appropriation to establish a center for criminal justice at his alma mater, Lamar University (located in his Texas congressional district).

Despite the charges of pork, the bill's progress was impeded primarily by the assault weapons ban and the inclusion of a provision that barred the use of statistics to help prove racial bias in criminal cases involving the death penalty. This latter measure alienated many members of the congressional Black Caucus, who would have otherwise provided key support for President Clinton. Because of the concern that the death penalty is applied disproportionately against black men, blacks in Congress were also dismayed by a provision adding more than fifty new federal crimes for which the death penalty could be applied.

Anxious to win final approval, and with an eye toward the fall elections, Clinton and his congressional allies pushed for an early vote in the House. This proved to be a serious tactical blunder because they had not lined up the necessary support. In a dramatic reversal on a procedural vote to adopt a rule for the bill, the House rejected the crime bill on 11 August by a vote of 225–210. Especially embarrassing was the fact that fifty-eight Democrats voted against the bill. As with other gun votes, opposition was strongest in the South. Sixty-four percent of the defecting Democrats (thirty-seven of the fifty-eight) were from the South; most of the rest came from strong gun states in the Midwest and West. Eleven Republicans supported the bill. Although twenty-seven members of the congressional Black Caucus supported Clinton on the vote, eleven did not (including the lone Republican member of the caucus, Gary Franks of Connecticut).

Under normal circumstances, a defeat on a rules vote would spell the end of the legislation. Yet President Clinton would not accept defeat, vowing to "fight and fight and fight until we win this battle for the American people." Clinton launched an intensive public campaign, enlisting the assistance of police organizations and several members of his cabinet. Congressional leaders vowed to bring back the bill, and in another departure from normal procedure, they negotiated a new version of the bill, this time cutting the bill's spending by about 10 percent ($3.3 billion), including Representative Brooks's $10 million allocation for Lamar University. In addition, in order to sway some moderate Republicans, a provision was added to allow evidence of previous sex crimes to be introduced in subsequent such trials. Throughout the negotiations process, many supporters of the bill urged Clinton to drop the assault weapons ban from it in order to ensure passage, but Clinton refused to budge on the matter. Throughout this period, the NRA lobbied intensively to kill the assault weapons provision.

On 21 August, after three days and two nights of negotiation, the revised bill was brought before the House in a highly unusual Sunday session. This time, with the help of moderate Republicans and four members of the Black Caucus—Cleo Fields (D-La.), Gary Franks (R-Conn.), John Lewis (D-Ga.), and Charles Rangel (D-N.Y.)—who were persuaded to vote with the president, the bill passed by a vote of 235–195 (after two other affirmative procedural votes for the bill). This time, forty-six Republicans supported the bill in a bipartisan effort that led many to proclaim "a new era of cooperation" between the parties. Key moderate Republicans, including junior House members, played an uncharacteristically major role in the negotiations process with the White House. Stubborn opposition from anti-gun control Democrats made such bipartisan bargaining necessary.

The bill then went to the Senate, where the bipartisan spirit quickly evaporated as opponents expressed dismay over the fact that the House had taken the highly unusual action of altering the original conference committee version. Bill opponents sought to bring back the original conference version, a move that would have effectively ended the bill's chances for 1994. In the Senate as well as the House, the primary focus of contention was the assault weapons ban.

On 23 August, Senate Minority Leader Robert Dole announced that forty Republicans (plus Dole himself) had agreed to block the crime bill, which would have killed the measure because a bloc of forty-one could prevent any move to end debate. Two days later, however, in a crucial procedural vote, bill supporters won the votes of sixty-one senators, with thirty-nine voting in opposition. Six Republicans defected to support the bill; one Democrat voted against it. The six Republicans were John Chafee (R.I.), John Danforth (Mo.), James Jeffords (Vt.), Nancy L. Kassebaum (Kans.), William Roth (Del.), and Arlen Specter (Pa.). The one defecting Democrat was Richard Shelby (Ala.). After an additional procedural vote, the bill was passed by the Senate, and Clinton signed the bill, H.R. 3355, on 13 September 1994 as Title XI of the Violent Crime Control and Law Enforcement Act (PL 103–322; 108 Stat. 1796).

In its final form, the assault weapons ban outlawed for ten years the sale and possession of nineteen specified types of weapons, as well as dozens of "copycat" weapons that possessed two or more characteristics of the nineteen named types. It also specifically exempted 661 sporting rifles and limited gun clips to those that could hold no more than ten bullets. Existing assault-style rifles were exempted from the ban, and Congress was given the power to review the inclusion of additional weapons under the terms of the measure.

Thus, in a five-year period, the assault weapons ban was submitted to a vote six times on the floor of the Senate and six times on the House floor. The significance of these votes is underscored by the virulent politics surrounding congressional deliberations (comparable to that described in this chapter for the other gun bills), the bypassing of usual procedures, and the admitted reluctance of many in Congress to deal with any gun control measure. As Representative Hughes noted about the gun issue, "It's one of those issues that members would be just as happy if it would go away. A lot of people have said to me, 'I hope we don't have to take it up next year.'"[36]

That prediction failed to come true. When Republicans won control of both houses of Congress in the 1994 elections, gun control foes found close allies among Republican leaders. Early in 1995, Senate Majority Leader Dole and House Speaker Newt Gingrich (R-Ga.) both publicly pledged to make repeal of the assault weapons ban a top priority. A vote was planned for late spring, but those plans were derailed by the terrorist bombing of a federal office building in Oklahoma City on 19 April. While the 170 people killed died from a fuel oil and fertilizer bomb rather than gunfire, public sentiment turned fiercely against the venomous antigovernment rhetoric that had accompanied efforts to repeal the weapons ban. This sensitivity was heightened because of evidence that the explosion was the work of one or more Americans who may have been motivated by a fierce antipathy to U.S. governmental authority (as represented by the federal office building). As time went on, support for repeal of the ban waned.[37]

By 1996, Majority Leader Dole had become the Republican frontrunner for the presidential nomination, which prompted him to downplay his earlier promise to seek repeal. Nevertheless, a vote to repeal the ban was brought to the floor of the House on 22 March 1996. The repeal passed by a vote of 239 to 173 (not enough to override an expected veto from President Clinton). As in other gun control votes, the parties split on the issue; 183 Republicans voted for repeal, with 42 voting against; 56 Democrats voted for repeal, and 130 against. This division of party loyalties was especially significant because party-line voting reached record high levels in 1995 and 1996. Finally, regional differences again emerged, in that a majority of northern Democrats voted against repeal, whereas a majority of southern Democrats voted for repeal. Of 69 southern Republicans, all but 4 voted for repeal. Despite the successful vote, it was clear by early 1996 that the Senate would not take up the measure because Dole realized that a prominent stand against the ban might hurt his chances in the presidential election. This ensured that the measure would never reach the president's desk during the 104th Congress. The vote was nevertheless held to fulfill the Republican promise to the NRA.[38]

In policy terms, critics derided the assault weapons ban as purely symbolic politics. Yet crime statistics revealed that assault weapons had a certain criminal appeal. Federal law enforcement officials reported that while assault weapons made up only about 1 percent of all weapons owned nationwide, 5.9 percent of weapons traced to crime use in 1990 were assault weapons; in 1993, the figure rose to 8.1 percent. An Urban Institute study found that assault weapons accounted for 8 percent of guns at crime scenes during a seven-year period in the 1990s, and the Violence Policy Center reported that one in ten law-enforcement officers killed in the line of duty died from an assault weapon. Another indication of the appeal of such weapons to criminals came in May 1996, when federal agents broke up a gun smuggling ring that involved efforts to smuggle Chinese AK–47 assault rifles into the U.S. The investigation was prompted when the weapons began turning up among members of violent California gangs. By 2001, four states (California, Connecticut, New Jersey, and New York), along with several cities, enacted their own bans on assault weapons.[39]

Yet for all the attention focused on assault weapons, another gun issue received even more attention in Congress during this time period: the debate over the imposition of a national waiting period for gun purchases.

The Brady Bill

From 1987 to 1993, gun control proponents placed their primary emphasis on the enactment of a national waiting period for handgun purchases. The purpose of such a rule would be twofold: first, to provide authorities with the opportunity to conduct a background check on the prospective purchaser in order to prevent handgun purchases by felons, the mentally incompetent, or others who should not have handguns; and second, to provide a cooling-off period for those who seek to buy and perhaps use a handgun in a fit of temper or rage. On its face, such a procedure certainly represents a modest degree of government regulation, for it merely postpones a handgun purchase by a few days and denies handguns only to those who everyone agrees should not have them. Yet the struggle over enactment of a waiting period took on epic proportions as a bitter power struggle between regulation opponents and proponents, where the ground being fought over was far less important than the struggle itself.[40]

Act One

The so-called Brady bill (named after James Brady, the former White House press secretary and subsequent gun control advocate who was seriously injured in the assassination attempt against President Reagan in 1981) was introduced in early 1987 in the Senate by Howard Metzenbaum and in the House by Rep. Edward F. Feighan (D-Ohio). It quickly became the top priority of HCI and Sarah Brady, James Brady's wife and HCI leader. The NRA opposed the measure, saying that it would simply be a prelude to stronger regulation, that it would not stop criminals from getting guns, and that it merely inconvenienced those entitled to guns. As late as the mid–1970s, however, the NRA had supported such a waiting period. This change can be taken as one evidence of the NRA's increasingly hard line on any and all gun controls.

The Brady bill was put up to a chamberwide vote for the first time in the House in September 1988, when opponents led by the NRA succeeded in defeating the bill (by substituting an NRA-backed amendment for the waiting period, approved by a vote of 228–182), despite a concerted effort by HCI and a coalition of police organizations called the Law Enforcement Steering Committee. By its own account, the NRA spent between $1.5 million and $3 million in the successful effort to kill the bill, mostly on a media campaign and grassroots efforts. Assessing the failed effort, Representative Feighan noted that at least two dozen House members had privately spoken of their support for the bill but had refused to vote for it, not because they feared losing their seats, but because of "the aggravation" that accompanied opposing the NRA (what was discussed in chapter 4 as the "hassle factor").[41]

Act Two

Two years later, both chambers voted to approve the Brady bill. Initial House approval for a seven-day waiting period came in May 1991 (by a 239–186 vote), with Senate approval (by a 71–26 vote) following a month later. Before passing the Brady bill, the House defeated an NRA-backed substitute, sponsored by Rep. Harley O. Staggers (D-W.Va.), that called instead for an instant computerized background check of prospective handgun purchasers. Such a system would, in theory, eliminate the need for waiting yet still bar gun purchases by those not eligible.

The problem with such a proposal, according to critics, is that successful operation of such a system would require that pertinent records from all the states be fully automated. Yet in 1991, only ten states had such automation; eight states still handled files manually, and nine states did not even maintain the necessary felony records. Moreover, according to an analysis by Congress's Office of Technology Assessment, the time lapse between the conclusion of a criminal case and its logging in state records runs from weeks to months. Thus the actual development of a viable system would take years and would cost hundreds of millions of dollars. The political strategy behind the Staggers proposal was based on the principle that a motion is easier to defeat if the opposition has something to offer in its place. By proposing an alternative of little or no feasibility, the NRA and its allies were offering a plan that seemed to offer a meaningful reform yet posed no actual change in gun purchasing procedures for many years to come.[42] The Staggers proposal became Brady bill opponents' chief rallying point.

The Senate version, approved in June 1991, differed from that of the House in two important respects. First, it called for a five-day, instead of seven-day, waiting period. Second, the Brady provision was attached to an omnibus crime bill, over which the two chambers wrangled throughout the year.

A conference version was hammered out in November that rolled the Brady provision (with a five-day waiting period) and a compromise crime bill together. The House narrowly approved that bill on 27 November. The Senate finally brought the compromise bill to the floor for a vote on 19 March 1992, but Republicans used the unique Senate device of the filibuster (i.e., unlimited debate) to force bill sponsors to withdraw the measure after a vote to end debate (to invoke "cloture") failed. Such a cloture vote to end a filibuster poses a special problem because it requires an extraordinary majority of sixty votes to pass, instead of the normal majority of fifty-one required for most Senate actions.

Democratic leaders brought the bill back a second time in the fall, but the failure to end a second filibuster in a vote on 2 October killed the bill. Majority Leader George Mitchell (D-Maine) also attempted unsuccessfully to force a separate vote on a seven-day waiting period. By this point, however, concern over the impending elections overshadowed further efforts.

President Bush publicly opposed the Brady bill throughout 1991 and 1992 but linked it with the larger crime bill, saying that he would sign the measure even if Brady was included—but only if the larger crime bill was to his liking. Bush's veto threat hung over the bill, yet it also opened the door to presidential approval because it provided a means whereby he could have signed the measure into law without seeming to abandon his inclination to oppose most gun control measures entirely. In the end, Bush's qualified veto threat had little effect on the outcome, except to the extent that it buttressed the cause of Senate Republicans, who succeeded in blocking the measure.[43]

Act Three

The Brady bill struggle climaxed in 1993 when supporters promoted a five-business-day waiting period. House Judiciary Committee approval was won on 4 November, despite the objections of committee chair and gun control opponent Jack Brooks, who also boosted the bill's chances by consenting with reluctance to separate the measure (H.R. 1025) from a new crime bill. Six days later, the full House approved the Brady bill after fending off several amendments (sponsored by Republicans and Representative Brooks) designed to weaken the bill. One such amendment, to phase out the waiting period after five years, was adopted. The final vote to pass the bill, H.R. 1025, was 238–189.

Following the lead of the House, the Senate separated the Brady bill (S. 414) from the larger crime package. The bill faced a Republican filibuster almost immediately, but this move was forestalled by an agreement between the political party leaders to allow floor consideration of a substitute version that included two NRA-backed provisions. The first called for all state waiting periods to be superseded by the federal five-day waiting period (twenty-four states had waiting periods of varying lengths in 1993; twenty-three also had background checks). This was objectionable to Brady supporters because many states had waiting periods longer than five days, and the move was seen as a violation of states' rights. This amendment was stricken from the bill by a Senate floor vote. The second measure called for ending the five-day waiting period after five years. It survived a vote to kill it. The Senate then faced another filibuster, which looked as though it would be fatal to the bill. Brady supporters and congressional allies all conceded that the bill was dead for the year. The postmortems proved to be premature, however, as within a couple of days the Republicans decided to end their opposition on 20 November, sensing a rising tide of impatience and no sense that they could win further concessions from Democratic leaders. The bill was passed that day by a 63–36 vote.[44]

The bill then went to a contentious House-Senate conference on 22 November. The House passed the conference version early the following morning. Senate Republican leader Robert Dole, however, balked at the compromise, calling it unacceptable. Senate Democratic leader George Mitchell threatened to reconvene the Senate after the Thanksgiving break in order to obtain final action. The two finally reached an accommodation, and the bill was approved in the Senate by voice vote on 24 November, with a promise to consider several modifications in early 1994. President Clinton signed the Brady Handgun Violence Prevention Act (PL103–159; 107 Stat. 1536) into law on 30 November.

As enacted, the Brady law codified a five-business-day waiting period for handgun purchases. It also authorized $200 million per year to help states improve and upgrade their computerization of criminal records, increased federal firearms license fees from $30 to $200 for the first three years and $90 for renewals, made it a federal crime to steal firearms from licensed dealers, barred package labeling for guns being shipped (to deter theft), required that state and local police be told of multiple handgun sales, and stated that police must make a "reasonable effort" to check the backgrounds of gun buyers.

In policy terms, the Brady law's consequences were expected to be modest. First, because the Brady law does not actually require local police to conduct background checks, the federal government cannot prosecute those who fail to do so. And the wide variations in state recordkeeping practices will result in differential application, at least until recordkeeping improves.

Second, state experiences with waiting periods showed that about 1–2 percent of prospective gun buyers were denied sales as the result of background checks, a figure that may be more significant than this percentage suggests, given that a 1991 Justice Department survey showed that roughly one-quarter of state prison inmates reported purchasing their guns legally. In 1992, for example, California turned away 5,763 gun applicants out of a total of more than 500,000 purchases. The ATF reported that it conducted about 90,000 Brady background checks each week, using the National Criminal Information Computer system. About 16 percent of those came up with criminal records, and 6 percent were convicted felons. While such laws seemed to have had no appreciable effect on overall crime rates, they have denied legal purchases to felons and provided the desired "cooling-off period."

After the Brady law went into effect, several surveys verified that the law was operating as expected. In its first three years, about 250,000 gun sales were blocked by the law. In addition, the increase in license fees for gun dealers decreased the number of dealers, from 285,000 before the law to 224,000 one year later (about 80 percent of these dealers were individuals with no storefront). By 1996, the number of licensed dealers had dropped to about 103,000; in 2002, there were still about 103,000 licensed dealers, according to the ATF.[45]

In 1998, the five-day waiting period lapsed, as per the terms of the law, and was replaced by the FBI's National Instant Criminal Background Check System (NICS). This system is designed to allow an immediate background check to occur, although the system has been hampered by gaps in information and other technical problems. The check must be completed within three days, but 95 percent of the background checks are completed within two hours, according to a U.S. Justice Department report. From 1994 to 2000, almost 600,000 handgun purchases have been blocked as the result of background checks. This represented a rejection rate of about 2.5 percent of all handgun purchases. In 2000, twenty-six states conducted their own background checks; the rest relied on FBI data. State checks resulted in a slightly higher rejection rate, probably owing to better and more complete state data. Even though waiting periods are no longer required by the national government, nineteen states have their own, ranging from a few days to several months. These states are Alabama, California, Connecticut, Florida, Illinois, Indiana, Kansas, Maryland, Massachusetts, Minnesota, Missouri, New Jersey, New York, North Carolina, Ohio, Rhode Island, South Dakota, Washington, and Wisconsin. Control proponents have argued for a restoration of a national three-day waiting period, in part because of the perceived value of a cooling off period before handgun purchases.

One area of gun sales continued to be omitted from nationally mandated background checks. In most places, "secondary market" gun sales by unlicensed individuals can occur without background checks. Generally referred to as the gun show loophole, these sales at gun shows, flea markets, and other unregulated venues account for as much as 40 percent of gun sales. As of 2000, eleven states required background checks for all handgun purchases, even those from unlicensed sellers.

In a final twist, foes of the Brady law, including the NRA, challenged its constitutionality—not as a violation of the Second Amendment, but as a violation of states' rights under the Tenth Amendment. In 1997, a sharply divided Supreme Court struck down the provision of the Brady law requiring local police to conduct background checks. In a 5–4 ruling in the case of *Printz* v. *U.S.* (521 U.S. 898), the Court held that Congress had overstepped its power, violating state police power. The ruling did not challenge the propriety of barring handgun sales to those with criminal backgrounds or those deemed mentally incompetent. In the aftermath of the case, President Clinton urged the states to continue to conduct the background checks.

Political Assessment

The political consequences of the Brady law far outstripped its policy consequences. As noted earlier, no gun control measure was put to a vote in either house from 1972 until 1988 (not including McClure-Volkmer, which was a measure to lift gun controls). From 1988 through 1993, eight floor votes were taken on the Brady bill alone (five were votes in favor, with three against; four in the House, and four in the Senate). A crucial swing in favor of the Brady bill occurred in the House between 1988 and 1991. About thirty-five House members actually switched their votes to support the bill, citing repugnance at the NRA's continued strong-arm tactics and the modest nature of the regulation being proposed. In addition, the 1991 House vote helped to deflate the NRA's image of invulnerability. According to Rep. Charles E. Schumer (D-N.Y.), a Brady supporter, "people realized that there's life after voting against the NRA."[46]

The common partisan pattern observed in other gun bill votes emerged here as well. More Democrats supported the Brady bill than Republicans, but both parties were split. In the House, 184 Democrats supported Brady, with 69 opposed (77 percent Democratic support); the Republican split was 54 in favor and 119 opposed (31 percent Republican support). Northern Democrats provided the greatest support for Brady (82 percent); southern Democrats provided the lowest Democratic support (55 percent).[47] As has been true with other gun bill votes, the strongest opposition came from southern, western, and rural representatives (rural districts are concentrated in the South and West), regardless of party. Strongest support came from urban representatives.

As with the other gun bills analyzed in this chapter, consideration of the Brady bill was fraught with contention from beginning to end. The version passed in 1993 had ten roll-call votes in the House and five in the Senate. Consideration was marked by intense lobbying, numerous filibusters in the Senate (despite its reputation, the filibuster is still relatively unusual), many attempts to amend the bill, use of conference committees, and limited presidential influence.

Outside Congress, popular support for the Brady bill continued to swell, especially as concerns over crime once again rose. Moreover, leaders of all ideological stripes voiced Brady bill support, including former Presidents Nixon, Ford, Carter, and Reagan, as well as conservatives such as William F. Buckley.

The election of Bill Clinton put a president in the White House who was much more sympathetic to the aims of gun control proponents. Still, the bill's near-passage in 1992 clearly suggested that time for enactment had come, and Clinton's primary focus in his campaign and his first year in office was on a plethora of other domestic policy issues, not including gun control. Indeed, many of Clinton's people were caught by surprise when Clinton began aggressively to promote gun control in late 1993.[48]

Finally, passage of the Brady law did have one effect predicted by the NRA: it opened the door to further regulations, to the extent that it showed the NRA could be beaten and depicted it as an extremist organization opposed to any regulation, no matter how modest or limited. Similarly, enactment was empowering for the Brady Campaign, police organizations, and others fighting for the control cause. But control opponents renewed their commitment to block further regulation and reaffirmed their resolve to fight on.[49] As the public turned its attention to other matters, the likelihood that further significant controls would be enacted began to diminish. Commenting on the NRA's continued ability to apply political pressure, one member of Congress noted that "it's a lobby that can put 15,000 letters in your district overnight and have people in your town hall meetings interrupting you."[50]

The Post-Columbine Reaction

The 20 April 1999 massacre at Columbine High School in Littleton, Colorado, was the most shocking in a series of high school shootings that occurred in the late 1990s (see chapter 3). In the aftermath of the incident, national shock and outrage put unprecedented pressure on Congress to respond. Senate leadership, headed by gun control foe Trent Lott (R-Mo.), seemed unsure about the Senate's mood on the issue, but yielding to pressure, he advanced a juvenile justice bill to which were added several gun control measures. On 12 May, the Senate rejected a measure to require background checks for gun show sales, but two days later, the Senate reversed itself and adopted the measure, although it was not as strong as Democratic leaders had sought. That same day, the Senate rejected a measure to bar internet sales of guns by unlicensed dealers. On 20 May, the Senate passed a bill that would have required background checks to occur within three days for firearms purchases at gun shows, flea markets, and pawn shops (closing the so-called gun show loophole), revocation of gun ownership for those convicted of gun crimes as juveniles, tougher penalties for juvenile offenders who used guns in crimes and also for those who provided such guns to juveniles, required sale of locking devices or boxes sold with all new handgun purchases, blocked legal immunity to those who sold guns to felons, and a ban on the import of high-capacity ammunition clips (those that could hold more than ten bullets). The final version included a tougher background check provision than had been added by Republicans on 14 May, which was adopted by an unusual 51–50 vote, when Vice President Al Gore, as president of the Senate, cast the tie-breaking vote for the amendment. The final package was approved by a

73–25 vote. As a measure of shifting sentiment, the Senate had defeated attempts to require gun locks and ban the import of high-capacity clips the previous year.

The Senate-passed bill met a chilly reception in the House of Representatives, although the initial reactions of House Speaker Dennis Hastert (R-Ill.) and House Judiciary Committee Chair Henry Hyde (R-Ill.) were positive, as both expressed support for many of the elements of the package. Yet Republican House leaders had long records of opposition to stronger gun laws, and House Majority Whip Tom DeLay (R-Tex.) led the NRA-backed counterattack. By early June, House Majority Leader Dick Armey (R-Tex.) and DeLay had publicly broken with Hastert, vowing to defeat the measure. After several weeks of bargaining and delay, during which time control foes marshaled their resources, the House took three decisive floor votes on 18 June. The first vote narrowly approved (218–211) a weakened gun control package that was sponsored by former NRA board member John Dingell (D-Mich.) and drafted with the guidance of the NRA. This version would have weakened the gun show background check system and opened the door to the interstate sale of handguns, thereby rolling back a restriction that had been on the books for thirty years. The second vote defeated (193–235) a version similar to the tougher Senate-passed bill sponsored by Rep. Carolyn Mc-Carthy (D-N.Y.). The final vote on the overall gun package was defeated (147–280) by a coalition of procontrol representatives who considered the bill too weak, and anticontrol representatives who opposed any new controls. The House thus sent to a House-Senate conference committee a juvenile justice bill without any gun control provisions. It was never reconciled with the Senate version, killing the legislation.

Political Assessment

House stalling tactics gave bill foes, led by the NRA, the time they needed to mobilize opposition and hope for declining public interest as schools let out, families went on vacation, and the country's attention began to turn to other matters. From mid-May to mid-June, the NRA spent $750,000 on mass mailings and $300,000 on phone banks. HCI spent about $350,000 on similar activities. Part of the effort to defeat the new measure included diverting attention away from gun control measures, and toward issues of media violence. Still, passage of the Senate bill marked the first successful effort to pass any new gun law since 1994, indicating the impact of public pressure. Following on the contentious political patterns of the other bills discussed in this chapter, chamber leaders were able to exercise relatively little control; committee preeminence, a hallmark of congressional activity, was contradicted. Extended and heated debate, numerous votes, procedural wrangling, and intense political pressures all marked the politics of this effort.[51]

The Bureau of Alcohol, Tobacco, and Firearms

The ATF traces its history back to 1791 when Treasury Secretary Alexander Hamilton created a tax on spirits that had to be collected by the department. That tax was ended in 1802 but was reintroduced to help finance the Civil War. Even then, the department had to hire people to track down tax evaders. In 1919, the enactment of Prohibition prompted creation of the Prohibition Unit, which then became the Bureau of Prohibition, still under Treasury. (It was this office under which Elliot Ness of "Untouchables" fame operated in the 1920s and 1930s.) The unit then became the Alcohol Tax Unit when Prohibition ended in 1933. The unit was renamed the Alcohol and Tobacco Tax Division in 1951 when it was given jurisdiction over newly instituted tobacco taxes. (By this time, it was a part of the Internal Revenue Service in Treasury.) Although first gaining jurisdiction over guns in 1942, arising from the gun regulations enacted in the 1930s, the agency was given important additional jurisdiction over guns—and its current title—in 1968 as a result of the Gun Control Act of that year, which required the ATF to issue licenses to firearms dealers and oversee proper recordkeeping. In 1972, the ATF was transferred from the IRS and given bureau status within Treasury.[52]

Although the bureau's headquarters are located in Washington, D.C., its operations are relatively decentralized, as most ATF personnel operate from regional offices around the country. The bureau is organized into two sections: regulatory enforcement and criminal enforcement. Matters dealing with gun regulations, including licensing, gun tracing, illegal firearms transport and possession, and explosives, are handled by criminal enforcement. Although long involved in criminal investigations, the ATF possesses neither the size nor the reputation of other federal law enforcement agencies such as the FBI or the Secret Service.

The central political question regarding the ATF's enforcement activities revolves around two contradictory charges. The NRA and its allies charge that the ATF ruthlessly and arbitrarily harasses honest gun owners and dealers and that the agency is a loose cannon. To that end the NRA has publicly and repeatedly attacked the ATF over the years. In the late 1970s and early 1980s, this campaign against the ATF became both mean and angry. In a 1981 NRA-produced film called *It Can Happen Here*, ATF agents were depicted as "Nazi gestapos" and "jackbooted fascists."[53] During congressional hearings the following year, Rep. John Dingell, also an NRA board member, called ATF agents "knaves and rogues" and said, "I would love to put them in jail. I would dearly love it." Of the agency, he said, "I think they are evil."[54]

The demonizing of the ATF reached a fever pitch in the mid–1990s, as the NRA and other opponents tarred the agency with claims of murder and persecution of allegedly innocent citizens. In a full-page newspaper ad run in several national papers in March 1995, the NRA said that the ATF "deserves public contempt." Rep. Harold Volkmer called the ATF "One of the most Rambo-rogue law enforcement agencies in the United States." In one instance, radio talk show host G. Gordon Liddy counseled his listeners to fire "head shots" at ATF agents who approached them because "they've [the agents] got a vest underneath." In 1995, more than 100 ATF agents received death threats, which in some instances included threats against agents' children. Many attributed these vituperative attacks to the NRA's bellicose rhetoric, even suggesting that such rhetoric might have contributed to extremist actions, including the bombing of the federal office building in Oklahoma City in 1995. A former NRA board member, David Edmondson, said of the NRA's attacks on the ATF that "I think these ads, which are going in a direction of radicalism and the militias, are embarrassing to the traditional market of the N.R.A.—Joe Gun Owner."[55]

In contrast, gun control proponents and others have argued that the ATF is a weak and relatively ineffective agency that has been buffeted by the prevailing political winds, especially those stirred up by the NRA. Its multiple and relatively unpopular agency purposes carve out a difficult bureaucratic mission. And given the characteristics of social regulatory agencies, we would expect agency behavior to conform more closely to this view than to that of ATF critics.

ATF Performance

Much of the reputed laxity of ATF enforcement can be traced to its stated objective of relying on voluntary compliance with many of the laws it is charged with enforcing. Yet the enforcement problem predates even the ATF's modern incarnation.

During congressional hearings in 1965, for example, Treasury Department officials acknowledged that only five employees were assigned full-time to enforce the 1934 and 1938 gun laws. In the previous thirty years, Treasury had obtained only one conviction involving the improper mailing of firearms to individuals in states that required purchase permits. An ATF representative reported that during 1980 the bureau had conducted only 103 investigations of firearms dealers and that only ten dealer licenses had been revoked. In 1985, the ATF fielded only 400 inspectors to monitor what were then more than 200,000 gun dealers. In 1994, about 250 agents were responsible for overseeing 280,000 dealers.[56]

To cite a different kind of regulatory lapse, in 1979 the ATF's firearms-technology branch examined the Ingram MAC–10 pistol and recommended that it be classified as a machine gun. This classification would have placed strict controls on the weapon under the National Firearms Act of 1934, but the recommendation was overturned by the agency's firearms-classification panel, which instead put it in the semiautomatic category, freeing it from significant regulation. At the time, fewer than 1,000 of these weapons had been produced. But in the next three years, production increased and the weapon was used in a variety of crimes, including the murder of a Missouri state trooper. In 1982, the ATF re-assessed the status of the weapon, but this time classified it as a machine gun (the weapon is easily converted to either semi- or fully automatic use).[57] But in the reclassification process, ATF exempted the 32,000 MAC–10s produced or sold before 1982. Subsequently, RPB Industries Inc. in Texas has produced a variation of the MAC–10.

In the mid–1980s, ATF and other government officials admitted that gun smuggling and other illegal gun trafficking had not been high enforcement priorities.[58] A 1994 investigation found that the United States was a major source of illegal gun shipments to other countries, in part because the ATF lacked the personnel to monitor the country's then 280,000 gun dealers. The Associated Press reported that Colombian drug lords, Japanese gangsters, Croatian nationalists, Irish gunrunners, Argentine and Philippine rebels, and Mexican drug gangs were among many international groups that had obtained arms from the mostly unregulated U.S. dealers. Government officials expressed concern that the illicit gun trade was on the verge of a significant expansion to nations of the former Soviet bloc.[59]

The Political Balancing Act

The key bureaucratic trait of the ATF is its dependence on executive branch superiors. Unlike other federal agencies, the ATF has no constituency to stand behind it in politically troubled times, nor does it possess statutory independence, as do independent regulatory agencies (e.g., the Food and Drug Administration).

During the Carter administration, political attacks on the ATF were largely fended off. In 1978, however, after the ATF announced plans to computerize its records to facilitate gun tracing—a task legally delegated to the agency—the NRA flooded Congress and the Treasury Department with angry mail aimed at what it labeled the "gun police." As a consequence, Congress denied ATF the $4.2 million appropriation to implement the program. When the ATF then said that it could still fund the program from other budget lines, Congress cut the agency's appropriation by that amount.[60]

ATF opponents found an ally in Ronald Reagan, who moved early in 1981 to abolish the agency entirely, a fate avoided only because of the intervention of Treasury Secretary Donald Regan, who did allow significant budget cuts. In the fall of 1981, Reagan proposed to shift some ATF responsibilities (such as tax collection) back to the IRS, with the ATF's special agents to be transferred to the Secret Service. At the time, the ATF employed 3,900 people and had an operating budget of $160 million.

The proposal initially met with approval from the NRA and dismay from the ATF. One employee commented, "The N.R.A. has finally won." The agency director said that the ATF was being "destroyed by cuts that are in large measure due to the N.R.A. campaign against us."[61] Despite the initial outcry, the ATF's days seemed numbered, until the NRA and its congressional allies realized that the cure might be worse than the disease (they were tipped off in part by the curious reticence of some gun control proponents to speak out against the plan). Instead of keeping gun control in the hands of a beleaguered, low-prestige agency, the new proposal would lodge this authority in the hands of the highly respected, efficient, and fully computerized Secret Service. Labels such as "jack-booted fascists" would never stick to the agency that guards the life of the president.

What followed was furious backpedaling. The plan was suddenly found to be "ill advised" and "unworkable." Representative Dingell claimed that the plan would sully whatever new agencies adopted the ATF mission and employees. "Mix dirty water with clean water . . . and you get dirty water every time," he said. The plan was thus killed, although the agency underwent further budget cuts.[62] According to *Congressional Quarterly*, the proposal died because it met with "fierce opposition from gun owners . . . led by the National Rifle Association, a frequent harsh critic of the BATF."[63] The NRA's subsequent "shrill attacks" on the Reagan administration for continuing to promote the plan before the final agreement to kill it earned the ire of Reagan adviser Edwin Meese, among others.

By the end of Reagan's administration, the ATF had grown to nearly the size it had maintained in the 1970s and had improved its reputation by successful investigations of abortion clinic bombings and crime activities of armed neo-Nazis and other extremist groups.[64] Even so, it still tread carefully in gun activities. For example, it stopped monitoring the thousands of gun shows held yearly around the country, despite the general acknowledgment that widespread illegal gun trafficking occurs at such shows. "If we wanted to," said ATF head Stephen Higgins, "we could go to a gun show and arrest people coming out and just line 'em up."[65]

The ATF suffered a serious loss of prestige in 1993 over its handling of a February 1993 raid on the heavily fortified and armed compound of the Branch Davidian cult near Waco, Texas. (Some have erroneously tied the ATF to the botched raid on Ruby Ridge, Idaho, in 1992, where the agency was not involved.) Four ATF agents were killed and twenty were wounded in an initial assault on the compound, leading to a two-month standoff until FBI agents stormed the fortress, when the cult leader ordered the structure burned to the ground, killing nearly all of those inside. A subsequent report sharply criticized the ATF for mishandling the raid and then lying to cover up its mistakes. Later in 1993, Vice President Al Gore headed a committee that proposed merging the ATF into the FBI (along with the

Drug Enforcement Agency). This time, the plan was not motivated by animus toward gun control but by concern for budget efficiency. The plan was dropped, however, and the new ATF director, former Secret Service Director John Magaw, worked to improve agency morale and effectiveness. Magaw's organizational reforms and a backlash of sympathy for the agency after the Oklahoma City bombing (in which ATF agents were killed, and which was also investigated by the ATF) helped the agency's reputation.[66]

The Clinton administration's support for gun controls meant an expanded mission for the ATF. In 1994, for example, ATF extended the prohibition on armor-piercing bullets to certain bullets that formerly could not be fired from handguns. Rapid-fire, "street sweeper" shotguns were subjected to strict ATF regulation on the directive of Treasury Secretary Lloyd Bentsen. Owners of the 18,000 such weapons in circulation were required to submit to registration, fingerprinting, and photographing (the weapon had been developed for military and riot-control purposes in South Africa). Dealers of such weapons were also subjected to new fees and regulations.[67]

Political Assessment

The NRA's depiction of the ATF as an out-of-control agency that has exceeded its mandate is a claim that is virtually without foundation.[68] While it has no doubt instituted some unjustified prosecutions (an inevitable consequence for any law enforcement agency), its overall record suggests a contrary conclusion. The exaggerated and even wild claims leveled by the NRA are explainable as (1) part of the NRA's political tactic of identifying and attacking an external "enemy" around which it can rally its partisans, (2) a political tactic to put the ATF on the defensive in an effort to curtail its watchdog activities, and (3) the NRA's long-time opposition to any and all government regulation of guns.

The ATF has labored under several bureaucratic and political handicaps. First, it has no native constituency to provide political support from outside the government. Similar agencies, such as the FBI, the Secret Service, and the CIA, have similar circumstances, yet these agencies have been able to compensate for this political deficiency by building strong national reputations for crime fighting and national security work that have insulated them from budget cuts and political attacks. The smaller ATF (its 1996 budget was $400 million, about one-fifth the size of the FBI's) has generally been considered a "second-string" enforcement agency, dealing with less glamorous elements of law enforcement. This becomes clear when the ATF is compared with other federal law enforcement agencies, including the FBI, the Drug Enforcement Agency, the Secret Service, Immigration and Naturalization, and the Bureau of Customs. In 1970, the ATF had the fourth largest budget; by 1995, it had the smallest budget of the six agencies.[69]

Second, the agency's disparate and seemingly marginal purposes have further undercut its bureaucratic standing. Stated more simply, an agency with a "glamorous" and clearly focused mission is more likely to be effective and respected than one whose mission is less well focused and less glamorous. Indeed, a key reason for the ATF's survival as a separate agency was that J. Edgar Hoover did not want agents whose job was tracking down illegal liquor to be a part of the FBI.[70] This problem is summarized by a derisive spinoff of the ATF's name: the Bureau of "Whiskey, Cigarettes, and Pistols."

Third, the agency lacks statutory independence, making it subject to the political preferences of the president and the secretary of the treasury. Thus, the agency's fortunes improved under sympathetic presidents such as Carter and Clinton and declined under less sympathetic presidents such as Reagan. Such a roller-coaster existence has undercut agency morale and therefore its effectiveness.

Fourth, the ATF does not possess the resources to do its job. For example, the agency is charged with regulating those who apply for and obtain federal firearms licenses (that is, a license to deal in guns, which allows the dealer to obtain guns at wholesale prices through the mail, and also exempts the dealer from background checks and waiting periods). The number of such licenses increased 59 percent from 1980 to 1993, yet the number of ATF inspectors actually dropped 13 percent during the same time. As a consequence, 90 percent of these applicants were never interviewed by an ATF inspector. In 1990, the ATF inspected only 2 percent of all gun dealers. Violations are frequently uncovered in the rare inspections that do occur, suggesting widespread violation of federal laws. Even with the dramatic drop in the number of licensed dealers, the ATF still lacks the necessary resources to conduct routine checks on most dealers. And the Firearms Owners Protection Act of 1986, discussed earlier, included a provision weakening the ATF's ability to regulate gun dealers. Clearly, the ATF's inability to carry out the law encourages much suspicious gun trafficking. Similarly, the ATF has been steadily pressured to deemphasize gun control activities, and concentrate instead on the war on drugs.[71] This analysis is confirmed by a close analysis of ATF appropriations patterns from 1970 to 1995, which reveals that ATF appropriations have grown more slowly than that of other, comparable federal law-enforcement agencies (including the FBI, Drug Enforcement Agency, Secret Service, Immigration, and Customs). As for charges that the ATF has recklessly used deadly force, a comparative analysis reveals that the ATF's record is no different from other federal law enforcement agencies' records. Further, the ATF is more strictly constrained by federal law than are other federal law-enforcement agencies. In short, "the ATF is not a powerful bureaucracy," but "the weak sister of federal law enforcement agencies."[72]

Like other agencies involved with social regulatory policy, the ATF has been whipsawed by its political opponents, congressional critics, and even others in the executive branch. Regardless of the course of future national gun control efforts, the ATF will continue to be subject to prevailing political winds.

Conclusion: Furious Politics, Marginal Policy

I noted at the start of this chapter that the proposal advanced by the Roosevelt administration in the 1930s, national gun registration, represented a far more ambitious policy goal than the celebrated (among control advocates) victory of proponents in the early 1990s, a waiting period for handgun purchases. Attendant to these lowering policy objectives has been the achievement of some legislative successes for control supporters. Yet the fury of gun politics has hardly abated. If anything, that fury has become more intense in recent decades. How do we explain the changes in policy focus from the 1930s to the 1990s and the divergent trends of sustaining-to-escalating political intensity versus the regressing policy objectives of control supporters (leaving aside the prospect of more ambitious policy objectives expected in the future)?

The first and most important response is to underscore the common political traits of national institutions as they struggle with social regulatory policy. As expected, Congress has been the primary focal point for efforts to revise national gun policy. Presidents have maintained interest in gun issues but have played a relatively marginal role. The ATF has behaved as an agency besieged. Its fate has hung on the preferences and disposition of its sole political benefactors, the president and the secretary of the treasury. All these institutions have assumed political roles when dealing with social regulatory policy that differ markedly from the common understanding of how these institutions behave: that is, the president leads, Congress follows, and federal agencies operate, within bounds, by their own discretion and organizational mission. That these three institutions behave in an entirely contrary fashion when it comes to gun control—Congress's role is preeminent, the president's role is marginal, and the federal agency is whipsawed by outside interests—speaks to the intractability of the issue and the power of the social regulatory framework.

Second, as to the political forces brought to bear on these national institutions, the NRA has obviously been the dominant actor. Yet its influence peaked with the McClure-Volkmer bill in 1986, and it has witnessed a relative decline in influence attributable to the improved ability of groups advocating gun control to counterbalance NRA influence, especially in the halls of Congress, and to enduring and increasing public support for every gun control idea that has received serious national attention (based on the fear of crime and the general belief that guns should be subject to greater government control, crime notwithstanding). This is not to underestimate the NRA's continued clout; the organization remains one of the most feared, and fearsome, interest groups in American politics.

The nature of interest-group politics is such that the energized and intense backers of the NRA have repeatedly proven the axioms that a highly motivated, intense minority operating effectively in the interest-group milieu will usually prevail in a political contest over a larger, relatively apathetic majority, and that it is easier to prevent policy enactment than cause it. With the exception of Mc-Clure-Volkmer, the NRA's political tack has been opposition to policy enactment. The difficult task for control proponents has been to "ratchet up" elements of the apathetic majority sufficiently to overcome the inertia of inaction. Yet if control supporters have been hampered by the greater difficulty of policymaking offense than defense, they have also benefited from a factor beyond their control—popular revulsion arising from a series of massacres in the late 1980s and 1990s, from Long Island to California, that served as a catalyst for change in the way political assassinations did in the 1960s.

Third, the sustained-to-escalating intensity of gun politics juxtaposed with regressing policy objectives is explainable by the prior success of the NRA in controlling political outcomes, including its notable, yet little-noticed, ability to keep gun issues off the legislative agenda altogether. *To control the agenda is also to control the outcome.* Gun control supporters needed to establish political credibility and puncture the NRA's image of invulnerability by logging a win, any win, against it. The more modest a policy proposal is, the more likely is success. And the NRA's absolutist position against all gun regulations meant that the policy ground was left entirely to control proponents, who could champion the most reasonable, modest, and incremental proposal imaginable.

The sea change in the gun policy struggle is best exemplified by the shift in agenda control in Congress. From 1972 to 1988, no bill to expand gun controls came to a vote on the floor of either house of Congress. From 1988 to 1993, thirteen floor votes on gun bills were taken (on assault weapons, banning handgun sales to minors, and the Brady bill). Of those, nine passed and four failed. The NRA's best strategy has always been to keep gun bills bottled up in committee, or otherwise off the floor of Congress, where bills receive wider public attention, and where control proponents are more able to tap into broad popular sentiments supporting stronger gun measures. Political scientist E.E. Schattschneider identified this phenomenon as expanding the scope of conflict in order to change the outcome (in this case, to the benefit of control supporters).[73]

The NRA's strategy to forestall this pattern broke down in the late 1980s. The fact that this political shift has occurred does not mean that the gun battle is over or that a political climax has been reached. Quite the contrary, the successes of control proponents promise instead more conflict, as control proponents move past marginal controls toward policy options first raised in the 1930s. In the final chapter, we turn to the policy prospects for gun control and a proposal for a new way to think about the gun issue.

CHAPTER 6

Gun Policy:
A New Framework

> The greater the difficulties, the greater is the task of a policy of restraint and
> the merit of those who . . . would know how to forego the "easy" solution,
> the "Gordian knot" solution of force, in favor of a peace that would be nei-
> ther appeasement and abdication nor the Carthaginian result of a war
> which might spell the destruction of our civilization.
> —**John H. Herz, "Idealist Internationalism and
> the Security Dilemma," *World Politics***

THE GUN CONTROL BATTLE is, above all, a struggle over public policy. As the many
elements and cases of the gun issue analyzed in this book reveal, the gun policy
struggle is one in which elephantine political forces battle over policy mice. This
conclusion is surely no surprise to anyone with a passing acquaintance with the
gun issue. At the same time, only a full understanding of the policy issue's scope
and its political consequences can hope to yield any sort of policy synthesis.

The purposes of this chapter are, first, to draw together the primary findings of the previous chapters, and second, to use them as a springboard to propose a new framework for conceptualizing the gun issue, based precisely on its
inflammatory nature, grounded as it is in the social regulatory policy dynamic.
I draw such a framework from an unlikely but entirely logical source—international relations. Before considering these primary purposes, however, we need
first to address one final, crucial matter: the relationship between federalism and
gun control.

Federalism: The Great Regulation Dilemma

America's 20,000 gun regulations belie the central, often ignored fact that nearly
all these regulations exist at the state and local levels. There is reason to believe
that some of these regulations have had an effect on behavior. Nevertheless, de-

spite our country's geographic size and diversity, the ease of long-distance travel means that the flow of arms from low-regulation to high-regulation states continues nearly unabated.[1] Therefore, the question of how state powers and regulations relate to national governmental powers and regulations (a practical definition of federalism[2]) undergirds any analysis of national gun policy.

The New York Case

The situation in New York State provides a classic example of the federalism dilemma. New York enacted the nation's first tough gun law in 1911. Known as the Sullivan Law, the measure imposed strict requirements on the sale, possession, and carrying of concealable weapons.[3] Despite resistance from rural upstate interests, the state has generally maintained among the toughest gun laws in the nation. In order to obtain a handgun license in New York, an individual must be at least twenty-one years old, have no felony convictions or other serious offenses or mental illness, be of "good moral character," submit photos and fingerprints, and pay an application fee of $170. The entire process can take as long as a year, and all licenses must be renewed every two years. Even so, guns continue to pose a major problem, especially in New York City. According to data compiled by the Bureau of Alcohol, Tobacco, and Firearms, 80 to 90 percent of the guns used in crimes throughout the state come from out of state. Virginia is the source for more than one-quarter of these guns, followed by Florida, Texas, Georgia, Connecticut, West Virginia, and Ohio. This flow of guns into New York is referred to as the "iron pipeline." According to the Brooklyn district attorney's office, half of all the guns recovered in this one New York City borough in 1999 came from Georgia, Virginia, and Florida alone.[4] All these states have more lax gun laws. Frustrated at the federal government's continued sporadic and ineffective enforcement efforts, New York began a cooperative effort with Virginia in 1993 to stem the flow of illegal guns between the two states. It also decided to devote more state resources to stemming the illicit gun trade.

New York's cooperative effort with Virginia showed some results. After Virginia imposed a limit of one handgun purchase per month in 1993, the percentage of Virginia-purchased handguns used in crimes fell by 61 percent in New York, 67 percent in Massachusetts, and 38 percent in New Jersey.[5] A 1997 congressional study found that four states—Florida, Georgia, South Carolina, and Texas—were the source for 25 percent of all guns seized in crimes nationwide, and that the ten states with the most lax gun laws accounted for more than half of out-of-state guns used in crimes in 1996. The nation's capital faces a similar problem. A 2000 ATF study found that half of all guns used in Washington, D.C., crimes were purchased from dealers in Maryland and Virginia. Yet the city has among the toughest gun laws in the nation.

This inherent federalism problem was recognized early in the twentieth century when progressives and other reformers proposed "model legislation" to be adopted by the states voluntarily to deal with gun regulation and other emerging national concerns. If the states could all be persuaded to adopt their own versions of model regulations, no federal action would be necessary. The problem with this theory, of course, was that its success depended on complete, or nearly complete, voluntary state compliance—an unattainable goal for almost any policy area. With the coming of the New Deal, the old inhibitions about federal regulation abated.

Recent State Activity

Paralleling an upswing in support for stronger regulations at the national level in the late 1980s and early 1990s, a flurry of state and local gun regulation efforts attracted wide attention. In a move that proved to be a political watershed, Maryland passed a measure (which also survived a tumultuous statewide referendum) in 1988 barring the sale of cheap handguns. California became the first state in the nation to enact an assault weapons ban in 1989, followed by New Jersey in 1990, Connecticut in 1993, and New York State in 2000, along with such cities as Los Angeles, Cleveland, Denver, Philadelphia, and New York City. In an effort to counter its reputation as a weapons bazaar, Virginia passed a measure limiting handgun purchases to one per month in 1993. The same year, Colorado and Florida passed a law barring juveniles from purchasing or possessing handguns. Controversial new gun control measures also cropped up in such traditionally anticontrol states as Texas and Utah.

As is true of parallel federal efforts, these state measures are more important for their political consequences (i.e., the defeat of gun control opponents) than for their policy impact.[6] Still, the upsurge in state action is unprecedented. According to the National Council of State Legislatures, about 1,000 gun control bills were introduced in state legislatures in 1993, a record number. The number of gun control bills introduced in just the first half of 1994 was over 2,000.[7]

A countertrend in the states has been a low-visibility but relatively successful effort by the NRA and its allies to enact state preemption legislation, designed to nullify or bar enactment of tougher gun laws by counties, cities, and other local jurisdictions. As of 1994, forty-two states had passed such legislation. The political motive for such action is that it allows regulation opponents to concentrate their efforts in state capitals, where conservative forces are traditionally stronger, rather than in scores of localities around the country.[8]

Gun Policy Alternatives

Without uniform state adoption of parallel laws, meaningful gun regulation must be federal. Neither the law nor the Constitution precludes a wide range of gun policy options. Yet a primary conclusion of this book is that a rational weighing of policy options bears even less relationship to actual policy outcomes for gun control than such a formulation does for most other policy areas.

In its simplest terms, the press for stronger gun laws from policy advocates and the general public is buttressed by two beliefs: (1) that such laws will contribute to a diminution of the crime problem, even if such a contribution is marginal; and (2) that guns are inherently dangerous implements of destruction, and that regardless of their impact on crime, guns should be subject to restrictions similar to any product or hazard that imposes comparable (or less) risk—especially given that guns, unlike products ranging from automobiles to knives, serve no other, counterbalancing purpose. This latter belief garners its chief support from the long-held view that government does and should do what it can to protect its citizens from harm that can be feasibly regulated. While the gun debate is typically framed in criminological terms, this reasoning makes clear that the gun problem is not just criminological, although fear of crime has provided much of the momentum for recent gun-law reforms. Any effort to define the gun issue solely in criminological terms ignores the larger, if more diffuse, issue of safety.

Opposing this view is the set of values, beliefs, and practices embodying the American gun culture, discussed in chapter 1. Buttressed today primarily by the hunting/sporting ethos, the gun culture resists further efforts at regulation. As public opinion polls reveal (see chapter 4), that resistance is based less on objections to the content of proposed regulation than on (1) the slippery-slope concern that regulation, whether reasonable or not, will inevitably lead to more regulation, and ultimately the banning of many, if not most, weapons (the NRA's primary clarion call); and (2) the subjective but deeply felt belief that such regulations may or do infringe on "rights." Even though no such rights infringement exists from a constitutional perspective (see chapter 2), the belief itself is an intense motivator for most.

Thus the very actions advocated by control proponents, animated by the desire to improve the safety and quality of American life, are viewed by control opponents as inimical to the same quality (although differently defined) of American life. It is a conundrum closely analogous to John L. Gaddis's analysis of why the Cold War evolved at the end of World War II, when he asserted that the very actions pursued by America and its allies in Europe to ensure security and forestall a new war were interpreted by the Soviet Union as provocative and warlike. Similarly, the Soviet Union's actions to develop a loyal ring of buffer nations for its own security were seen by the West as provocative and warlike.[9]

What I have described is the inherent problem of social regulatory policy, where the clash of values plays itself out in the political, and especially legislative, arena. An additional insight arising from social regulatory policy analysis is that even if the weight of policy rationality lies with regulation proponents, no meaningful policy resolution can afford to ignore the sensibilities of those whose barricades are the gun culture. It is certainly possible that, with the long-term projected decline of hunting (discussed in chapter 1) and of rural populations (and therefore related cultural norms), the control coalition may eventually succeed in rolling over the NRA and its allies to adopt sweeping national gun control reform of the sort found in other Western nations. Yet that outcome seems unlikely in the foreseeable future, for the simple reason that control opponents have resisted such a fate until now, despite having been in the numerical and opinion minority almost from the beginning of the modern gun control fight.

Thus we return to the likelihood of a protracted standoff between the two sides, with a possible slight advantage favoring control proponents, based on an extension of the direction of the policy trend in recent years.

The Barriers to Gun Control

As chapter 2 concluded, there is no constitutional barrier to stricter gun laws, even including a ban on the possession of handguns. The weight of criminological analysis assessed in chapter 3 leads to the conclusion, based on the preponderance of admittedly incomplete evidence, that gun control is a functional approach to the problems posed by guns in society.[10] Chapters 4 and 5 analyzed the political forces brought to bear on the state of gun policy, noting the political successes of gun control foes and the rising influence of control supporters, as well as the long-standing public support for tougher gun laws. The often reluctant national institutional players—Congress, the president, ATF—have found themselves reacting to political tides that literally seem to wash over the nation's capital like periodic, fierce storms blown in from the Atlantic. The bottom-line conclusion for the state of gun control policy is that barriers to further regulation are fundamentally political.

The primary substantive argument opposing further gun regulations is that such regulations will only make it more difficult for law-abiding citizens to obtain weapons, especially for purposes of self-defense, whereas criminals will continue to gain access to weapons regardless of the law. Remember that this individualistic view of the role of the citizen is deeply rooted in the nation's past, as described in chapter 1.

The Good Guy–Bad Guy Myth

This assertion contains within it one fallacy—that one can readily differentiate between "good guys" and "bad guys"; stated differently, the assumption is that guns in the hands of good guys are good, whereas guns in the hands of bad guys are bad. If the latter are controlled (through deterrence or imprisonment, for example), the problem is essentially solved.

Yet the statistics on gun-related deaths discussed in chapter 3 make clear that this Hollywood-cultivated dichotomy bears little relation to reality for most gun-related homicides, in that many homicides are the result of impulsive actions taken by individuals who have little or no criminal background or who are known to the victims. A study of murder trends in 1988 found that 64 percent of murderers were friends or acquaintances of the victims, and 16 percent were members of the victims' families. Only 20 percent of murders were committed by strangers. According to the government's Uniform Crime Reports from 1991, almost half of all murders that year (two-thirds of which were committed with guns) were committed by an acquaintance or relative of the victim. More than one-quarter of all women murdered were killed by boyfriends or husbands. Arguments precipitated 32 percent of all murders. Only 21 percent of murders resulted from the commission of felonies such as arson, robbery, and the like. Handguns were used six times as often as long guns (rifles and shotguns).[11]

These trends are exemplified in journalistic tallies of gun deaths. An examination of the eleven gun fatalities that occurred during the month of January 1989 in San Jose, California, noted that four of the deaths involved justified police shootings; four were murders of spouses or roommates, all arising from domestic disputes; two were accidental shooting deaths; and one was a suicide.[12] A Time magazine compilation of all 464 gun deaths that occurred nationwide during the week of 1–7 May 1989 found that the majority of the murders "typically involved people who loved, or hated, each other—spouses, relatives or close acquaintances." Only 13 of the gun deaths were law enforcement related, 14 were self-defense, 22 were accidents, and 216 were suicides.[13]

The good guy–bad guy myth thus evaporates when most murders are examined. Even when we consider that gun crimes such as murder are more likely to be committed by persons with criminal backgrounds, we are still left with the conclusion that such individuals ought not to have ready access to guns. This becomes even more apparent when suicides and gun accidents (fatal and nonfatal) are added to the cumulative harm caused by guns. For gun use (especially nonfatal gun use) in other crimes, such as robbery and theft, the good guy–bad guy principle retains some usefulness, because such crimes (especially when guns are involved) are infrequently attributable to impulse and are almost never attributable to accident. Nevertheless, the consequences of a citizenry armed to stave off crime would inevitably result in more gun crimes and gun deaths, based on existing patterns of gun use.

The Armed Citizen

To return to the argument against gun control, one can still plausibly argue that widespread citizen possession of guns for self-defense retains logic at both the societal and individual levels. On the societal level, one may argue that a cumulative deterrent effect may arise from an armed civil society and that some crimes will be thwarted, even though death is more likely to occur when victims resist or are armed. Indeed, some might be more than willing to accept such a trade-off. On the individual level, it seems commonsensical that a crime victim has a better chance of self-protection and crime suppression if the citizen is armed. During the 1992 Los Angeles riots, for example, some store owners saved their places of business by the display and even use of weapons. Yet this bit of apparent common sense is never held up to examination in the gun debate. That is, to have any meaningful effect, such an arming process must take place systematically, on a societal scale. We must then ask, what is the cumulative consequence of an implicit or explicit policy that encourages civilian arming to counteract crime and lawlessness in a modern, developed society? An answer to this question can be found in international relations theory.

The Security Dilemma

Students of international relations concern themselves with how nations behave and interact. Not surprisingly, a central concern of these analysts is armed conflict—in particular, the causes and prevention of war. Throughout history, nations have been forced to rely on themselves, sometimes with the help of allied nations, to ward off the aggressions of other nations. Unlike citizens or communities within a nation, sovereign nations usually operate within an international framework of anarchy, meaning that nations must look out for themselves.[14] (Note that this definition of anarchy is not the one popularly used, in which indiscriminate disorder, confusion, and mayhem are the norm.) International relations expert Kenneth Waltz notes that "self-help is necessarily the principle of action in an anarchic order."[15]

Anarchy in the international system prevails because of the absence of any authoritative governing body or structure. As international security expert Bruce Russett writes: "There is no higher authority, such as a world government, to which they [nations] can appeal for protection. Rather, they must try to provide security through policies that heavily emphasize military strength and military deterrence."[16] International politics is, quite simply, "politics in the absence of government."[17]

The great dilemma of this behavior among nations is that as nations arm and fortify themselves in an effort to stave off conflict, they in turn fan the flames of insecurity in other nations. Emphasizing the universality of this problem, international expert John Herz wrote of

the "security dilemma" of men, or groups, or their leaders. Groups or individuals . . . concerned about their security from being attacked, subjected, dominated, or annihilated . . . [s]triving to attain security from such attack . . . are driven to acquire more and more power in order to escape the impact of the power of others. This, in turn, renders the others more insecure and compels them to prepare for the worst. Since none can ever feel entirely secure in such a world of competing units, power competition ensues, and the vicious circle of security and power accumulation is on.[18]

As security analyst Robert Jervis says, "the means by which a state tries to increase its security decrease the security of others."[19] This, in a nutshell, is the "security dilemma."

When a nation takes actions that it considers to be purely defensive (and therefore not threatening to other nations), some of those actions may be perceived by other nations as an offensive threat to their security. If, for example, a nation builds up its army to deter an attack from a neighboring nation, the neighboring nation is likely to assume that the buildup is designed for attack, not defense, and to respond by increasing its forces, an action that may accelerate the first nation's buildup, and so on, until war breaks out. A classic example of such a cycle is that preceding World War I, as described in Barbara Tuchman's revealing book *The Guns of August*.

One might suppose that such a cycle could be prevented if nations developed solely defensive weapons. But there are two problems with this solution. First, virtually all weapons can be construed as having an offensive purpose (although some defensive *actions* may avoid this problem). Second, even those weapons considered purely defensive, such as antimissile missiles (the Patriot missile, used during the 1991 Persian Gulf War, is one example), can be considered threatening to other nations because they suggest that the nation developing them may use them to defend its territory against retaliation in the aftermath of an initial offensive strike. For this reason, defensive weapons are often considered destabilizing in a balance-of-power situation.[20]

Thus, the classic response to the security dilemma is for nations "to expand their *individual* power."[21] Yet the cumulative consequence of this seemingly rational response to international anarchy is the escalation of arms races and an ever-increasing likelihood of war.

Arms races are problematic for three reasons: they are costly and wasteful, they ratchet up the degree of destruction likely to occur if conflict does break out, and they are a primary cause of war. While arms races are not necessarily the sole causes of war, the historical correlation between the two is very high. And arms races are undeniably a bad way to prevent conflict.[22]

These threats to security have driven nations to form alliances, make treaties, and engage in other actions to reduce the likelihood of war. The most prominent such example is the formation of the United Nations at the end of World War II. Central to this effort in recent years has been negotiation of arms control agreements designed to limit the development and spread of nuclear arms, although the security dilemma is not unique to the nuclear age. In fact, arms control "is virtually as old as weapons themselves."[23]

As international security specialists well understand, the constant threat posed by the security dilemma would be no threat at all if a powerful international authority existed that could impose order, and accompanying standards of behavior, on the nations of the world. It is precisely because international systems are "decentralized and anarchic," whereas domestic political systems are "centralized and hierarchic,"[24] that one does not find anarchy to be a prevalent mode of interaction within most nations. Obviously, such an authority exists within the borders of the United States.

The Security Dilemma and the Gun Debate

The startling parallels between the behavior of nations and that of citizens within the United States is less surprising when one considers the primeval need for order, described at the start of chapter 1, as the first purpose of governments. The desire to own guns for the purpose of self-defense underscores the government's inability to provide a greater degree of public order. The domestic "anarchy" many fear is the anarchy of elements of the inner city, the darkened lonely street, the random killer, the vicious rapist.

The problem of widespread gun ownership and proliferation in society lies precisely in the facts that individual gun ownership for self-defense seems rational for the individual, even though its cumulative consequence is likely to be more detrimental than helpful to societal order; and that guns can be used as easily for offense (e.g., to commit a robbery) as for defense (e.g., to thwart a robbery). Although the purpose of a gun purchase may be defensive, it is impossible for others to feel secure unless they already feel trust in the gun owner. No matter how defense-minded the gun owner, the very act of gun ownership and especially gun display is invariably offensive in nature. As a Spanish diplomat noted between the two world wars: "A weapon is either offensive or defensive according to which end of it you are looking at."[25] As one international security expert observed, the only way to ensure that others would interpret gun ownership as purely defensive in nature would be somehow to chain the gun to one's house.[26] Even then, the dangers of suicide and accident would persist.

Bearing in mind the differences between international and domestic political systems, the applicability of the security dilemma to the American gun situation is dramatically illustrated by the standoff and conflagration that consumed the Branch Davidian compound near Waco, Texas, in early 1993. The fringe group had amassed an enormous quantity of arms and explosives, insisting that they were for defensive purposes only. One can accept their claim of defense and still understand why the mere acquisition of these materials aroused alarm among government officials and others. This is admittedly an extreme example, but it almost precisely parallels the security dilemma in international politics.

Offense versus Defense

The mere act of gun possession, then, is offensive *regardless of intent*, because weapons are inherently offensive and because it is "hard to convince most people that they [through weapons acquisitions] may be inadvertently threatening others."[27] Bearing this in mind, one can still refine the distinction by borrowing from international relations the principle that weapons may be distinguished by their relative degree of offensive or defensive capability, applying the distinction to different types of guns.

Handguns pose an even greater offensive risk than long guns because of their concealability, portability, and ease of use. Supporting this proposition is the fact that even though long guns are easier to obtain and outnumber handguns nationwide by a ratio of roughly 2 to 1, handguns are more than three times as likely to be used in violent crime as long guns.[28] In 1992, for example, handguns were used in more than 930,000 violent crimes. Handguns are the weapon of choice for criminals. Moreover, the most frequently cited reason for handgun ownership is self-protection, whereas those who own long guns cite hunting and sporting purposes as the primary reason for ownership. Obviously, long guns may have offensive and defensive purposes as well, but just as international relations specialists distinguish between weapons that have more versus less offensive capabilities, one may do the same when considering types of weapons owned by Americans.

Following this line of logic, assault weapons may also be considered to pose a greater offensive threat than other long guns. Even though assault weapons are infrequently used by criminals and constitute a relatively small percentage of total firearms, they have gained in popularity among drug traffickers, urban gangs, extremist groups, and others in recent years and have gained considerable notoriety when used in highly publicized mass killings. Especially popular among criminals are assault-style semiautomatic pistols, such as the Tec–9.[29] Sales to law-abiding citizens have also increased in recent years. As discussed in chapter 5, assault weapons are distinguishable from other semiautomatic weapons, and they are generally considered to have no legitimate hunting or sporting use. Yet the firepower they deliver (that is, the ability to fire a bullet per trigger pull from clips that can hold thirty rounds or more) makes them useful for offensive purposes, as reflected in the military basis for their development.[30] Moreover, physicians report more serious injuries from assault weapons than from handguns (because of the greater muzzle velocity of bullets fired from assault weapons, the bullets' tendency to tumble and thus cause more damage, and the assault weapons' ability to fire more bullets before reloading) and an upsurge of such wounds requiring treatment in urban hospital emergency rooms.

For the defense-minded citizen, gun acquisition is not the only available means of defense. The citizen seeking self-protection can instead turn to an array of indisputably defensive *actions* designed to increase personal safety and yet, unlike guns, pose no offensive capability or threat. As discussed in chapter 3, these include installation of better street lighting, bars on windows, and home alarm systems; utilization of guard dogs; and formation of neighborhood alliances.

Based on the security dilemma principle, a national policy that encourages and implements weapons ownership as a recognized means of self-defense invites a domestic arms race. Of the three problems with arms races mentioned earlier, the first, cost, is probably the least significant for the American gun issue. A government policy encouraging civilian gun possession could easily make weapons available at prices affordable to most. The second and third problems, however—escalation of the degree of destruction and increase in the likelihood of conflict—are severe problems for the domestic arms race advocates.

Escalation

As the security dilemma posits, arms proliferation among citizens would inexorably lead to an escalation of gun-related violence, injuries, and deaths.[31] Writers who emphasize the desirability of widespread weapons ownership and carrying among the civilian population never consider, for example, that aside from a likely rise in incidental injuries and deaths, such a policy would invite criminals, as well as law-abiding citizens now more fearful of their safety, to carry more and more destructive weapons.[32] This pattern of mutual escalation is predicted by the security dilemma.

Such a phenomenon is observable in the rearming of police forces around the country, where the traditional six-shot service revolver has been replaced by higher-capacity semiautomatic handguns, notably 9-mm pistols capable of holding fifteen- to nineteen-round clips. From the mid–1980s to 1990, nearly half of America's police forces made the switch. By 1995, the 9-mm was found in nearly all police forces. The reason for the switch is that police have found themselves increasingly outgunned, especially as street violence and semiautomatic weapons have proliferated. Echoing the parallel to international relations, the executive director of the Police Executive Research Forum said, "We've got a full-blown arms race going on in the streets today." Yet police authorities have been concerned about the consequences of this arms escalation. Police in New York City have been "firing too many shots" with the new semiautomatic pistols, according to authorities, which in turn has led to increased training.[33]

Some might be tempted to cite this phenomenon as a justification for arming citizens to assist the police. Yet it must be noted that the great majority of police officers nationwide never fire their guns in the line of duty, so it would be a mistake to exaggerate the actual threat to police and the public. Beyond this, containment is a key to arms control, and unlike the international sphere, the powers of the state can be brought to bear against those who either own or use weapons improperly, as a means of limiting the arms race. That is, to escalate a domestic arms race beyond law enforcement officers, whose specific and professional function is the maintenance of societal order, to the general population is to make a quantum leap in the abnegation of government authority over the maintenance of public order. The option of arms escalation among the general population also invites comparable escalation by the criminal population, and it widens the scope of those participating in the escalation process and therefore also the scope of gun-related mayhem. As Jervis notes, "there is no policy and level of arms that is mutually satisfactory [to opposing sides]."[34] Such an approach would feed, not reduce, the security dilemma. This does not mean that citizens have no role in the law enforcement process, but that widespread gun carrying is neither the only nor the most desirable option. Indeed, the fact that police organizations have lined up consistently in favor of gun control in recent years provides clear evidence that police are not sanguine about more widespread gun ownership, even among the most law-abiding segments of the population.

To summarize, despite the difficult plight faced by law enforcement agencies, to bring citizens into a domestic arms race against crime would, as the security dilemma predicts, (1) invite and broaden an arms race that could only result in a dramatic escalation of violence (both intentional and unintentional) and cultivate anarchy of the sort found in the international system and in some inner cities, and (2) undercut the legitimate role of the state as arbiter of public order. The Hobbesian world within nations such as Lebanon in the 1980s, Somalia in 1992, and Rwanda in 1994 are extreme, if exemplary, cases where the state's responsibility to maintain order was passed on de facto to its respective citizens. The resulting chaos and carnage are adequate testimonials to the virtue of leaving the maintenance of public order to the state.

To take a less extreme and more specific example, Texas state law has long included a provision sanctioning citizen use of deadly force against intruders and thieves during nighttime hours. On 25 February 1994, an automobile repossessor was shot and killed by and in front of the home of the man whose vehicle he was repossessing for failure to keep up with his car payments. The shooter, Jerry Casey, admitted that he was not acting in self-defense when he killed the repossessor with a .30–30 telescopic rifle, and there seemed little doubt that Casey knew why his Ford truck was being towed away. Even though the repossessor was acting legally, no charges were brought against Casey by the district attorney of Harris County, who argued that state law did and should protect such a use of deadly force by citizens because of its general deterrent value to crime.[35]

A similar circumstance arose in Colorado, which enacted a "make-my-day" law in 1985, allowing citizens to use deadly force against anyone who unlawfully enters a dwelling if the occupant believes a crime is being or might be committed. A year after the law's passage, state residents were horrified when a man who shot and killed a young couple and a third person in a neighborhood dispute was held immune from prosecution under that law.[36]

These examples hint at the broader consequences of a population armed with recognized discretion for the purpose of deterring crime. To return to the good guy–bad guy myth, the Texas instance in particular involved two "good guys"—one, a repo man simply doing his job; the other, a citizen without a past criminal record who committed a murder that the state would not prosecute under a law sanctioning wide citizen discretion to use deadly force as a means of deterring and thwarting crime.

Even if one accepts the good guy–bad guy myth, the security dilemma underscores the simple lesson, extracted from countless wars over many centuries, that people (and nations) with the best of intentions still find themselves inevitably drawn into escalating arms races and conflicts when they have no overarching government or authority in which to vest the responsibility for public order. The Texas law just described, enacted at a time when the existing government could provide little help to ward off horse thieves, enmeshes American citizens a little more deeply in the security dilemma.

The self-defense question begs the most important issue distinguishing international politics from domestic politics: Americans have a government that possesses the legitimacy, power, resources, and above all the obligation to address the crime and related defense problems. Admittedly, a government of limited powers that places great store in individual rights and liberties is also limited in the solutions it can pursue. Such is the price of living in a free society. Yet living under a government means also that the individual accedes to the authority and legitimacy of the state.

Concealed Carry Laws

As discussed in chapter 3, thirty-one states have enacted laws allowing qualified citizens to carry concealed weapons. A primary argument on behalf of such laws is the claim that private citizens should have the right to protect themselves with firearms if necessary. While the consequences of such laws are yet to be fully understood (and clearly the consequences will be marginal in states where few citizens seek such permits), a key distinction is made between "may carry" and "shall carry" laws. That is, states with a "may carry" law give the government considerable discretion over who may obtain a carry permit, so that only those who can demonstrate both a compelling need and the necessary skill are given such permits. Not surprisingly, relatively few such permits are granted. "Shall carry" laws, in contrast, stipulate that the government must grant carry permits as long as the applicants meet a set of prespecified criteria. Permits are easier to obtain in such circumstances.

A study of three states (Florida, Mississippi, and Oregon) that changed their laws from "may carry" to "shall carry" concluded that homicide rates rose as the result of the relaxation of carry laws. Part of the explanation for the rise in homicides is that criminals are more likely to carry weapons if they believe that average citizens are more likely to be armed.[37] Thus, regardless of whether one supports or opposes gun carry laws (whether limited or permissive), observed behavior supports the arms race principle.

A similar lesson comes from recent practices of police departments around the country. Police forces in general dislike concealed carry laws and have been moving more aggressively to deter weapons carrying, especially in urban areas. Police in such cities as New York, Indianapolis, and Kansas City have directed patrol officers to watch for any infractions that might allow for stop and search of individuals and of cars. Kansas City reported a 49 percent drop in gun crimes in the areas where this policy was carried out and a 65 percent increase in gun seizures. New York City reported a 41 percent drop in handgun murders in precincts where this was tried, surpassing a 31 percent drop in the overall murder rate. Criminologists such as James Q. Wilson have become strong advocates for this kind of police tactic.[38] Returning to the international relations framework, police forces are applying an effective arms control strategy.

As the French philosopher Jean-Jacques Rousseau observed, "Man loses, through the social contract, his natural liberty, along with an unlimited right to anything that he is tempted by and can get. He gains civil liberty . . . which is limited by the general will." A policy that surrenders a significant degree of state police power to individuals pushes society toward, rather than away from, the chaotic state of nature.

Nonproliferation and Arms Control

A rejection of the armed-citizen argument returns us to the original question of this chapter and book, government regulation of guns. Just as some visualize an idyllic world without armies or nuclear weapons, some envision a nation without guns. While some might argue on behalf of citizen disarmament, it is clear that a host of practical and other problems all but eliminate the citizen disarmament option, just as world nuclear disarmament can only be considered a fantasy. The most obvious of these problems is the sheer number of weapons in

America, along with the difficulty of tracking and retrieving them. Moreover, the current state of armament among the general population is the product of a long and deeply rooted social tradition that cannot simply be legislated out of existence. Indeed, such a tradition is entitled to respect.

A logical policy framework that balances competing values and preferences between hostile opponents is, to borrow again from international relations theory, *nonproliferation* of new weapons and technologies, combined with *arms control* for existing weapons. Nonproliferation is designed to fend off the proliferation of new, more destructive weapons, based on the assumption that it is far easier and more practical to block the distribution of new types of weapons *before* they flood the market than after.

Such a strategy is justifiable for limiting the criminological use of guns because of the inherent desirability of applying brakes to the domestic arms race, and because the active life of guns used in crime may actually be substantially less than for guns not used in crime.[39] The effort to regulate assault weapons (especially assault-style pistols) falls loosely into this category. Although such weapons have been available, the purpose of regulation would be to stem their distribution before they become more widespread.

Critics of those seeking such regulations have argued that because assault weapons represent only a small percentage of weapons used in crimes, there is no reason to regulate or restrict their acquisition. Yet their destructive capabilities, offensive nature, and superfluousness to hunting and sporting purposes undercut this argument, even if they are never used in crime. The fact that many such weapons are being adopted for criminal purposes simply emphasizes the desirability of applying the nonproliferation principle to assault weapons before they spread further.

The effort in the 1980s to ban armor-piercing bullets (see chapter 5) represents another, more successful effort along these lines. More recently, Senator Daniel Patrick Moynihan (D-N.Y.) spearheaded an effort to ban hollow-point pistol bullets (except for use by the police and the military), designed to expand on impact into a sharp-edged, starlike pattern that causes considerable damage to the victim. These bullets were designed for police use because they provide greater stopping power, yet are less likely to pass through the body of the intended target and hit a bystander. Like armor-piercing ammunition, these bullets were designed solely to increase the damage to individuals or targets being shot. A similarly destructive bullet was developed in 1994 by Signature Products Corp. of Huntsville, Alabama. Because this bullet was made from a plastic material (a polymer), it escaped existing federal regulations. According to the company's chief executive officer, the bullet was developed because the company had lost business with the end of the Cold War. According to the developer, the bullet "causes a horrific wound."[40]

Arms control has played a vital role in limiting the international nuclear arms race. At the same time, it has offered no panacea and has been most important as a means "to avoid the most provocative actions and limit the most provocative weapons."[41]

Applied to gun regulation, the arms-control principle similarly attempts to impose a greater degree of security by controlling guns' deployment, characteristics, uses, safety, and the like. Most recent gun regulation efforts, including those discussed in chapter 5, fall into this category. That is, they are relatively modest measures generally designed to create a greater degree of stability. Even though these measures are, in policy terms, marginal, they make sense in an arms-control framework, just as international arms agreements may call for only marginal substantive changes yet are still important for their contribution to international security. An example of a new weapons technology that calls for strict regulation is the Barrett .50-caliber sniper rifle. Weighing about twenty-eight pounds, this weapon is highly accurate from more than a mile away, and it must be fired while resting on a bipod. Designed for military applications, the weapon was used by U.S. Marines to knock out Iraqi armored vehicles during the 1991 Persian Gulf War. A 1995 RAND Corporation report noted that the weapon was highly effective against parked aircraft and has the capability of piercing reinforced armor used to protect airplanes, fuel tanks, toxic chemicals, and ground facilities. The NRA has thwarted efforts by Congress to regulate or restrict civilian purchase of the weapons, arguing that they are used legitimately for sharpshooting. Yet the rifles also have been found in the possession of right-wing American terrorists and even Muslim extremists. In fact, in the 1980s, American companies sold at least twenty-five such rifles to Osama bin Laden's group al Qaeda – although at the time, America was supporting the Afghani war against the Soviet Union. Yet as of 2002, these sniper rifles are easier to obtain than handguns, and they are now produced by at least fifteen different companies.[42] Recent efforts to impose more stringent regulations and fees on gun dealers and to institute meaningful regulation of gun shows are obvious and previously overlooked means to impose greater control over the general flow of guns into the national market. While gun control opponents view these and other efforts as simply a prelude to disarmament—and indeed this is surely the intent of at least a few proponents of gun control—disarmament is a separate and distinct purpose. *The only way to reconcile the fears of control opponents with the efforts of control proponents is to recognize the fundamental distinction between arms control and disarmament.*

To deprive citizens of assault weapons and to make handgun acquisition extremely difficult, to cite two control objectives, are justifiable from a security dilemma perspective. Yet the achievement of these objectives could and should occur only with a concomitant guarantee of ownership protection of traditional hunting and sporting weapons for hunters, target shooters, collectors, and sports enthusiasts. It would mean, for example, that a hunter could use a standard semiautomatic hunting rifle but not an AK–47. Those inordinately concerned with home protection and seeking a gun for this purpose would need to turn to a shotgun, for example, plus an array of home security devices and techniques, in preference to a handgun.

An express bargain could be negotiated along these lines: gun control supporters would affirm that their goal excludes gun disarmament, and would expressly recognize the legitimate hunting and sporting traditions in America. Gun control foes, in turn, would accept a degree of regulation, but they could be secure in the knowledge that such regulation would not extend to confiscation or disarmament, yet would include arms control that focused on handguns and on new, exotic weaponry.

It is obvious that many control opponents, and especially the NRA, would recoil from any such agreement, although the NRA would be shrewd to press for, say, exclusive control over mandatory national gun training programs for all gun owners in exchange for its support of a limited menu of gun regulations. Given the drift of events and changing national demography, the time may come when the NRA and its allies face the prospect of accepting either such an agreement or a more draconian (from their perspective) alternative. One can indeed argue that the hunting/sporting tradition legitimately warrants protection, but no such protective agreement can ignore the multiplicity of gun issues and problems that beset the American consciousness.

The theoretical elegance of an arms-control approach to this security dilemma problem is that it provides a structure through which bargaining and accommodation can take place between opposing, hostile interests. It offers no magic solution, but an ongoing process with which both sides can learn to live. That is, it offers a key to the social regulatory paradox.

Notes

Chapter 1. Policy Definition and Gun Control

1. See "Gun Law Failures," NRA Institute for Legislative Action, 1982. The 20,000 figure traces back to Richard Hofstadter, "America as a Gun Culture," *American Heritage* 21 (October 1970): 85.

2. American history is of course pockmarked by civil strife, from the Whiskey Rebellion of 1794 to the 1992 Los Angeles riots following the Rodney King incident. Our greatest threat to public order, the Civil War, nearly destroyed the United States. Despite these and other instances, however, American society has been among the most ordered, despite its size, diversity, and democratic values.

3. The philosophical and practical problems of balancing order and freedom are nicely discussed in Theodore J. Lowi and Benjamin Ginsberg, *American Government: Freedom and Power* (New York: Norton, 1994).

4. Samuel Huntington, *Political Order in Changing Societies* (New Haven: Yale University Press, 1968), 7–8.

5. Thomas R. Dye, *Understanding Public Policy* (Englewood Cliffs, N.J.: Prentice Hall, 1984), 2. Dye insightfully discusses the many efforts to define public policy properly (efforts he understandably labels "exasperating"). He concludes that the debate tends to divert attention away from the actual study of policy and that despite apparent differences, competing definitions tend ultimately to converge on a common understanding.

6. See Carl J. Friedrich, *Constitutional Government and Democracy* (Boston: Little, Brown, 1941), 88–89. See also Theodore J. Lowi, *The End of Liberalism* (New York: Norton, 1979), 273. According to the *Oxford English Dictionary*, "policy" and "police" share the Latin root *politia*. Henry C. Black defined police power as securing "generally the comfort, safety, morals, health, and prosperity of its citizens by preserving the public order, preventing a conflict of rights in the common intercourse of the citizens, and insuring to each an uninterrupted enjoyment of all privileges conferred upon him or her by the general laws." *Black's Law Dictionary* (St. Paul, Minn.: West, 1983), 603.

7. Lowi and Ginsberg, *American Government*, 76.

8. Larry N. Gerston, Cynthia Fraleigh, and Robert Schwab, *The Deregulated Society* (Pacific Grove, Calif.: Brooks/Cole, 1988), 66. See also Joyce M. Mitchell and

William C. Mitchell, *Political Analysis and Public Policy* (Chicago: Rand McNally, 1969), 207–9.

9. Lowi and Ginsberg, *American Government*, 640.

10. Bear in mind that the use of words such as *control* and *coercion* when applied to the government is not meant to be pejorative. Governments may exert too much control, or use it perniciously, but government control through the exercise of coercion is indispensable to modern society and is inherently neither positive nor negative.

11. This discussion is a simplified version of Lowi's arenas-of-power scheme. A more detailed examination can be found in Theodore J. Lowi, "American Business, Public Policy, Case Studies, and Political Theory," *World Politics* 16 (July 1964): 677–715; idem, "Four Systems of Policy, Politics, and Choice," *Public Administration Review* 32 (July/August 1972): 298–310; Robert J. Spitzer, *The Presidency and Public Policy: The Four Arenas of Presidential Power* (University, Ala.: University of Alabama Press, 1983); idem, "Promoting Policy Theory: Revising the Arenas of Power," *Policy Studies Journal* 15 (June 1987): 675–89; and Randall B. Ripley and Grace A. Franklin, *Congress, the Bureaucracy, and Public Policy* (Pacific Grove, Calif.: Brooks/Cole, 1991).

12. This rank ordering is confirmed in Theodore J. Lowi, "Decision Making vs. Policy Making," *Public Administration Review* 30 (May/June 1970): 314–25; Lowi, "Four Systems of Policy"; Spitzer, *Presidency and Public Policy*; and Ripley and Franklin, *Congress, the Bureaucracy, and Public Policy*.

13. For more on this distinction, see William Lilley III and James C. Miller III, "The New 'Social Revolution,'" *Public Interest* 47 (Spring 1977): 52–53; Lester M. Salamon, "Federal Regulation: A New Arena for Presidential Power?" in *The Illusion of Presidential Government*, ed. Hugh Heclo and Lester M. Salamon (Boulder, Colo.: Westview, 1981), 150–51; Gerston, Fraleigh, and Schwab, *The Deregulated Society*, 27–34; and James Q. Wilson, ed., *The Politics of Regulation* (New York: Basic Books, 1980).

14. Gerston, Fraleigh, and Schwab, *Deregulated Society*, 23.

15. Raymond Tatalovich and Byron Daynes, "Introduction: Social Regulation and Moral Conduct," in *Moral Controversies in American Politics*, ed. Tatalovich and Daynes (Armonk, N.Y.: M.E. Sharpe, 1998), xxx. See also their article, "Moral Controversies and the Policymaking Process: Lowi's Framework Applied to the Abortion Issue," *Policy Studies Review* (February 1984): 207–22.

16. This corresponds to the distinction between "style" and "position" issues arising from the study of public opinion. Style issues, such as social regulation, are defined as those dealing with matters of taste and manner derived from cultural, religious, or ethnic values (and thus tap stronger and deeper feelings). Position issues, paralleling economic regulation, involve material or economic benefits. The distinction comes from Bernard R. Berelson, Paul F. Lazarsfeld, and William N. McPhee, *Voting* (Chicago: University of Chicago Press, 1954), 184. See also Robert E. Lane and David O. Sears, *Public Opinion* (Englewood Cliffs, N.J.: Prentice Hall, 1964), 75–76.

17. Claude Blair, ed., *Pollard's History of Firearms* (New York: Macmillan, 1983), 27–33 and passim.

18. The Consumer Product Safety Commission maintains data on injuries treated in hospital emergency rooms that patients say are related to various products, excluding firearms.

19. Leslie McAneny, "Americans Tell Congress: Pass Brady Bill, Other Tough Gun Laws,"

Gallup Poll Monthly 330 (March 1993): 5. See also Osha Gray Davidson, *Under Fire: The NRA and the Battle for Gun Control* (New York: Holt, 1993), 142–43; "Guns in America: National Survey on Private Ownership and Use of Firearms," *National Institute of Justice*, May 1997; Bureau of Justice Statistics, *Sourcebook of Criminal Justice Statistics* 1999 (Washington, D.C.: Government Printing Office, 2000), 138.

20. Some see a parallel between efforts to regulate guns and the country's experiment with Prohibition in the 1920s, when public policy was altered to try to end the consumption of alcoholic beverages. A good, brief summary of the policy problems raised by Prohibition is found in Cynthia E. Harrison, "Appendix: The Prohibition Experience," in *The Abortion Dispute and the American System*, ed. Gilbert Y. Steiner (Washington, D.C.: Brookings Institution, 1983).

21. The concept of culture, arising from anthropology, is defined as "knowledge, belief, art, morals, law, custom, and any other capabilities and habits acquired by man as a member of society"; "the essential core of culture consists of traditional . . . ideas and especially their attached values." Milton Singer, "Culture," in *International Encyclopedia of the Social Sciences*, ed. David L. Sills (New York: Macmillan, 1968), 3:527, 528. These and other offered definitions conform to what is described in this and other works as the culture of guns.

22. The gun culture is recognized, barring interpretive quibbles, by such gun control proponents as Robert Sherrill, *The Saturday Night Special* (New York: Charterhouse, 1973), 324; Carl Bakal, *The Right to Bear Arms* (New York: McGraw-Hill, 1966), chap. 5; Hofstadter, "America as a Gun Culture," 4–11, 82–85; and Franklin E. Zimring and Gordon Hawkins, *The Citizen's Guide to Gun Control* (New York: Macmillan, 1987), chap. 7. Among gun control opponents, see, for example, David B. Kopel, *The Samurai, the Mountie, and the Cowboy* (Buffalo, N.Y.: Prometheus Books, 1992), 419–22; and James D. Wright, Peter Rossi, and Kathleen Daly, *Under the Gun: Weapons, Crime, and Violence in America* (New York: Aldine, 1983). One gun control opponent, William R. Tonso, attempts to argue that there is no unique American gun culture, but winds up using the synonym "gun attachment" to summarize his observation that "firearms come close to being central to the lifestyles of large numbers of Americans." See *Gun and Society* (Washington, D.C.: University Press of America, 1982), 11, 15.

23. Erik Eckholm, "A Basic Issue: Whose Hands Should Guns Be Kept Out Of?" *New York Times*, 3 April 1992; and Bob Herbert, "Deadly Data on Handguns," *New York Times*, 2 March 1994.

24. See, for example, Hugh Davis Graham and Ted Robert Gurr, *Violence in America: Historical and Comparative Perspectives* (New York: Bantam Books, 1970); William E. Burrows, *Vigilante!* (New York: Harcourt Brace Jovanovich, 1976); and Zimring and Hawkins, *Citizen's Guide to Gun Control*.

25. Richard Slotkin notes about cultural myth making that it "exists 'for the culture' that it serves, and we therefore speak of it as if it were somehow the property or production of the culture as a whole. But the actual work of making and transmitting myths is done by particular classes of persons." *Gunfighter Nation: The Myth of the Frontier in Twentieth-Century America* (New York: Atheneum, 1992), 8.

26. Michael A. Bellesiles, "The Origins of Gun Culture in the United States, 1760–1865," *Journal of American History* 83 (September 1996), 426, 428; Bellesiles,

Arming America: The Origins of a National Gun Culture (New York: Alfred A. Knopf, 2000). Bellesiles's book won the Bancroft Prize in history in 2001, but the volume was also severely criticized, especially in the author's apparent mishandling of probate records analysis. See "Forum: History and Guns," *William and Mary Quarterly* 59 (January 2002): 203–68.

27. Quoted in Daniel J. Boorstin, *The Americans: The Colonial Experience* (New York: Vintage, 1964), 350.

28. Alden Hatch, *Remington Arms in American History* (New York: Rinehart, 1956), 5; see also Jervis Anderson, *Guns in American Life* (New York: Random House, 1984), 12; and Leonard Kriegel, "A Loaded Question: What Is It about Americans and Guns?" *Harper's*, May 1992, 45–51.

29. Lee Kennett and James LaVerne Anderson, *The Gun in America* (Westport, Conn.: Greenwood, 1975), 48. Even during early instances of urban unrest before and after the Revolution, citizens rarely carried or used guns (pp. 48–49). See also Bellesiles, "Origins of Gun Culture."

30. Hatch, *Remington Arms in American History*, 29. See also Kennett and Anderson, *Gun in America*, 138–41; and Hofstadter, "America as a Gun Culture," 82.

31. According to the 1991 National Survey of Fishing, Hunting, and Wildlife-associated Recreation, as cited in Daniel J. Decker, Jody W. Enck, and Tommy L. Brown, "The Future of Hunting—Will We Pass On the Heritage?" Paper presented at the 2d Annual Governor's Symposium on North America's Hunting Heritage, Pierre, S.D., 24–26 August 1993, 2. The U.S. Bureau of Census reported about 14 million hunters in 1991 and 1996, indicating that hunting as a percentage of the population is declining.

32. Reported in Ted Kerasote, *Bloodties: Nature, Culture, and the Hunt* (New York: Random House, 1993), 211–12. Kerasote, an author and hunter, provides as eloquent a defense of hunting as any. He asks: "Can a cultural being ethically participate in these natural cycles, cycles that may entail taking the lives of individual animals, animals who are as bright, as bold, and tenderly aware of sunshine and storm as we are? Can one be both cultural and natural?" (178). Kerasote's answer is yes. "Hunting, along with procreation," he says, "is the oldest expression of our genetic nature" (xix).

33. See Decker, Enck, and Brown, "The Future of Hunting."

34. Kennett and Anderson, *Gun in America*, 43–48, 58; and Boorstin, *The Americans*, 352–57.

35. A thorough analysis of the militias in the post-colonial period is found in John K. Mahon, *The American Militia: Decade of Decision, 1789–1800* (Gainesville: University of Florida Press, 1960). See also Hofstadter, "America as a Gun Culture," 83; and James M. McPherson, *Battle Cry of Freedom* (New York: Oxford University Press, 1988), 317.

36. Kennett and Anderson, *Gun in America*, 38–42. First developed in Lancaster, Pennsylvania, in the early 1700s, this American rifle was lighter and less ornamental, had a longer barrel, and fired a smaller-caliber bullet loaded with a greased patch, making it easier to use and more accurate at longer distances than the guns brought over from Europe (pp. 38–39).

37. Jack Rohan, *Yankee Arms Maker* (New York: Harper and Brothers, 948), 298.

38. James Wycoff, *Famous Guns That Won the West* (New York: Arco, 1968), 5–6. See also

Harold F. Williamson, *Winchester: The Gun that Won the West* (Washington, D.C.: Combat Forces Press, 1952), 3; Martin Rywell, *The Gun That Shaped American Destiny* (Harriman, Tenn.: Pioneer Press, 1957), 4; and James B. Trefethen and James E. Serven, *Americans and Their Guns: The National Rifle Association Story Through Nearly a Century of Service to the Nation* (Harrisburg, Pa.: Stackpole Books, 1967). Carl Russell asserted that "the gun had a greater influence in changing the primitive ways of the Indian than any other object brought to America by the white man." Of far greater consequence to the life of Native Americans, however, was the spread of European diseases accompanying the massive influx of European settlers, whose sheer numbers exceeded the significance of their weapons. *Guns on the Early Frontier* (Berkeley: University of California Press, 1957), vii.

39. Lewis Atherton, *The Cattle Kings* (Bloomington: Indiana University Press, 1961).

40. Richard Shenkman, *Legends, Lies, and Cherished Myths of American History* (New York: Morrow, 1988), 112. See also Robert R. Dykstra, *The Cattle Towns* (New York: Knopf, 1968).

41. For an excellent analysis of vigilantism, see Craig B. Little and Christopher Sheffield, "Frontiers and Criminal Justice: English Private Prosecution Societies and American Vigilantism in the Eighteenth and Nineteenth Centuries," *American Sociological Review* 48 (December 1983): 796–808.

42. Ray Allen Billington, *Westward Expansion: A History of the American Frontier* (New York: Macmillan, 1974), 587.

43. Joe B. Frantz and Julian Ernest Choate Jr., *The American Cowboy: The Myth and the Reality* (Norman: University of Oklahoma Press, 1955), 78.

44. Billington, *Westward Expansion*, 787. See also Frank Richard Prassal, *The Western Peace Officer* (Norman: University of Oklahoma Press, 1972), 22, and the numerous works cited by Billington.

45. An excellent summary treatment of this subject is found in Billington, *Westward Expansion*, chap. 30. For a more general treatment of western violence, see W. Eugene Hollon, *Frontier Violence* (New York: Oxford University Press, 1974). Hollon notes that "of all the myths that refuse to die, the hardiest concerns the extent of the unmitigated bloodletting that occurred in the Western frontier during the closing decades of the nineteenth century" (p. x).

46. Richard Slotkin, *The Fatal Environment: The Myth of the Frontier in the Age of Industrialization, 1800–1890* (New York: Atheneum, 1985), 15–16. See also Slotkin's other two authoritative works on the myth of the frontier, *Regeneration through Violence* (Middletown, Conn.: Wesleyan University Press, 973); and *Gunfighter Nation*.

47. This is a primary theme of Richard Slotkin's trilogy. As film director Joel Schumacher noted, "Guns are as much a part of the movies as they are of American culture." Quoted in Jeff Silverman, "Romancing the Gun," *New York Times*, 20 June 1993. Silverman argues that guns are increasingly eroticized and prominently featured in American movies, a fixation that persists despite Hollywood's liberal leanings.

48. Tom W. Smith, "The 75% Solution: An Analysis of the Structure of Attitudes on Gun Control, 1959–1977," *Criminology* 71 (Fall 1980): 309, 311.

49. Wright, Rossi, and Daly, *Under the Gun*, 112–20; Gregg Lee Carter, *The Gun Control Movement* (New York: Twayne, 1997).

50. Josh Sugarmann, *National Rifle Association: Money, Firepower and Fear* (Washington, D.C.: National Press Books, 1992), 27.

51. For more on these incidents, see Davidson, *Under Fire*, 3–19, 272–73.

52. Ibid., 194. According to Davidson, one leader of gun control forces called the Brady bill "a nice, innocuous piece of legislation." During the 1970s, even the NRA supported a waiting period (p. 194).

53. Dye, *Understanding Public Policy*, 14.

54. Theodore J. Lowi, "The State in Politics: The Relation between Policy and Administration," in *Regulatory Policy and the Social Sciences*, ed. Roger G. Noll (Berkeley: University of California Press, 1985), 68. See also Lowi, "What Political Scientists Don't Need to Ask about Policy Analysis," *Policy Studies Journal* 2 (1973): 61–67.

55. This list is a summary of the hypothesized political patterns of social regulatory policy described in Tatalovich and Daynes, "Conclusion: The Social Regulatory Policy Process," in *Moral Controversies in American Politics*, 258–70.

Chapter 2. The Second Amendment

1. Lucilius A. Emery, "The Constitutional Right to Keep and Bear Arms," *Harvard Law Review* 28 (March 1915): 473.

2. See, for example, Alan M. Gottlieb, *The Rights of Gun Owners* (Ottawa, Ill.: Green Hill, 1981).

3. "The Fight to Bear Arms," *U.S. News & World Report*, 22 May 1995, 29. See also James D. Wright, "Public Opinion and Gun Control: A Comparison of Results from Two Recent National Surveys," *Annals of the American Academy of Political and Social Science* 455 (May 1981): 37; and Nelson Lund, "The Second Amendment, Political Liberty, and the Right to Self-Preservation," *Alabama Law Review* 39 (1987): 105.

4. Mary Ann Glendon, *Rights Talk: The Impoverishment of Political Discourse* (New York: Free Press, 1991), 3–4.

5. Ibid., 8, 12, 14, 77, 171. Glendon's analysis parallels that of Robert N. Bellah et al., who discuss the self-expressive and self-gratifying qualities of modern Americans in *Habits of the Heart: Individualism and Commitment in American Life* (Berkeley: University of California Press, 1985).

6. State right-to-bear-arms provisions, and a more detailed examination of the Second Amendment, are found in Robert J. Spitzer, *The Right to Bear Arms: Rights and Liberties under the Law* (Santa Barbara, Calif.: ABC-CLIO, 2001).

7. Thomas Babington Macaulay, *The History of England from the Accession of James II*, 5 vols. (New York: Crowell, 1879), 1:117, 269.

8. Quoted in Roy G. Weatherup, "Standing Armies and Armed Citizens: An Historical Analysis of the Second Amendment," *Hastings Constitutional Law Quarterly* 2 (Fall 1975): 973.

9. Lois Schworer, "To Hold and Bear Arms: The English Perspective," in *The Second Amendment in Law and History*, ed. Carl T. Bogus (New York: New Press, 2001), 226. See also Emery, "The Constitutional Right to Keep and Bear Arms," 473–77; Peter Buck Feller and Karl L. Gotting, "The Second Amendment: A Second Look," *Northwestern University Law Review* 61 (March/April 1966): 48–49; Joyce Lee Malcolm, *To Keep and Bear Arms* (Cambridge, Mass.: Harvard University Press, 1994);

Wilbur Edel, *Gun Control* (Westport, Conn.: Praeger, 1995), 1–9; and Ralph J. Rohner, "The Right to Bear Arms: A Phenomenon of Constitutional History," *Catholic University of America Law Review* 16 (September 1966): 53–84.

10. Feller and Gotting, "Second Amendment," 48–49; Rohner, "Right to Bear Arms," 58; David T. Hardy, *Origins and Development of the Second Amendment* (Southport, Conn.: Blacksmith, 1986), 35; Lawrence D. Cress, "The Right to Bear Arms," in *By and for the People: Constitutional Rights in American History*, ed. Kermit L. Hall (Arlington Heights, Ill.: Harlan Davidson, 1991), 64–66; *National Commission on the Causes and Prevention of Violence* (Washington, D.C.: Government Printing Office, 1969), App. J; and Carl T. Bogus, "The Hidden History of the Second Amendment," *U.C. Davis Law Review* (Winter 1998): 375–86.

11. Macaulay, *History of England*, 1:269.

12. Keith Ehrman and Dennis A. Henigan, "The Second Amendment in the Twentieth Century: Have You Seen Your Militia Lately?" *University of Dayton Law Review* 15, (1989): 8–10. Firearms have been closely regulated in Britain from medieval times to the present.

13. Daniel J. Boorstin, *The Americans: The Colonial Experience* (New York: Vintage, 1964), 356; and Stephen Halbrook, *That Every Man Be Armed: The Evolution of a Constitutional Right* (Oakland, Calif.: Independent Institute, 1984), 58.

14. Lee Kennett and James L. Anderson, *The Gun in America* (Westport, Conn.: Greenwood, 1975), 61. See also Stephen Halbrook, "To Keep and Bear Their Private Arms," *Northern Kentucky Law Review* 10 (1982): 13–39.

15. Richard L. Perry, ed., *Sources of Our Liberties* (New York: American Bar Foundation, 1959), 7th in series, 34; 11th in series, 11.

16. Clinton Rossiter, *Seedtime of the Republic* (New York: Harcourt, Brace and World, 1953), 386–87. John K. Mahon defines militia (composed of "irregulars" or "citizen soldiers") as adult male citizens of fighting age (between eighteen and forty-five) obligated to enroll with the government for military service, serve for a few months every year, meet or train rarely when there was no impending emergency, only partially covered by military law, and usually under state command. Professional soldiers were volunteers who enlisted for several years, served even in peacetime, were under federal control, and were fully subject to military law. *The American Militia: Decade of Decision, 1789–1800* (Gainesville: University of Florida Press, 1960), v.

17. According to the historian James Flexner, "Utopian thinking backed the political preferences of state leaders by postulating that the best fighting force would be made up of militiamen who exerted their God-given natural gifts as they took turns defending their fields." *Washington: The Indispensable Man* (New York: New American Library, 1984), 111.

18. Merrill Jensen, *The New Nation* (New York: Vintage, 1965), 30. Despite common impressions to the contrary, service in colonial militias was not universal. See John Shy, *A People Numerous and Armed* (New York: Oxford University Press, 1976), 21–33; and Don Higginbotham, "The Federalized Militia Debate: A Neglected Aspect of Second Amendment Scholarship," *William and Mary Quarterly* 55 (January 1998): 39–58.

19. Boorstin, *The Americans*, 355–56; and Mahon, *American Militia*, 3.

20. Quoted in Weatherup, "Standing Armies and Armed Citizens," 979–80. At a later

point, Washington said of the militias that they ". . . consume your provisions, exhaust your stores, and leave you at last in a critical moment." Quoted in Mahon, *American Militia*, 5. According to Washington, the militia "system" was "sinking the cause" of the Revolution. See Flexner, *Washington*, 85; also 67, 83–84, 111.

21. During the Revolution, Congress was extremely reluctant to accede to General Washington's repeated requests for a larger professional force because of the fear that it "weakened the soldiers' state ties and seemed a possible instrument of tyranny." Flexner, *Washington*, 111.

22. Max Farrand, *The Framing of the Constitution of the United States* (New Haven, Conn.: Yale University Press, 1913), 49. Charles Pinckney argued that the states would see the wisdom of some degree of federal control over the state militias. For himself, Pinckney had "but a scanty faith in Militia. There must be (also) a real military force—This alone can (effectually answer the purpose.) The United States had been making an experiment without it, and we see the consequence in their rapid approaches toward anarchy [a reference to Shays's rebellion]." Max Farrand, ed., *The Records of the Federal Convention of* 1787, 4 vols. (New Haven: Yale University Press, 1966), 2:332. Theodore J. Lowi and Benjamin Ginsberg assert that "it is quite possible that the Constitutional Convention of 1787 in Philadelphia would never have taken place at all except for . . . Shays's Rebellion." *American Government: Freedom and Power* (New York: Norton, 1994), 34.

23. Farrand, *Records of the Federal Convention*, 2:326.

24. Ibid, 2:388. See also 1:465; 3:616–17.

25. Ibid., 4:59.

26. Ibid., 3:319.

27. Ibid., 3:420.

28. Ibid., 3:209.

29. Bernard Schwartz, *The Bill of Rights: A Documentary History*, 2 vols. (New York: Chelsea House, 1971), 2:773, 831.

30. New York, New Hampshire, North Carolina, and Rhode Island all recommended a bill of rights, including wording regarding militias and the right to bear arms.

31. Schwartz, *Bill of Rights*, 2:842. Other states that tacked on militia-related wording when they approved the Constitution used similar language.

32. Mahon, *American Militia*, 6. See also the remarks of Luther Martin to the Maryland ratifying convention in Farrand, *Records of the Federal Convention*, 3:207–8.

33. Helen E. Veit, Kenneth R. Bowling, and Charlene Bangs Bickford, eds., *Creating the Bill of Rights* (Baltimore: Johns Hopkins University Press, 1991), x, xiv, xv, 12, 30, 38, 48. Unlike the House, the Senate met in secret, so no official debate records exist. Supreme Court Chief Justice Warren Burger wrote that the Second Amendment "must be read as though the word 'because' was the opening word" of the amendment. "The Right to Bear Arms," *Parade*, 14 January 1990, 5.

34. Veit, Bowling, and Bickford, *Creating the Bill of Rights*, 182, 183–84, 198–99.

35. Ibid., 182. Gerry's reference to "the late revolution" was to Britain's Glorious Revolution of 1688.

36. For the common law basis of personal self-protection, see, for example, Joel Samaha, *Criminal Law* (Minneapolis/St. Paul: West, 1993), chap. 6. The irrelevance of such activities as hunting, sporting, and personal protection to the Second Amendment

are discussed in Andrew D. Herz, "Gun Crazy: Constitutional False Consciousness and Dereliction of Dialogic Responsibility," *Boston University Law Review* 75 (January 1995): 65–67.

37. 1 U.S. Stat. 271 (1792). The Act went on to direct that "commissioned officers shall severally be armed with a sword or hanger and espontoon, and that from and after five years from the passing of this act, all muskets for arming the militia as herein required, shall be of bores sufficient for balls of the eighteenth of a pound. And every citizen so armed, and providing himself with the arms, ammunition, and accoutrements required as aforesaid, shall hold the same exempted from all suits, distresses, executions or sales, for debt or for the payment of taxes."

38. Farrand, *Records of the Federal Convention*, 2:385. This wording, of course, allowed the government to provide arms, which it has done since the mid-nineteenth century.

39. Mahon, *American Militia*, 21–22, 25. On the other hand, militia forces suffered their most devastating defeat in American history at the hands of Native Americans, known as St. Clair's defeat, in 1791. See Arthur M. Schlesinger Jr. and Roger Bruns, eds., *Congress Investigates: A Documented History*, 1792–1974, 5 vols. (New York: Chelsea House, 1983), 1:3–101.

40. Local militias continued to gather for "musters" throughout much of the nineteenth century, but such gatherings were primarily social occasions that were important for their entertainment, sporting, and social consequences at a time when Americans had few forms of amusement or entertainment. See Mahon, *American Militia*, 67–68; and William Riker, *Soldiers of the States: The Role of the National Guard in American Democracy* (Salem, N.H.: Ayer, 1979; first published 1957).

41. Ehrman and Henigan, "The Second Amendment in the Twentieth Century," 36; Mahon, *American Militia*, 48–49, 66–67.

42. Donald M. Snow and Dennis M. Drew, *From Lexington to Desert Storm* (Armonk, N.Y.: M.E. Sharpe, 1994), 261–62. See also Frederick B. Wiener, "The Militia Clause of the Constitution," *Harvard Law Review* 54 (December 1940): 188–89.

43. Stephen Skowronek, *Building a New American State* (Cambridge, England: Cambridge University Press, 1982), 315, n. 17.

44. James D. Richardson, *Messages and Papers of the Presidents*, 11 vols. (Washington, D.C.: Bureau of National Literature, 1913), 9: 66–70.

45. 32 Stat. 775–80 (1903), also known as the Dick Act.

46. 39 Stat. 166 (1916); see 197–203.

47. 32 U.S.C. 7014–16 (1959). The National Guard is today paid and equipped by the national government.

48. See 10 U.S.C. 311 (1983). The organized militia today includes the National Guard and the Naval Militia.

49. There was a militia call-up at the start of the Civil War, but as the Civil War historian James M. McPherson noted: "By the 1850s the old idea of militia service as an obligation of all males had given way to the volunteer concept." Those militia outfits still meeting at all "spent more time drinking than drilling." *Battle Cry of Freedom* (New York: Oxford University Press, 1988), 317.

50. According to the constitutional scholar Frederick B. Wiener, "the Second Amendment, which purportedly guarantees the right to bear arms, is now substantially a dead letter in the face of police power necessities and a recession from the frontier."

"Militia Clause of the Constitution," 186. This history and interpretation of militias is confirmed in *Maryland* v. *U.S.* (381 U.S. 41; 1965) and in *Perpich* v. *Department of Defense* (496 U.S. 334; 1990).

51. 92 U.S. at 553. The only dissenter in the case was Justice Clifford. The three men in this case were charged under the Force Act of 1870, a civil rights act that made it a federal crime to conspire to intimidate or injure citizens in order to prevent them from exercising their constitutional rights.

52. The case was *Chicago, Burlington and Quincy Railroad Co.* v. *Chicago*, 166 U.S. 226 (1897), in which eminent domain from the Fifth Amendment was applied to the states using the Fourteenth Amendment.

53. Justice Hugo Black argued for total incorporation, but the idea never found wide acceptance on the Court or elsewhere. Daniel A. Farber, William N. Eskridge Jr., and Philip Frickey say, for example, that "the Supreme Court never accepted Justice Black's theory as a matter of constitutional interpretation." *Constitutional Law* (St. Paul, Minn.: West, 1993), 398. See Black's dissenting opinion in *Adamson* v. *California*, 332 U.S. 46 (1947), at 68–123.

54. In *Twining* v. *New Jersey* (211 U.S. 78; 1908), the Supreme Court cited Presser to underscore that the Second Amendment was not incorporated: "The right of trial by jury in civil cases, guaranteed by the 7th Amendment . . . and the right to bear arms, guaranteed by the 2nd Amendment (*Presser* v. *Illinois* . . .), have been distinctly held not to be privileges and immunities of citizens of the United States, guaranteed by the 14th Amendment against abridgment by the states" (at 98). The court has never reversed its decision to leave the Second Amendment out of the incorporation process. Because the Second Amendment confers a right on states, there would be no reason to incorporate it in any case, as it true of the Ninth and Tenth Amendments.

55. "[T]he right of the people to keep and bear arms (art. 2) is not infringed by laws prohibiting the carrying of concealed weapons" (281–82). The Court also ruled in *Patsone* v. *Commonwealth* (232 U.S. 138 [1914]) that a Pennsylvania law prohibiting unnaturalized, foreign-born persons from possessing firearms was constitutional.

56. Lund, "The Second Amendment, Political Liberty, and the Right to Self Preservation," 109. Sawed-off shotguns were used in trench warfare during World War I.

57. 307 U.S. 174; 26 U.S.C. 1132c. One reason the Court may not have addressed these broad issues more completely is that the defendants did not send a representative to argue their side before the Supreme Court in oral argument.

58. *Adams* v. *Williams* did not involve the Second Amendment as an issue. In it, Justice William O. Douglas objected to what he considered an illegal search of a suspect, which uncovered a gun. This prompted Douglas to question the ease with which Americans can obtain guns: "A powerful lobby dins into the ears of our citizenry that these gun purchases are constitutional rights protected by the Second Amendment. . . . There is under our decisions no reason why stiff state laws governing the purchase and possession of pistols may not be enacted. There is no reason why pistols may not be barred from anyone with a police record. There is no reason why a State may not require a purchaser of a pistol to pass a psychiatric test. There is no reason why all pistols should not be barred to everyone except the police." Douglas then cited *U.S.* v. *Miller* as precedent, and discussed the history behind the Second

Amendment. Justice Thurgood Marshall joined in the dissent. *Lewis* v. *U.S.* involved a man convicted for unlawfully possessing a weapon under the Omnibus Crime Control and Safe Streets Act of 1968. In his majority opinion, Justice Harry Blackmun recognized the propriety of the gun control provisions in the act, saying that they did not violate the Second Amendment: "These legislative restrictions on the use of firearms are neither based upon constitutionally suspect criteria, nor do they trench upon any constitutionally protected liberties. See *United States* v. *Miller*."

59. *U.S.* v. *Nelson,* 859 F.2d 1318 (8th Cir. 1988), at 1320. The other federal court of appeals cases include:

Cases v. *U.S.,* 131 F.2d 916, 922–23 (1st Cir. 1942), cert. denied sub nom   *V e - lazquez* v. *U.S.,* 319 U.S. 770 (1943);

U.S. v. *Tot,* 131 F.2d 261, 266 (3d Cir. 1942), reversed on other grounds, 319 U.S. 463 (1943);

U.S. v. *Johnson,* 441 F.2d 1134, 1136 (5th Cir. 1971);

Stevens v. *U.S.,* 440 F.2d 144, 149 (6th Cir. 1971);

U.S. v. *McCutcheon,* 446 F.2d 133, 135–36 (7th Cir. 1971);

U.S. v. *Decker,* 446 F.2d 164 (8th Cir. 1971);

U.S. v. *Synnes,* 438 F.2d 764 (8th Cir. 1971), vacated on other grounds, 404 U.S. 1009 (1972);

Cody v. *U.S.,* 460 F.2d 34, 36–37 (8th Cir. 1972), cert. denied, 409 U.S. 1010 (1972);

Eckert v. *City of Philadelphia,* 477 F.2d 610 (3d Cir. 1973), cert. denied 414 U.S. 839 (1973);

U.S. v. *Day,* 476 F.2d 562, 568 (6th Cir. 1973);

U.S. v. *Johnson,* 497 F.2d 548, 550 (4th Cir. 1974);

U.S. v. *Swinton,* 521 F.2d 1255 (10th Cir. 1975), cert. denied, 424 U.S. 918 (1976);

U.S. v. *Warin,* 530 F.2d 103, 106 (6th Cir. 1976), cert. denied, 426 U.S. 948 (1976);

U.S. v. *Graves,* 554 F.2d 65, 66–67 (3d Cir. 1977);

U.S. v. *Oakes,* 564 F.2d 384, 387 (10th Cir. 1977), cert. denied, 435 U.S. 926 (1978);

Quilici v. *Village of Morton Grove,* 695 F.2d 261, 270 (7th Cir. 1982), cert. denied, 464 U.S. 863 (1983);

Thomas v. *Members of City Council of Portland,* 730 F.2d 41 (1st Cir. 1984);

U.S. v. *Toner,* 728 F.2d 115 (2d Cir. 1984);

Farmer v. *Higgins,* 907 F.2d 1041 (11th Cir. 1990), cert. denied, 498 U.S. 1047 (1991);

U.S. v. *Hale,* 978 F.2d 1016 (8th Cir. 1992), cert. denied, 507 U.S. 997 (1993);

Fresno Rifle & Pistol Club v. *Van de Camp,* 965 F.2d 723 (9th Cir. 1992);

U.S. v. *Friel,* 1 F.3d 1231 (1st Cir. 1993);

Love v. *Pepersack,* 47 F.3d 120, 124 (4th Cir. 1995);

U.S. v. *Farrell,* 69 F.3d 891 (8th Cir. 1995);

Hickman v. *Block,* 81 F.3d 168 (9th Cir. 1996), cert. denied, 519 U.S. 912 (1996);

U.S. v. *Rybar,* 103 F.3d 273 (3d Cir. 1996), cert. denied, 522 U.S. 807 (1997);

U.S. v. *Wright,* 117 F.3d 1265, 1273 (11th Cir. 1997), cert. denied, 522 U.S. 1007 (1997);

Peoples Rights Organization, Inc. v. *City of Columbus,* 152 F.3d 522, 539 (6th Cir. 1998);

Gillespie v. *City of Indianapolis,* 185 F.3d 693 (7th Cir. 1999), cert. denied, 528 U.S. 1116 (2000);

U.S. v. *Napier,* 233 F.3d 394 (6th Cir. 2000);

U.S. v. *Metcalf,* 221 F.3d 1336 (6th Cir. 2000);

U.S. v. *Finitz,* 234 F.3d 1278 (9th Cir. 2000), cert. denied, 121 S. Ct. 833 (2001);

U.S. v. *Hancock,* 231 F.3d 557 (9th Cir. 2000), cert. denied, 121 S. Ct. 1641 (2001).

U.S. v. *Baer,* 235 F.2d 561 (10th Cir. 2000);

U.S. v. *Lewis,* 236 F.3d 948 (8th Cir. 2001);

U.S. v. *Haney,* 264 F.3d 1161 (10th Cir. 2001).

In a case appealed to the Supreme Court from New Jersey, *Burton* v. *Sills,* 394 U.S. 812 (1969), a challenge to a gun law alleging a violation of the Second Amendment was "dismissed for want of a substantial federal question."

Some of these cases, federal and state, are found in edited form in Earl R. Kruschke, *The Right to Keep and Bear Arms* (Springfield, Ill.: Charles C. Thomas, 1985).

60. Burger, "Right to Bear Arms," 4–6. Burger describes the militia-based history of the Second Amendment, noting that a "huge national defense establishment has taken over the role of the militia of 200 years ago" (p. 5).

61. See John Levin, "The Right to Bear Arms: The Development of the American Experience," *Chicago-Kent Law Review* 48 (Fall-Winter 1971): 159–62; and Dennis A. Henigan, "Arms, Anarchy and the Second Amendment," *Valparaiso University Law Review* 26 (1991): 108–9, 127. State court decisions that discuss a right to bear arms beyond militia activity are considered in David I. Caplan, "The Right of the Individual to Bear Arms: A Recent Judicial Trend," *Detroit College of Law Review* 4 (Winter 1982): 789–823; and Stephen Halbrook, *A Right to Bear Arms* (Westport, Conn.: Greenwood, 1989). Thirty-five state constitutions make some mention of a right to bear arms.

62. *Quilici* v. *Village of Morton Grove,* 532 F.Supp. 1169 (1981); 695 F.2d 261. See also Eric S. Freibrun, "Banning Handguns: *Quilici* v. *Village of Morton Grove* and the Second Amendment," *Washington University Law Quarterly* 60 (Fall 1982): 1087–1118. Residents are not denied their handguns, but must keep them in licensed gun clubs. The ordinance does not affect long guns.

63. *Quilici* v. *Village of Morton Grove,* 695 F.2d 261 (1982). The federal district court and court of appeals also found the law to be consistent with the Illinois state constitution (Article 1, sec. 22), which recognizes "the right of the individual citizen to keep and bear arms."

64. Joseph Story, *Commentaries on the Constitution* (Durham, N.C.: Carolina Academic Press, 1987; first pub. 1833), 708; and Thomas M. Cooley, *General Principles of Constitutional Law* (Boston: Little, Brown, 1898), 298–99. Cooley's book did not include discussion of the important *Presser* case until the subsequent (fourth) edition of this book, published in 1931, which buttressed the standard interpretation found in the writings of other constitutional scholars. Both Story and Cooley describe the broader, more general nature of keeping and bearing arms arising from the old-style unorganized militias and musters of the pre–Civil War era.

65. Irving Brant, *The Bill of Rights* (Indianapolis: Bobbs-Merrill, 1965), 486.

66. Robert A. Rutland, *The Birth of the Bill of Rights* (Chapel Hill: University of North Carolina Press, 1955), 229.

67. See *American Law Reports, Federal* (Rochester, N.Y.: Lawyers Co-Operative, 1983), 700–729. In 1975, the American Bar Association endorsed the understanding that the Second Amendment is connected with militia service. See Lund, "The Second Amendment, Political Liberty, and the Right to Self-Preservation," 105.

68. Neither the Ninth nor the Tenth amendments has been incorporated, as it is entirely unnecessary. The Ninth deals with enumeration of rights belonging directly to the people, and the Tenth already reserves powers to the states.

69. See Richard C. Cortner, *The Supreme Court and the Second Bill of Rights* (Madison: University of Wisconsin Press, 1981), 279.

70. Neil A. Lewis, "At the Bar," *New York Times*, 5 May 1995; "The Fight to Bear Arms," 36.

71. According to Andrew D. Herz, five writers account for twenty-five articles that seek other interpretations of the Second Amendment. "Gun Crazy," 138. NRA lawyer Stephen P. Halbrook alone had written three books and thirteen law journal articles on gun control and the Second Amendment as of the end of the 1990s. Bogus, "Hidden History of the Second Amendment," 318.

    The National Rifle Association has provided at least some of the support for this writing. A group formed in 1992 by individuals seeking to promote other interpretations of the Second Amendment, called Academics for the Second Amendment (ASA), asserted in a 1995 open letter that "The Second Amendment does not guarantee merely a 'right of the states,' but rather a 'right of the people,' a term which . . . is widely understood to encompass a personal right of citizens." The organization further states that "Our primary goal is to give the 'right to bear arms' enshrined in the Bill of Rights its proper, prominent place in Constitutional discourse and analysis." This group received $6000 from the NRA, out of a total of $90,000 raised by the group. The ASA's president, Joseph Olson, serves on the NRA's governing board. In 1992, the NRA's Firearms Civil Rights Legal Defense Fund contributed $5000 to cover the expenses for academics who attended the ASA conference that year. In 1993, the NRA's Legal Defense Fund contributed $99,000 "for undisclosed 'right to bear arms research and education.'" Scott Heller, "The Right to Bear Arms," *Chronicle of Higher Education*, 21 July 1995, A12.

    Further, the NRA offered a first prize of $25,000 for its 1994–95 essay contest titled "Stand Up for the Second Amendment." The annual contest "seeks publication-quality law review pieces on gun-rights issues." Herz, "Gun Crazy," 138, n. 358.

    A group of lawyers has created a comparable organization, called the Lawyer's Second Amendment Society (LSAS), which seeks to promote the idea that the Second Amendment "guarantees a personal right to keep and bear arms." Based in California, LSAS has also established a legal defense fund to appeal gun control cases. It publishes a newsletter, "The Liberty Pole."

72. See, for example, Don B. Kates, "Handgun Prohibition and the Original Meaning of the Second Amendment," *Michigan Law Review* 82 (November 1983): 206. The first law journal article taking the individualist view was published in 1960; prior to 1960, the conventional or court-based view of the Second Amendment discussed in this chapter appeared in thirteen law journal articles published from 1874 to 1959. See Robert J. Spitzer, "Lost and Found: Researching the Second Amendment," *Chicago-Kent Law Review* 76(2000): 349–401; Spitzer, *The Right to Bear Arms*, 72.

73. For example, Stuart R. Hays, "The Right to Bear Arms, a Study in Judicial Misinterpretation," *William and Mary Law Review* 2 (1960): 381–406; Caplan, "Right of the Individual to Bear Arms"; Robert E. Shalhope, "The Ideological Origins of the Second Amendment," *Journal of American History* 69 (December 1982): 599–614;

Robert J. Cottrol, "The Second Amendment: Invitation to a Multi-Dimensional Debate," in *Gun Control and the Constitution*, 3 vols. (New York: Garland, 1993), 1: ix-xi; and Halbrook, *That Every Man Be Armed*. An indication of the weakness of this argument is seen in an effort in 1989 to codify the "individualist" interpretation of the Second Amendment in a concurrent resolution introduced in the House of Representatives by Representative Philip Crane (R-Ill.). It read in part: "Whereas the Framers of the second amendment to the Constitution and those who ratified the second amendment intended that the individual retain the right to keep and bear arms in order to protect life, liberty, and property and to protect our Nation from those who would attempt to destroy our freedom: Now, therefore, be it Resolved . . . That it is the sense of the Congress that the Constitution provides that all individual citizens have the right to keep and bear arms, which right supersedes the power and authority of any government." No such resolution would be necessary if the verdict of history, law, and the courts supported this proposition to begin with. See Subcommittee on Crime, Judiciary Committee, House of Representatives, "Semiautomatic Assault Weapons Act of 1989," 101st Cong., 1st sess., hearings 5 and 6 April 1989 (Washington, D.C.: Government Printing Office, 1989), 53–54.

74. To pick an example, Stephen Halbrook quotes Patrick Henry as saying during the Virginia ratifying convention: "The great object is, that every man be armed. . . . Every one who is able may have a gun." This quote would seem to support the view that at least some early leaders advocated general popular armament aside from militia purposes. Yet here is the full quote from the original debates: "May we not discipline and arm them [the states], as well as Congress, if the power be concurrent? so that our militia shall have two sets of arms, double sets of regimentals, &c.; and thus, at a very great cost, we shall be doubly armed. *The great object is, that every man be armed.* But can the people afford to pay for double sets of arms, &c.? *Every one who is able may have a gun.* But we have learned, by experience, that, necessary as it is to have arms, and though our Assembly has, by a succession of laws for many years, endeavored to have the militia completely armed, it is still far from being the case" (emphasis added). It is perfectly obvious that Henry's comments are in the context of a discussion of the militia, and of the power balance between the states and Congress.

75. See 10 U.S.C. 311 (1983). Current code lists the lower age as seventeen, but in colonial times, the age range was of necessity wider.

76. This also puts to rest the assertion of some that the phrase "the people" in the Second Amendment somehow means all of the people, as is the case when the phrase appears in other parts of the Bill of Rights. Obviously, the Second Amendment is talking about only those people who could serve in a militia.

77. For example, William Van Alstyne, "The Second Amendment and the Personal Right to Bear Arms," *Duke Law Journal* 43 (April 1994): 1243, n. 19.

78. Stephen P. Halbrook, for example, claims that the *Presser* case "plainly suggests that the second amendment applies to the States through the fourteenth amendment" when in fact the court said precisely the opposite. "To Keep and Bear Their Private Arms," *Northern Kentucky Law Review* 10 (1982): 85. Sanford Levinson asks why the *Cruikshank* and *Presser* cases should be considered as legal precedent, because they occurred before the Supreme Court began the incorporation process in 1897. The obvious answer is because the courts have chosen not to incorporate the Second

Amendment and still consider the two cases binding precedent. "The Embarrassing Second Amendment," *Yale Law Journal* 99 (December 1989): 653. Some argue that the Fourteenth Amendment should be used to incorporate the Bill of Rights in totality, even though the courts have refused to do so. See, for example, Akhil Reed Amar, "The Bill of Rights and the Fourteenth Amendment," *Yale Law Journal* 101 (April 1992): 1193–1284.

David C. Williams extolls "the corruption-battling functions" of early militia service and the bearing of arms, arguing that such service "trained one in a life of virtue, both self-sacrificing and independent." Yet this characterization bears no relationship to the actual behavior of militias during the Revolution or after. "Civic Republicanism and the Citizen Militia: The Terrifying Second Amendment," *Yale Law Journal* 101 (1991): 556, 579–81.

79. Judith V. Best, *The Case against Direct Election of the President* (Ithaca, N.Y.: Cornell University Press, 1975).

80. Robert J. Cottrol, for example, says that the Supreme Court has shown "reluctance" to examine Second Amendment questions. "Second Amendment Debate," xxxii. Levinson says analysts "marginalize" the amendment. "Embarrassing Second Amendment," 640. Lund says that the Supreme Court has "ignored" the Second Amendment and that the courts are "uncomfortable" with it. "Second Amendment, Political Liberty, and the Right to Self-Preservation," 103.

81. See, for example, David I. Caplan, "Restoring the Balance: The Second Amendment Revisited," *Fordham Urban Law Journal* 5 (Fall 1976): 52; Robert Dowlut, "The Right to Bear Arms: Does the Constitution or the Predilection of Judges Reign?" *Oklahoma Law Review* 36 (Winter 1983): 67; Don B. Kates, "The Second Amendment and the Ideology of Self-Protection," *Constitutional Commentary* 9 (1992): 87–104; and Lund, "Second Amendment, Political Liberty, and the Right to Self-Preservation," 118, 130.

82. See Samaha, *Criminal Law*, chap. 6.

83. American Law Institute, *Model Penal Code and Commentaries* (Philadelphia: American Law Institute, 1985), vol. 1, pt. 1, pp. 380–81. See also the definition of self-defense in Henry C. Black, *Black's Law Dictionary* (St. Paul, Minn.: West, 1983), 707.

84. Robert E. Shalhope says the Second Amendment protects weapons possession for Americans in part "for the purpose of keeping their rulers sensitive to the rights of the people." Would this make, say, Lee Harvey Oswald, John Wilkes Booth, and David Koresh true democrats? "The Ideological Origins of the Second Amendment," *Journal of American History* 69 (December 1982): 614. See also Halbrook, *That Every Man Be Armed*, 68, 194–95; Lund, "The Second Amendment, Political Liberty, and the Right to Self-Preservation," 111–16; Wayne LaPierre, *Guns, Crime, and Freedom* (Washington, D.C.: Regnery, 1994), 19–20; and Glenn H. Reynolds, "The Right to Keep and Bear Arms under the Tennessee Constitution," *Tennessee Law Review* 61 (Winter 1994): 668–69. For a more complex discussion, see Williams, "Civic Republicanism and the Citizen Militia," 588–94.

85. Roscoe Pound, *The Development of Constitutional Guarantees of Liberty* (New Haven: Yale University Press, 1957), 90–91. See also Wendy Brown, "Guns, Cowboys, Philadelphia Mayors, and Civic Republicanism: On Sanford Levinson's 'The Embarrassing Second Amendment,'" *Yale Law Journal* 99 (December 1989): 661–67.

86. Saul Cornell, *Whose Right to Bear Arms Did the Second Amendment Protect?* (Boston: Bedford/St. Martin's, 2000), 19–20. Stuart R. Hays goes so far as to cite with approval the Civil War as an instance of "the right to revolt when the laws of the government began to oppress." Whatever one thinks of that conflict, the effort of southern states to break away from the Union was not within the bounds of the Constitution but an attack on the document, and was a threat to the Union's continued existence. "Right to Bear Arms," 382.

87. The Calling Forth Act states as its purpose "to provide for calling forth the Militia to execute the laws of the Union, suppress insurrections and repel invasions." Section 1 of the act says "in case of an insurrection in any state, against the government thereof, it shall be lawful for the President of the United States, on application of the legislature of such state, or of the executive (when the legislature cannot be convened) to call forth such number of the militia of any other state or states, as may be applied for, or as he may judge sufficient to suppress such insurrection." Section 2 says "That whenever the laws of the United States shall be opposed, or the execution thereof obstructed, in any state, by any combinations too powerful to be suppressed by the ordinary course of judicial proceedings . . . it shall be lawful for the President of the United States to call forth the militia of such state to suppress such combinations, and to cause the laws to be duly executed. And if the militia of a state . . . shall refuse, or be insufficient to suppress the same, it shall be lawful for the President, if the legislature of the United States be not in session, to call forth and employ such numbers of the militia of any other state or states most convenient thereto."

88. See, for example, Robert J. Cottrol and Raymond T. Diamond, "The Second Amendment: Toward an Afro-Americanist Reconsideration," *Georgetown Law Journal* 80 (1991): 309–61; and Stefan B. Tahmassebi, "Gun Control and Racism," *George Mason University Civil Rights Law Journal* 1 (Winter 1990): 67–99. Blacks were undeniably deprived of the fundamental right of self-protection, pertaining to, but not limited to, weapons possession. Yet extension of weapons ownership to a subdominant group in society at a time when the group was deprived of most other basic freedoms and protections would in all likelihood be a formula for racial annihilation, as was the case with Native Americans: it would give the dominant group an excuse to attack. A discussion of women and the Second Amendment can be found in Jeffrey R. Stone, Richard A. Epstein, and Cass R. Sunstein, eds., *The Bill of Rights in the Modern State* (Chicago: University of Chicago Press, 1992).

89. Cottrol and Diamond, "The Second Amendment," 335.

90. Bogus, "Hidden History of the Second Amendment." See also idem, "Race, Riots, and Guns," *Southern California Law Review* 66 (May 1993): 365–88.

91. Subcommittee on the Constitution, Judiciary Committee, U.S. Senate, "The Right to Keep and Bear Arms," 97th Cong., 2d sess. (Washington, D.C.: Government Printing Office, February 1982), 14.

92. Ibid.

93. In *Lewis*, the Senate report took Justice Blackmun's affirmation of *U.S. v. Miller* to mean only that convicted felons may be deprived of rights, when in fact Blackmun was affirming the militia-based understanding of the Second Amendment as it was laid out in *Miller*. Here is how the Senate report discussed *Lewis*: "a footnote in *Lewis* v. *United States*, indicated only that 'these legislative restrictions on the use of

firearms'—a ban on possession by felons—were permissible. But because felons may constitutionally be deprived of many of the rights of citizens, including that of voting, this dicta reveals little." Here's the full quote from *Lewis*: "These legislative restrictions on the use of firearms are neither based upon constitutionally suspect criteria, nor do they trench upon any constitutionally protected liberties. See *United States* v. *Miller* . . . (the Second Amendment guarantees no right to keep and bear a firearm that does not have 'some reasonable relationship to the preservation or efficiency of a well regulated militia')." Contrary to the Supreme Court's own rulings, the report also argues wrongly that *Cruikshank* has been rendered irrelevant because it occurred before the Court began the incorporation process.

To cite another example of bad analysis, Robert E. Shalhope says that of the four key Supreme Court cases, only *U.S.* v. *Miller* "relate[s] gun ownership to the militia." Shalhope, "Ideological Origins of the Second Amendment," 600. This is manifestly untrue, as *Presser* gives this extended attention, and *Cruikshank* makes reference to "internal police," a synonym for the militia.

94. According to the historian Ralph Ketcham, "the anti-federalists saw in the enlarged powers of the central government only the familiar threats to the rights and liberties of the people." *The Anti-Federalist Papers and the Constitutional Convention Debates* (New York: New American Library, 1986), 16.

95. Garry Wills, "To Keep and Bear Arms," *New York Review of Books*, 21 September 1995, 68. Wills's article is as careful and detailed an account of the meaning of the words behind the Second Amendment as exists in print.

Chapter 3. The Criminological Consequences of Guns

1. Michael Moriarty, "Get Rid of Guns, Says Father of Boy Killed in Accident," *Syracuse Post-Standard*, 16 October 1989; and John O'Brien, "Family: Lax Gun Rules Led to Death," *Syracuse Post-Standard*, 26 April 1991.

2. "Women Find Security Behind a Gun," *Syracuse Herald American*, 9 September 1990. Marion Hammer later became the first female president of the National Rifle Association.

3. Robert Reinhold, "After Shooting, Horror but Few Answers," *New York Times*, 19 January 1989; and Osha Gray Davidson, *Under Fire: NRA and the Battle for Gun Control* (New York: Holt, 1993), 3–19.

4. Gary Taubes, "Violence Epidemiologists Test the Hazards of Gun Ownership," *Science* 258 (9 October 1992): 213–15; and Jane Gross, "Joining War over Guns, New Voices: Physicians," *New York Times*, 16 November 1993.

5. Murray Edelman, *The Symbolic Uses of Politics* (Urbana: University of Illinois Press, 1964), 121. Edelman also says that "language is not an independent variable but a catalyst in the shaping of perception. . . . People can potentially see an issue in several alternative lights, and the language form itself evokes some one of the potentialities." *Politics as Symbolic Action* (Chicago: Markham, 1971), 68.

6. Neil A. Lewis, "N.R.A. Takes Aim at Study of Guns as Public Health Risk," *New York Times*, 26 August 1995.

7. "U.S. Easily Leads World in Gun-Related Deaths," *New York Times*, 17 April 1998. See also Albert J. Reiss Jr. and Jeffrey A. Roth, eds., *Understanding and Preventing Violence*

(Washington, D.C.: National Academy Press, 1993); Jack Levin and James A. Fox, *Mass Murder: America's Growing Menace* (New York: Plenum, 1985); and Fox Butterfield, "Experts Explore Rise in Mass Murder," *New York Times*, 19 October 1991.

8. Peter Applebome, "Verdict in Louisiana Killing Reverberates Across Nation," *New York Times*, 26 May 1993.

9. David E. Sanger, "After Gunman's Acquittal, Japan Struggles to Understand America," *New York Times*, 25 May 1993; and Adam Nossiter, "Judge Awards Damages in Japanese Youth's Death," *New York Times*, 16 September 1994. America's gun habits continued to receive considerable attention in Japan. The country closely followed the enactment of the Brady bill in 1993, and its passage in November was front-page news throughout the country. Japan also began distributing pamphlets to Japanese planning to visit the United States, discussing how to avoid danger and explaining such phrases as "Freeze" and "Get your hands up." "Japan Hopes Brady Bill Is First Step," *Syracuse Post-Standard*, 76 November 1993.

10. See Philip J. Cook, "The Technology of Personal Violence," in *Crime and Justice: A Review of Research*, ed. Michael Tonry (Chicago: University of Chicago Press, 1991), 4, 6–7, 28; Marianne W. Zawitz, "Guns Used in Crime," U.S. Department of Justice, Bureau of Justice Statistics, July 1995; and Philip J. Cook and Jens Ludwig, *Gun Violence: The Real Costs* (New York: Oxford University Press, 2000), viii.

   I do not propose to answer the chicken-and-egg question of whether guns cause or are merely incidental to violence. In all probability, the actual relationship incorporates elements of both. But one need not resolve this dilemma to note that the two are closely and inextricably linked in both image and fact. The homicide rate began to rise dramatically in the 1960s, as did the production and sale of handguns, which play a disproportionately large role in gun injuries and deaths.

11. Francis X. Clines, "As Gunfire Gets Closer, Fear Comes Home," *New York Times*, 12 December 1993; and Richard L. Berke, "Fears of Crime Rival Concern over Economy," *New York Times*, 23 January 1994.

12. Bob Herbert, "Deadly Data on Handguns," *New York Times*, 2 March 1994; Erik Eckholm, "A Basic Issue: Whose Hands Should Guns Be Kept Out Of?" *New York Times*, 3 April 1992; Zawitz, "Guns Used in Crime"; and "Guns by the Numbers," *Washington Post*, 13 April 2001.

13. Based on death rates in the 1980s and early 1990s, some predicted that gun deaths would exceed auto fatalities by the year 2000, since gun deaths rose 60 percent from 1968 to 1991, whereas auto fatalities declined 21 percent during the same time period. From 1985 to 1991, among 15- to 24-year-olds, auto deaths increased 18 percent, but gun deaths rose 40 percent. In 1991 gun deaths exceeded those from cars in California, New York, Texas, Louisiana, Nevada, Virginia, and the District of Columbia. The rates were tied in Maryland and nearly identical in Michigan. This prediction has not been realized, however, owing to declines in crime rates in the late 1990s, and the leveling off of automobile deaths. "Guns Gaining on Cars as Bigger Killer in U.S.," *New York Times*, 28 January 1994; and "Guns Surpassing Cars as Nation's Top Killer," *Syracuse Post-Standard*, 28 January 1994.

14. Garen J. Wintemute, Stephen Teret, and Jess F. Kraus, "The Epidemiology of Firearm Deaths among Residents of California," *Western Journal of Medicine* 146 (March 1987): 374–77; Sabra Chartrand, "Gunshot Wounds Labeled Epidemic,"

New York Times, 11 June 1992; "After Dark," *Economist*, 5 March 1994, 25–26; and "Guns and Crime," Crime Data Brief, U.S. Department of Justice, April 1994.

15. Philip J. Hilts, "Gunshots Killing More Teen-Agers," *New York Times*, 10 June 1992; "Study: Firearms Killed 4,200 Teens in 1990," *Syracuse Post-Standard*, 24 March 1993; "Guns Are No. 2 Cause of Death among the Young, Data Show," *New York Times*, 9 April 1996; Cook and Ludwig, *Gun Violence*, 18; Gregg Lee Carter, "Dueling Statistics," *Forum for Applied Research and Public Policy* (Winter 2000): 70; Office of Juvenile Justice and Delinquency Prevention, *Report to Congress on Juvenile Violence Research*, U.S. Department of Justice, July 1999, x.

16. Quoted in "As Cities Reach Record Number of Killings, Youths Play Grim Role," *New York Times*, 1 January 1994; Office of Juvenile Justice and Delinquency Prevention, *Challenging the Myths*, U.S. Department of Justice, Juvenile Justice Bulletin, February 2000, 5.

17. See, for example, James D. Wright, Peter H. Rossi, and Kathleen Daly, *Under the Gun: Weapons, Crime, and Violence in America* (New York: Aldine de Gruyter, 1983), 170. Policy expert Philip Cook has produced an estimate of a little more than five injuries for every gun death, based on a variety of data sources. See "The Case of the Missing Victims: Gunshot Woundings in the National Crime Survey," *Journal of Quantitative Criminology* 1 (1985): 91–102; and Cook, "Technology of Personal Violence," 12, According to a 1993 report issued by the New York State Legislative Commission on Science and Technology, the nationwide ratio of gun injuries to deaths is closer to 7.5 to 1. Luther F. Bliven, "Committee Studies Report on Firearms Crime," *Syracuse Post-Standard*, 1 June 1993.

   A new system for reporting all firearms injuries is in the process of being implemented, but the system is not expected to be operational until 2003. Under the current system, many firearms-related injuries are not reported. In New York City, for example, hospitals are not required to report gunshot injuries treated in emergency rooms or on an outpatient basis.

18. Nancy Gibbs, "Up in Arms," *Time*, 20 December 1993, 21; Reiss and Roth, *Understanding and Preventing Violence*, 256; Cook and Ludwig, *Gun Violence*, 11.

19. Erik Eckholm, "Ailing Gun Industry Confronts Outrage over Glut of Violence," *New York Times*, 8 March 1992; and Erik Eckholm, "A Little Gun Control, a Lot of Guns," *New York Times*, 15 August 1993. See also "Guns in America: National Survey on Private Ownership and Use of Firearms," *National Institute of Justice*, May 1997; Bureau of Justice Statistics, *Sourcebook of Criminal Justice Statistics 1999* (Washington, D.C.: Government Printing Office, 2000), 138–39; Philip J. Cook and Mark H. Moore, "Guns, Gun Control, and Homicide," in *Homicide: A Sourcebook of Social Research*, ed. M. Dwayne Smith and Margaret A. Zahn (Thousand Oaks, Calif.: Sage), 278.

20. Franklin E. Zimring, "Firearms, Violence and Public Policy," *Scientific American* 265 (November 1991): 50. Cook offers similar numbers. See "Technology of Personal Violence," 23; Zawitz, "Guns Used in Crime," 2; "Handgun Use Rose in 1993, Reports Show," *New York Times*, 10 July 1995; Josh Sugarmann, *Every Handgun is Aimed at You* (New York: The New Press, 2001).

21. Philip J. Cook, "Guns and Crime: The Perils of Long Division," *Journal of Policy Analysis and Management* 1 (1981): 120–25. When divided out, however, the per year

use of handguns in crime as a percentage of all handguns is small, as guns have a long shelf life. Gary Kleck provides an estimate of .9 percent of handguns involved in crime in any one year, a figure consistent with Cook's estimate. *Point Blank: Guns and Violence in America* (New York: Aldine de Gruyter, 1991), 44.

22. For more on the relationship between handguns and crime, see Bureau of Alcohol, Tobacco and Firearms, *Project Identification: A Study of Handguns Used in Crime* (Washington, D.C.: Bureau of Alcohol, Tobacco, and Firearms, 1976); Comptroller General of the United States, *Handgun Control: Effectiveness and Costs* (Washington, D.C.: General Accounting Office, 6 February 1978); and Bureau of Justice Statistics, "Handgun Crime Victims," *Special Report* (Washington, D.C.: U.S. Department of Justice, July 1990). On the importance of bullet caliber and speed, see Jeremy J. Hollerman, "Gunshot Wounds," *American Family Physician* 37 (1988): 231–46; Franklin E. Zimring, "The Medium Is the Message: Firearm Calibre as a Determinant of Death from Assault," *Journal of Legal Studies* 1 (January 1972): 97–124; Sugarmann, *Every Handgun Is Aimed at You.*

23. From a 1978 survey, reported in Wright, Rossi, and Daly, *Under the Gun,* 96.

24. Cook, "Technology of Personal Violence," 28–29.

25. The study by James D. Wright and Peter H. Rossi is based on self-administered questionnaires to 1,874 prisoners in ten states. The sample was not random but was based (for reasons the authors discuss) on convenience. Thus the group studied cannot be considered representative of prisoners, or of those who do or do not use guns in crimes. Nor does it reflect those who use guns illegally but are not caught and imprisoned. Still, it is an important research effort. *Armed and Considered Dangerous: A Survey of Felons and Their Firearms* (New York: Aldine de Gruyter, 1986). As Daniel D. Polsby noted, those in prison "are remarkable neither for honesty nor acute introspection." "Reflections on Violence, Guns, and the Defensive Use of Lethal Force," *Law and Contemporary Problems* 49 (Winter 1986): 97. See also Gary S. Green, "Citizen Gun Ownership and Criminal Deterrence: Theory, Research, and Policy," *Criminology* 25 (February 1987): 70–71.

26. Wright and Rossi, *Armed and Considered Dangerous,* 15–17, 128.

27. Gary Kleck and Karen McElrath, "The Effects of Weaponry on Human Violence," *Social Forces* 69 (March 1991): 669–92; and Philip J. Cook and Mark H. Moore, "Gun Control," in *Crime,* ed. James Q. Wilson and Joan Petersilig (San Francisco: ICS Press, 1995), 272–75.

28. Franklin E. Zimring, "Is Gun Control Likely to Reduce Violent Killings?" *University of Chicago Law Review* 35 (Summer 1968): 721–37. See also Zimring, "Medium Is the Message"; Philip J. Cook, "The Effect of Gun Availability on Robbery and Robbery Murder: A Cross Section Study of Fifty Cities," in *Policy Studies Review Annual,* ed. Robert H. Haveman and B. Bruce Zellner (Beverly Hills, Calif.: Sage, 1979); Cook, "Robbery Violence," *Journal of Criminal Law and Criminology* 78 (Summer 1987): 357–76; and Franklin E. Zimring and Gordon Hawkins, *Crime Is Not the Problem* (New York: Oxford University Press, 1997). Wright, Rossi, and Daly are more cautious in their support of this principle. *Under the Gun,* 203, 209.

29. In 1989, for example, the success rate for noncommercial robberies was 70 percent when guns were used, 55 percent when knives were used, and 49 percent when clubs or other instruments were used. Cook, "Technology of Personal Violence," 21.

30. Leonard Berkowitz and Anthony Le Page, "Weapons as Aggression-Eliciting Stimuli," *Journal of Personality and Social Psychology* 7 (October 1967): 202–7; Berkowitz, "Impulse, Aggression and the Gun," *Psychology Today* 2 (September 1968): 19–22; and Berkowitz, "How Guns Control Us," *Psychology Today* 15 (June 1981): 11–12.

31. Alfred Blumstein and Richard Rosenfeld, "Assessing the Recent Ups and Downs in U.S. Homicide Rates," *National Institute of Justice Journal* 237 (October 1998): 10.

32. Philip J. Cook, "The Effect of Gun Availability on Violent Crime Patterns," *Annals of the American Academy of Political and Social Science* 455 (May 1981): 63–79; Cook, "Technology of Personal Violence," 4, 28; Kleck and McElrath, "Effects of Weaponry on Human Violence"; Franklin E. Zimring, "Reflections on Firearms and the Criminal Law," *Journal of Criminal Law and Criminology* 46 (Fall 1995): 7; Franklin E. Zimring and Gordon Hawkins, *Crime Is Not the Problem* (New York: Oxford University Press, 1997).

33. Gerald D. Robin, *Violent Crime and Gun Control* (Highland Heights, Ky.: Academy of Criminal Justice Sciences, 1991), 3–4. An important factor in at least some such incidents may be alcohol. For more on the link between alcohol and homicide, see Robert N. Parker and Linda-Ann Rebhun, *Alcohol and Homicide: A Deadly Combination of Two American Traditions* (Albany, N.Y.: SUNY Press, 1994).

34. On policymakers and guns, see Kleck, *Point Blank*, 223. Percentages are from John Henry Sloan et al., "Firearm Regulations and Rates of Suicide," *New England Journal of Medicine* 322 (8 February 1990): 369. On increasing use of guns in female suicides, see Wright, Rossi, and Daly, *Under the Gun*, 167–68.

35. J.J. Card, "Lethality of Suicidal Methods and Suicide Risk: Two Distinct Concepts," *Omega* 5 (1974): 37–45; and Kleck, *Point Blank*, 258.

36. Kleck, *Point Blank*, 225, 226; and Cook, "Technology of Personal Violence," 24.

37. See Mark S. Kaplan, Margaret E. Adamek, and Scott Johnson, "Trends in Firearm Suicide among Older American Males: 1979–1988," *Gerontologist* 34 (February 1994): 59–65; Cook and Ludwig, *Gun Violence*, 23.

38. As Cook observes, "Surely someone who purposefully points a gun at a vital area and pulls the trigger expects to die." "Technology of Personal Violence," 25.

39. Ronald V. Clarke and David Lester, *Suicide: Closing the Exits* (New York: Springer Verlag, 1989), vii. The difficulties of studying displacement are discussed on pp. 76–77.

40. Arthur L. Kellerman et al., "Suicide in the Home in Relation to Gun Ownership," *New England Journal of Medicine* 327 (13 August 1992): 467.

41. Robert E. Markush and Alfred A. Bartolucci, "Firearms and Suicide in the United States," *American Journal of Public Health* 74 (1984): 123–27; David Lester, "An Availability-Acceptability Theory of Suicide," *Activitas Nervosa Superior* 29 (1987): 164–66; and David Lester, "Restricting the Availability of Guns as a Strategy for Preventing Suicide," *Biology and Society* 5 (1988): 127–29.

42. Card, "Lethality of Suicide Methods and Suicide Risk"; Richard Seiden, "Suicide Prevention: A Public Health/Public Policy Approach," *Omega* 8 (1977): 267–76; Myron Boor, "Methods of Suicide and Implications for Suicide Prevention," *Journal of Clinical Psychology* 37 (1981): 70–75; Clarke and Lester, *Suicide*; Kellerman et al., "Suicide in the Home in Relation to Gun Ownership"; Garen J. Wintemute et al., "Mortality among Recent Purchasers of Handguns," *New England Journal of Medicine* 341 (November 1999): 1583–89.

In his tabular synthesis of the existing literature, Kleck summarizes a lengthy list of studies. Yet he fails to include any of the studies listed here, all of which militate against his arguments, and he omits others as well. *Point Blank*, 265–67.

43. Clarke and Lester, *Suicide*, 72; see also chaps. 4 and 5 of this book.

44. Kellerman et al., "Suicide in the Home in Relation to Gun Ownership." Rather than rely on aggregate statistics, this study was based on an intensive analysis of the counties incorporating Memphis, Tennessee, and Seattle, Washington, from 1987 to 1990.

45. Sloan et al., "Firearm Regulations and Rates of Suicide." This study was based on a comparison of the counties incorporating Seattle, Washington, and Vancouver, British Columbia, Canada.

46. Cook, "Technology of Personal Violence," 26.

47. David A. Brent, Joshua A. Perper, and Christopher J. Allman, "Alcohol, Firearms, and Suicide among Youth," *Journal of the American Medical Association* 257 (26 June 1987): 3369; and Jane E. Brody, "Suicide Myths Cloud Efforts to Save Children," *New York Times*, 16 June 1992. For more on suicide and children, see Cynthia R. Pfeffer, *The Suicidal Child* (New York: Guilford Press, 1986).

48. Brody, "Suicide Myths Cloud Efforts to Save Children."

49. Ibid.

50. Mark L. Rosenberg, James A. Mercy, and Vernon N. Houk, "Guns and Adolescent Suicides," *Journal of the American Medical Association* 266 (4 December 1991): 3030.

51. David A. Brent et al., "The Presence and Accessibility of Firearms in the Homes of Adolescent Suicides: A Case-Control Study," *Journal of the American Medical Association* 266 (4 December 1991): 2989–95; Rosenberg, Mercy, and Houk, "Guns and Adolescent Suicides," 3030; Sean Joe and Mark S. Kaplan, "Firearm-Related Suicide among Young African-American Males," *Psychiatric Services* 53 (March 2002): 332–34.

52. Brent, Perper, and Allman, "Alcohol, Firearms, and Suicide among Youth," 3372. This finding was based on an earlier analysis of the blood and urine of suicide victims in Australia.

53. Wright, Rossi, and Daly, *Under the Gun*, 168–70; Cook, "Technology of Personal Violence," 8, 12–13. According to one study, the ratio of accidental gun injury to accidental gun death in 1992 was 13 to 1. See Joseph L. Annest et al., "National Estimates of Nonfatal Firearm-Related Injuries," *Journal of the American Medical Association* 273 (14 June 1995): 1751.

54. Zimring, "Firearms, Violence and Public Policy," 52; Wright, Rossi, and Daly, *Under the Gun*, 169; and Garen J. Wintemute et al., "When Children Shoot Children," *Journal of the American Medical Association* 257 (12 June 1987): 3107–9; Cook and Ludwig, *Gun Violence*, 27. See Kleck, *Point Blank*, 309. Kleck rails against those who use the word "children" to apply to those up to the age of eighteen, viewing the use of the term as serving "no purpose other than the propagandistic one of duping people into believing that accidental gun deaths are common among small children" (p. 277).

According to the *Britannica World Language Dictionary*, child is defined as "a young person of either sex at any age less than maturity, but most commonly one between infancy and youth." Clearly, the concern is with "minors," those who have not reached the age of majority, generally eighteen.

55. Wintemute et al., "When Children Shoot Children."
56. David McDowall and Colin Loftin, "Collective Security and Fatal Firearm Accidents," *Criminology* 23 (August 1985): 401, 403.
57. See Kleck, *Point Blank*, chap. 7. Kleck places little emphasis on the nonfatal injury rate.
58. Douglas A. Smith and Craig D. Uchida, "The Social Organization of Self-Help: A Study of Defensive Weapon Ownership," *American Sociological Review* 53 (February 1988): 94–102. See also McDowall and Loftin, "Collective Security and Fatal Firearm Accidents," 401–16. A useful discussion of self-defense and its relationship to deterrence is found in Green, "Citizen Gun Ownership and Criminal Deterrence."
59. Cook, "Technology of Personal Violence," 57–58. According to the National Crime Survey, from 1979 to 1987, burglaries were successful when the victim was home in 33 percent of the instances, compared to a success rate of 14 percent when the victim used a gun.
60. See Wright and Rossi, *Armed and Considered Dangerous*, 148. But see also Cook, "Effect of Gun Availability on Robbery and Robbery Murder"; and Cook, "Technology of Personal Violence," 60. In two actual instances where localities promoted gun possession to combat crime, Orlando, Florida, and Kennesaw, Georgia, the available data provide no reliable evidence that crime patterns were altered. Gary Kleck and David J. Bordua note that the rape rate dropped at the time of the Orlando intervention program. "The Factual Foundation for Certain Key Assumptions of Gun Control," *Law and Policy Quarterly* 5 (1983): 271–98. But Gary Green found fault with the city's police data on which the study was based, noting that the rape rate was reported at zero three years before the city program and that it recorded drops even larger than that attributed to the Orlando gun program before the program was implemented. "Citizen Gun Ownership and Criminal Deterrence," 73–75. For the Kennesaw case, see Kleck, "Crime Control through the Private Use of Armed Force," versus Cook, "Technology of Personal Violence," 61.
61. For example, Green, "Citizen Gun Ownership and Criminal Deterrence," 70–77; and Zawitz, "Guns Used in Crime," 3.
62. Kleck, *Point Blank*, 107, Kleck produced a figure of 645,000 defensive handgun uses in 1980, compared to 580,000 criminal handgun uses in the same year, leading him to conclude that the two uses balance each other out. "Crime Control through the Private Use of Armed Force," *Social Problems* 35 (February 1988): 1–21. The NRA's *American Rifleman* reported in its January 1994 issue that Kleck was now estimating "as many as 2.4 million defensive uses of firearms each year in America." "Gary Kleck Honored," 7.
63. Kleck's estimate assumes that the National Crime Victimization Survey, which in past years reported an average of about 55,000 defensive uses of guns per year, somehow failed to report another 945,000 defensive uses of guns per year. Kleck relied primarily on a 1981 Hart poll and a 1990 Mauser survey that asked if members of the respondents' households had used a handgun (the Mauser survey included any gun) for protection any time at work, home, or elsewhere, in the previous five years. The results, based on extrapolation from the sample, suggested that guns had been used for self-defense about 3 million times over five years. Yet such recall data is inherently unreliable in survey research, and the vagueness of the question makes the results highly

suspect. The additional surveys he cites as corroborating pose even greater problems, for example, by failing to distinguish between uses against animals versus people or by extending the retrospective period to "ever." Moreover, self-protection was defined so broadly that it would include such circumstances as investigating a noise in the basement. In essence, Kleck makes no distinction between actual and imagined instances of self-defense uses of guns. The numerous problems with Kleck's data are ironic in the light of his harsh criticism of the methodologies of those with whom he disagrees. *Point Blank*, 105–8, 146, 467–68. Kleck amplifies such criticisms in *Targeting Guns* (New York: Aldine DeGruyter, 1997). See also Cook, "Technology of Personal Violence," 54–55; and Robin, *Violent Crime and Gun Control*, 62.

The Kleck and Gertz poll, reported in "Armed Resistance to Crime," improves on the previous suspect polls, yet the survey's reliability is suspect because it was conducted privately (although the telephoning was done by a professional telephone polling firm) rather than by a professional survey organization, such as Gallup. Further, response validity was not verified by an outside, impartial expert unconnected with the research project. Kleck and Gertz dismiss the idea that their respondents would lie, yet they fail to consider another alternative—that their respondents believed they had encountered a serious self-defense instance, when in fact the belief might not jibe with the objective circumstances. That is, the self-defense belief might not coincide with an actual protection instance that would not have occurred without a gun. Philip Cook suggests, "It is quite possible that most 'self-defense' uses occur in circumstances that are normatively ambiguous: chronic violence within a marriage, gang fights, robberies of drug dealers, encounters with groups of young men who simply appear threatening." Cook and Moore, "Gun Control," 272.

An additional problem raised by Kleck's inability to verify the legitimacy of the alleged gun defense incidents is illustrated by the results of a study of gun ownership among urban gang members, in which self-protection was the most commonly cited reason for gun ownership. Most would question the legitimacy of such undoubtedly sincere sentiments expressed by members of urban gangs. See Beth Bjerregaard and Alan J. Lizotte, "Gun Ownership and Gang Membership," *Journal of Criminal Law and Criminology* 86 (Fall 1995): 37–58. See also Richard D. Alba and Steven E. Messner, "*Point Blank* Against Itself: Evidence and Inference about Guns, Crime, and Gun Control," *Journal of Quantitative Criminology* 11 (1995): 391–410; William Wells, "The Nature and Circumstances of Defensive Gun Use," *Justice Quarterly* 19 (March 2002): 127–57.

64. Cook, "Technology of Personal Violence," 56, 61–62. According to the data Cook obtained, from 1979 to 1987 an average of 6.8 million residential burglaries occurred per year. Of those, someone was home in about a million instances. Some kind of self-defensive action was taken in half these instances. Residents used guns in about 3 percent of the instances (a knife or other weapon was used in 2 percent). This yields a figure of 32,000 uses of guns. This figure is added to the 50,000 other defensive uses of guns to produce the 80,000 total. The 32,000 figure is significant because Kleck argues that most defensive gun uses occur in the home. See also Wright, Rossi, and Daly, *Under the Gun*, 149. Cook's numbers of defensive gun uses, and those of the National Crime Victimization Survey, have remained relatively constant at 80,000 to 85,000 per year. See Cook and Moore, "Gun Control," 270–72.

65. David Hemenway, "Survey Research and Self-Defense Gun Use: An Explanation of Extreme Overestimates," *Journal of Criminal Law and Criminology* 87 (Summer 1997): 1430–45; Tom W. Smith, "A Call for a Truce in the DGU War," *Journal of Criminal Law and Criminology* 87 (Summer 1997): 1462–69; and "Guns in America."

66. Gary Kleck and Marc Gertz, "Armed Resistance to Crime: The Prevalence and Nature of Self-Defense with a Gun," *Journal of Criminal Law and Criminology* 86 (Fall 1995): 150–87; Kleck and Gertz, "The Illegitimacy of One-Sided Speculation," *Journal of Criminal Law and Criminology* 87 (Summer 1997): 1460.

67. Gordon Witkin, "Should You Own a Gun?" *U.S. News & World Report*, 15 August 1994, 28. Cook went on to observe, "I don't understand why people would be so much more forthcoming with Kleck's survey callers than with the government's. I find that absurd." See also Dennis A. Henigan, E. Bruce Nicholson, and David Hemenway, *Guns and the Constitution* (Northampton, Mass.: Aletheia Press, 1995), 62–64.

68. Tom W. Smith, "A Call for a Truce in the DGU War," *Journal of Criminal Law and Criminology* 87 (Summer 1997): 1465. See also Kleck and Gertz, "The Illegitimacy of One-Sided Speculation"; Hemenway, "Survey Research and Self-Defense Gun Use," 1430–45; Philip J. Cook, Jens Ludwig, and David Hemenway, "The Gun Debate's New Mythical Number," *Journal of Policy Analysis and Management* 16 (Summer 1997): 463–69; Carter, "Dueling Statistics"; Deborah Homsher, *Women and Guns* (Armonk, N.Y.: M.E. Sharpe, 2002), 88.

69. According to one study, among robbery victims who used guns for self-defense, 17 percent reported injury, compared with an overall injury rate of 33 percent. Reiss and Roth, eds., *Understanding and Preventing Violence*, 266. See also Robin, *Violent Crime and Gun Control*, 70.

70. Reiss and Roth, eds., *Understanding and Preventing Violence*, 267 (based on data from the FBI); and Sue M. Holmes, "Weapons That Will Not Fire for Just Anybody," *Cortland Standard*, 19 April 1995.

71. Mike McAndrew, "Taking Aim under Fire," *Syracuse Post-Standard*, 13 March 1996.

72. Robert E, Drinan, "The Good Outweighs the Evil," in *The Gun Control Debate*, ed. Lee Nisbet (Buffalo, N.Y.: Prometheus Books, 1990), 58.

73. Arthur L. Kellerman and Donald T. Reay, "Protection or Peril? An Analysis of Firearm-Related Deaths in the Home," *New England Journal of Medicine* 314 (12 June 1986): 1557–60. For similar findings covering 1958 through 1973, see N.B. Rushforth et al., "Accidental Firearm Fatalities in a Metropolitan Area," *American Journal of Epidemiology* 100 (1975): 499–505.

74. Arthur L. Kellerman et al., "Gun Ownership as a Risk Factor for Homicide in the Home," *New England Journal of Medicine* 329 (7 October 1993): 1084–91. The study covered 1987 through 1992 for Washington State and Tennessee, and 1990 through 1992 for the Ohio county. The analysis was of 444 homicides committed in the home out of a total of 1,860 committed in the three counties during the time periods cited.

75. John Henry Sloan et al., "Handgun Regulations, Crime, Assaults, and Homicide," *New England Journal of Medicine* 319 (10 November 1988): 1260.

76. Arthur L. Kellerman et al., "Weapon Involvement in Home Invasion Crimes," *Journal of the American Medical Association* 273 (14 June 1995): 1759–62. Wintemute et al., "Mortality among Recent Purchasers of Handguns"; Mathew Miller, Deborah Azrael, and David Hemenway, "Firearm Availability and Unintentional Firearm

Deaths, Suicide, and Homicide among 5–14 Year Olds," *Journal of Trauma* 52 (February 2002): 267–75; Mark Duggan, "More Guns, More Crime," *Journal of Political Economy* 109 (October 2001): 1086–1114. David McDowall and Brian Wiersema report that from 1987 to 1990, fewer than two crimes in a thousand met armed resistance from victims. "The Incidence of Defensive Firearm Use by U.S. Crime Victims," *American Journal of Public Health* 84 (1994): 1982–84.

77. B. Bruce-Briggs, "The Great American Gun War," in *The Gun Control Debate*, 65. For more on self-defense, see Philip Cook, "The 'Saturday Night Special': An Assessment of Alternative Definitions from a Policy Perspective," *Journal of Criminal Law and Criminology* 72 (Winter 1981): 1741; and Robert Weissberg, *Public Opinion and Popular Government* (Englewood Cliffs, N.J.: Prentice Hall, 1976), 129.

78. Robert A. Sprecher, "The Lost Amendment," *American Bar Association Journal* 51 (June 1965): 668.

79. Larry Pratt, "Gun Laws Cost Lives," *Syracuse Post-Standard*, 8 January 1994. Pratt is vice president of the Gun Owners Foundation.

80. David McDowall, Colin Loftin, and Brian Wiersema, "Easing Concealed Firearms Laws: Effects on Homicide in Three States," *Journal of Criminal Law and Criminology* 86 (Fall 1995): 193–206; Center to Prevent Handgun Violence, "Legal Action Report," February 1998; "License to Kill, and Kidnap, and Rape, and Drive Drunk," Violence Policy Center, March 1999. See John R. Lott Jr. and David B. Mustard, "Crime, Deterrence, and Right-to-Carry Concealed Handguns," *Journal of Legal Studies* 26 (January 1997): 1–68, which argues that more gun carrying reduces crime.

81. Robert J. Spitzer, "More Permits Mean Less Crime . . . Maybe, but Not in Cities," *Los Angeles Times*, 19 February 1996. See also James Q. Wilson, "Just Take Away the Guns," *New York Times Magazine*, 20 March 1994; Rebecca Voelker, "States Debate 'Carrying Concealed Weapons' Laws," *Journal of the American Medical Association* 273 (14 June 1995): 1741; L. Sherman, J.W. Shaw, and D.P. Rogan, *The Kansas City Gun Experiment* (Washington, D.C.: National Institute of Justice, 1995); D.M. Kennedy, A.M. Piehl, and A.A. Braga, "Youth Violence in Boston," *Law and Contemporary Problems* 59 (1996): 147–96; Michael Janofsky, "Decline in Gun Violence Bypasses Philadelphia," *New York Times*, 10 May 1998; Bob Herbert, "A Winning Strategy," *New York Times,* 7 March 2002.

82. John R. Lott Jr., *More Guns, Less Crime* (Chicago: University of Chicago Press, 2000). Lott's argument appeared in an earlier coauthored article, Lott and Mustard, "Crime, Deterrence, and Right-to-Carry Concealed Handguns."

83. Dan A. Black and Daniel S. Nagin, "Do Right-to-Carry Laws Deter Violent Crime?" *Journal of Legal Studies* 27 (January 1998): 209–19; Kleck, *Targeting Guns*, 372. Kleck's discussion refers to Lott and Mustard, "Crime, Deterrence, and Right-to-Carry Concealed Handguns." Kleck does argue that the Lott study undercuts other studies showing that concealed carry laws produce an *increase* in crime, particularly murder. See also Jens Ludwig, "Guns and Numbers," *Washington Monthly* (June 1998), 50–51; Daniel W. Webster et al., "Flawed Gun Policy Research Could Endanger Public Safety," *American Journal of Public Health* 87 (June 1997): 918–21.

84. Hashem Dezhbakhsh and Paul H. Rubin, "Lives Saved or Lives Lost?" *American Economic Review Papers and Proceedings* 88 (May 1998): 468–74. Their analysis was based on Lott and Mustard, "Crime, Deterrence, and Right-to-Carry Concealed Handguns." My thanks to Mark Prus and Kathleen Burke for their insights on this matter.

85. Lott, *More Guns, Less Crime,* chapter 3. Bureau of Justice Statistics, *Sourcebook of Criminal Justice Statistics* 1999, 138–39; Kleck, *Targeting Guns,* 98–99; Harry Henderson, *Gun Control* (New York: Facts on File, 2000), 230.

86. Ted Goertzel, "Myths of Murder and Multiple Regression," *Skeptical Inquirer,* January/February 2002, 19–21; Duggan, "More Guns, More Crime." Goertzel's article argues that econometric modeling has failed to live up to its promise of resolving such controversial national issues as gun control and capital punishment.

87. Lott, *More Guns, Less Crime,* 24–25, 112.

88. Jens Ludwig, "Do Carry-Concealed Weapons Laws Deter Crime?" *Spectrum* 70 (Spring 1997): 29.

89. A 1977 survey of Florida felons found that guns were obtained in private transactions in about one-third of the instances, one-quarter through theft, one-quarter through retail purchase, and the rest through gifts or borrowing. Reported in Wright and Rossi, *Armed and Considered Dangerous,* 182. In their own survey, Wright and Rossi found that among inmates reporting having handguns before their incarceration, 43 percent were purchases, 32 percent thefts, 8 percent were borrowed, 8 percent gifts, and 7 percent trades. Among those who had had long guns, the figures were comparable: 42 percent purchases, 23 percent thefts, 22 percent gifts, and 6–7 percent borrow or trade. These figures do not mean that all those surveyed used guns in the commission of crimes, but merely report ownership patterns. See also Wright, Rossi, and Daly, *Under the Gun,* 119; and Steven Brill, *Firearm Abuse: A Research and Policy Report* (Washington, D.C.: Police Foundation, 1977), 103.

90. Mark H. Moore, "Keeping Handguns from Criminal Offenders," *Annals of the American Academy of Political and Social Science* 455 (May 1981): 96, 105, 106. The numbers cited here are averages of Moore's data.

91. Drinan, "Good Outweighs the Evil," 58. See also Robin, *Violent Crime and Gun Control,* 42–43. Most guns are stolen when thieves come across them in the process of committing burglaries aimed at other items.

    The figure of 500,000 guns stolen per year is consistent with that reported in Osha Gray Davidson, "Hot Guns, Cold Cash," *New York Times,* 21 February 1994.

92. Moore, "Keeping Handguns from Criminal Offenders," 92–109. Second study reported in Cook, "Technology of Personal Violence," 60.

93. David McDowall, "Firearm Availability and Homicide Rates in Detroit, 1951–1986," *Social Forces* 69 (June 1991): 1085–1101; James Lindgren, "Organizational and Other Constraints on Controlling the Use of Deadly Force by Police," *Annals of the American Academy of Political and Social Science* 455 (May 1981): 110–19; and Wilson, "Just Take Away the Guns," 47.

94. George D. Newton and Franklin E. Zimring, *Firearms and Violence in American Life* (Washington, D.C.: Government Printing Office, 1970); Llad Phillips, Harold L. Votey Jr., and John Howell, "Handguns and Homicide: Minimizing Losses and the Costs of Control," *Journal of Legal Studies* 5 (April 1975): 463–78; and Joseph Magaddino and Marshall H. Medoff, "An Empirical Analysis of Federal and State Firearm Control Laws," in *Firearms and Violence,* ed. Don B. Kates Jr. (San Francisco: Pacific Institute, 1984), 255. The Newton and Zimring study has been criticized for not analyzing causality or considering other social forces.

95. Cook, "Technology of Personal Violence," 44.

96. Franklin E. Zimring, "Firearms and Federal Law: The Gun Control Act of 1968," *Journal of Legal Studies* 4 (January 1975): 196.
97. Fox Butterfield, "Cities Finding a New Policy Limits Guns," *New York Times*, 20 November 1994; Fox Butterfield, "New Data Point Blame at Gun Makers," *New York Times*, 28 November 1998.
98. Wright, Rossi, and Daly, *Under the Gun*, 149. See also Matthew G. Yeager, "How Well Does the Handgun Protect You and Your Family?" in *Gun Control Debate*, 234.
99. David Hemenway, Sara J. Solnick, and Deborah R. Azrael, "Firearms and Community Feelings of Safety," *Journal of Criminal Law and Criminology* 86 (Fall 1995): 121–32; D. Hemenway, D. Azrael, and M. Miller, "National Attitudes Concerning Gun Carrying in the United States," *Injury Prevention* 7 (December 2001): 282–85.
100. David Olinger, "Massacre Energizes Gun Debate but Not Lawmakers," *Denver Post*, 19 April 2000; Robert J. Spitzer, *The Right to Bear Arms* (Santa Barbara, Calif.: ABC-CLIO, 2001), 1–2.
101. Robert J. Spitzer, "The Gun Dispute," *American Educator*, Summer 1999, 10–15; James Alan Fox and Marianne W. Zawitz, "Homicide Trends in the United States," Bureau of Justice Statistics Crime Data Brief, January 1999, NCJ 173956.
102. Patricia King and Andrew Murr, "A Son Who Spun Out of Control," *Newsweek*, 1 June 1998, 33; Timothy Egan, "From Adolescent Angst to Shooting Up Schools," *New York Times*, 14 June 1998; Ford Fessenden, "How Youngest Killers Differ," *New York Times*, 9 April 2000; Jack M. Bergstein et al., "Guns in Young Hands," *Journal of Trauma* 41 (November 1996): 794–98.
103. Kleck says, "Prospective violent offenders unable to easily obtain handguns would presumably seek substitutes, and for many of them the most satisfactory substitute would be a long gun." *Point Blank*, 91. Kleck thus concedes, although not explicitly, that some prospective criminals would not turn to long guns if handguns were less available. This is an assumption supported by existing patterns of gun use, as discussed in this chapter.

Chapter 4. Political Fury: Gun Politics

1. For more material on the rhetoric of gun control, see Andrew Jay McClurg, "The Rhetoric of Gun Control," *American University Law Review* 42 (Fall 1992): 53–113; and Raymond S. Rodgers, "The Rhetoric of the NRA," *Vital Speeches of the Day*, 1 October 1983, 758–61.
2. Larry J. Sabato, "How Direct Mail Works," in *Campaigns and Elections*, ed. Sabato (Glenview, Ill.: Scott, Foresman, 1989), 96. See also R. Kenneth Godwin, *One Billion Dollars of Influence* (Chatham, N.J.: Chatham House, 1988).
3. The literature on social movements supports this analysis. See, for example, Neil J. Smelser, *Theory of Collective Behavior* (New York: Free Press, 1963); Michael Useem, *Protest Movements in America* (Indianapolis, Ind.: Bobbs-Merrill, 1975); Robert J. Spitzer, *The Right to Life Movement and Third Party Politics* (Westport, Conn.: Greenwood, 1987); and Kay Lehman Schlozman and John T. Tierney, *Organized Interests and American Democracy* (New York: Harper and Row, 1986), 52.
4. Raymond Tatalovich and Byron Daynes, "Conclusion," in *Social Regulatory Policy*, ed. Tatalovich and Daynes (Boulder, Colo.: Westview, 1988), 213.

5. Other groups that have worked or are working against gun control laws include the Citizens Committee for the Right to Keep and Bear Arms (which includes a research arm, the Second Amendment Foundation), formed in 1971 by a group of gun enthusiasts who felt that the NRA was not being tough enough on the gun issue; and the Gun Owners of America (GOA), founded in 1975. The GOA is headed by Larry Pratt, and it claims a membership of 150,000. Other gun control proponent groups have included the National Alliance for Handgun Control Education, the National Alliance Against Violence, the Gun Safety Institute, and the Medical Council on Handgun Violence. The National Coalition to Ban Handguns (now the Coalition to Stop Gun Violence) receives brief treatment in this chapter. Its affiliate organization is the Educational Fund to End Handgun Violence. More recently, the Violence Policy Center, headed by Josh Sugarmann, has engaged in high-visibility research to promote gun control arguments. Because of the money required to have a direct impact on the political process, these groups have focused most of their efforts on education/propaganda activities. Robert J. Spitzer, "Gun Control: Constitutional Mandate or Myth?" in Tatalovich and Daynes, *Social Regulatory Policy*, 117–21; "Leading the Call to Arms," *Time*, 20 April 1981, 27; and Ted Gest, "Little Think Tank; Big Impact," *U.S. News & World Report*, 6 December 1993, 26.

6. L. Sandy Maisel, ed., *Political Parties and Elections in the United States*, 2 vols. (New York: Garland, 1991), 2:687.

7. Edward L. Schapsmeier and Frederick H. Schapsmeier, *Political Parties and Civic Action Groups* (Westport, Conn.: Greenwood, 1981), 310.

8. Carol Skalnik Leff and Mark H. Leff, "The Politics of Ineffectiveness: Firearms Legislation 1919–38," *Annals of the American Academy of Political and Social Science* 455 (May 1981): 60; Lee Kennett and James LaVerne Anderson, *The Gun in America* (Westport, Conn.: Westview, 1975), 138–41, 205–6; and Richard L. Worsnop, "Gun Control," *CQ Researcher*, 10 June 1994, 512.

9. Osha Gray Davidson, *Under Fire: The NRA and the Battle for Gun Control* (New York: Holt, 1993), 29–30.

10. Edward F. Leddy, *Magnum Force Lobby* (Lanham, Md.: University Press of America, 1987), 147, 197. The content analysis of the magazine spans 1926 through 1983.

11. Neil A. Lewis, "N.R.A. Meets Call for Gun Control with a Muzzle," *New York Times*, 12 March 1992; "NRA Loading Up over Gun Issue," *Cortland Standard*, 27 March 1989; Fox Butterfield, "Aggressive Strategy by N.R.A. Has Left Its Finances Reeling," *New York Times*, 26 June 1995; Richard Keil, "NRA Loses 300,000 Members since January," *Cortland Standard*, 2 August 1995; Jill Smolowe, "Go Ahead, Make Our Day," *Time*, 29 May 1995, 18–24; Michael Powell, "The Revival of the NRA," *Washington Post National Weekly Edition*, 28 August 2000.

12. Jack L. Walker Jr., *Mobilizing Interest Groups in America* (Ann Arbor: University of Michigan Press, 1991), 31. See also Graham K. Wilson, "American Interest Groups in Comparative Perspective," in *The Politics of Interests*, ed. Mark P. Petracca (Boulder, Colo.: Westview, 1992), 82.

13. The NRA concedes as much. See James Trefethen and James E. Serven, *Americans and Their Guns* (Harrisburg, Pa.: Stackpole Books, 1967).

14. Davidson, *Under Fire*, 22, 27–28. As Kennett and Anderson noted about the NRA,

"Government sales of surplus arms were a vital element in the organization's growth." *Gun in America*, 205.

15. Josh Sugarmann, *National Rifle Association: Money, Firepower and Fear* (Washington, D.C.: National Press Books, 1992), 111.

16. Robert Sherrill, *The Saturday Night Special* (New York: Charterhouse, 1973), 219–23; and Bill Keller, "Powerful Reputation Makes National Rifle Association a Top Gun in Washington," *CQ Weekly Report*, 9 May 1981, 799.

17. Sugarmann, *National Rifle Association*, 111.

18. Brooke A. Masters, "Rifle Program under Fire on Hill," *Washington Post*, 26 July 1989; Pete Stark, "Army Division Serves as NRA Recruiting Tool," *Syracuse Post-Standard*, 12 March 1990; James W. Davis, "We've Heard of Targeted Subsidies, but . . . ," *New York Times*, 20 June 1990; "The Democrats' Big Guns," *New York Times*, 18 October 1993; and George Will, "Termination Is Not a Viable Concept within Congress," *Cortland Standard*, 12 November 1993.

19. Paul Rauber, "Home on the Rifle Range," *Sierra*, May/June 1994, 42–43.

20. "The NRA Member Guide," 20; and Jan Hoffman, "Fund Linked to N.R.A. Gave $20,000 for Goetz's Defense," *New York Times*, 16 April 1996. The NRA established the fund in 1978.

21. Sugarmann, *National Rifle Association*, 87.

22. These activities are carefully chronicled in Carl Bakal, *The Right to Bear Arms* (New York: McGrawHill, 1966), chap. 6.

23. Michael J. Harrington, "The Politics of Gun Control," in *American Politics, Policies, and Priorities*, ed. Alan Shank (Boston: Allyn and Bacon, 1984), 146.

24. B.B. Drummond Ayres Jr., "Gun Maker on MayLem: That Is Not Our Doing," *New York Times*, 19 March 1994.

25. Sugarmann, *National Rifle Association*, 88.

26. Erik Eckholm, "Ailing Gun Industry Confronts Outrage over Glut of Violence," *New York Times*, 8 March 1992; Tom Diaz, *Making a Killing* (New York: The New Press, 1999).

27. Joseph P. Fried, "9 Gun Makers Called Liable For Shootings," *New York Times,* 12 February 1999; Sharon Walsh, "The NRA Fires Back," *Washington Post,* 8 March 1999; Robert J. Spitzer, "Gun Industry Doesn't Know What's Good For It," *Syracuse Post-Standard,* 20 April 1999; Michael Janofsky, "Pressured by Suits, Gun Makers Turn to Political Effort," *New York Times,* 19 January 2000; Fox Butterfield, "Suit against Gun Makers Gains Ground in Illinois," *New York Times,* 3 January 2002; Carl T. Bogus, "Gun Litigation and Societal Values," *Connecticut Law Review* 32 (Summer 2000): 1353–78.

28. Sugarmann, *National Rifle Association*, 89–99; Drummond Ayres Jr., "U.S. to Seek Rise in Fee for Gun Dealers," *New York Times*, 4 January 1994. The license fee increase was part of the Brady law, passed by Congress in November 1993.

29. Michael Barone, Grant Ujifusa, and Douglas Matthews, *The Almanac of American Politics* (Boston: Gambit, 1972), 321, 679. As is so often the case in interest-group politics, Clark and Tydings were hampered by other factors in their reelection bids that probably outweighed the NRA's role.

30. Quoted in Davidson, *Under Fire*, 39.

31. Peter H. Stone, "Under the Gun," *National Journal*, 5 June 1993, 1335.

32. Quoted in Davidson, *Under Fire*, 149.

33. Davidson, *Under Fire*, 151–52.

34. Joan Biskupic, "Handgun-Control Advocates Keep on Shooting Blanks," *CQ Weekly Report*, 2 December 1989, 3313–14. For example, NRA advertising erroneously reported that bills before Congress in 1989, S.747 and S.386, would require gun owners to pay a $200 tax for certain types of guns. The NRA also claimed falsely that semiautomatic weapons owners would be required to submit to fingerprinting and an FBI investigation.

35. Michael Blood, "Organizations Spend Millions On Partisan 'Communications,'" *Cortland Standard*, 13 January 1994. See also Ted Gest, "Battle over Gun Control Heats Up Across U.S.," *U.S. News & World Report*, 31 May 1982, 35

36. Carol Matlack, "Under Assault," *National Journal*, 22 April 1989, 980.

37. Stone, "Under the Gun," 1336, and data provided by the Federal Election Commission; Kelly D. Patterson and Matthew M. Singer, "The National Rifle Association in the Face of the Clinton Challenge," in *Interest Group Politics*, ed. Allan J. Cigler and Burdett A. Loomis (Washington, D.C.: CQ Press, 2002), 68–71; James Dao, "N.R.A. Tightens Its Embrace of Republicans with Donations," *New York Times*, 26 April 2000; James Dao, "National Rifle Association Unleashes Attack on Gore," *New York Times*, 21 May 2000. NRA spending to elect or defeat members of Congress is not necessarily devoted to appeals dealing with the gun issue. In two House races in 1992, for example, the NRA sponsored vigorous campaigns to unseat incumbents who supported a waiting period for handgun purchases. Yet these NRA-financed campaigns never mentioned gun control; instead, they focused on other issues, such as the balanced budget amendment and flag-burning. See Richard E. Cohen, "NRA Draws a Bead on Incumbents," *National Journal*, 19 September 1992, 2134.

38. Peter H. Stone, "Is the NRA Bleeding Internally?" *National Journal*, 13 March 1993, 626–27. This was a spurious argument to some extent, as the ratio of initial cost to dues payment tends to follow this pattern for most organizations. Organizations make back their money through renewals and ancillary contributions or purchases, although the NRA's member renewal rate has been low in recent years. See, for example, Andrew S. McFarland, *Common Cause* (Chatham, N.J.: Chatham House, 1984), 81. See also Jack Anderson, *Inside the NRA* (Beverly Hills, Calif.: Dove Books, 1996), 31–34; Robert Dreyfuss, "Good Morning, Gun Lobby!" *Mother Jones*, July/August 1996, 38–47; and Barbara Vobejda, "NRA Is Said to Lay Off Dozens," *Washington Post*, 23 September 1996.

39. Butterfield, "Aggressive Strategy by N.R.A. Has Left Its Finances Reeling"; and David C. Morrison, "From the K Street Corridor," *National Journal*, 8 July 1995, 1774.

40. "NRA Rated 'Risky,'" *Syracuse Post-Standard*, 5 June 1995.

41. Katharine Q. Seelye, "National Rifle Association Is Turning to World Stage to Fight Gun Control," *New York Times*, 2 April 1997; Raymond Bonner, "U.S., in a Shift, Backs U.N. Move to Curb Illicit Trade in Guns," *New York Times*, 25 April 1998; and Raymond Bonner, "U.N. Panel May Approve Limit on Guns Despite N.R.A. Pleas," *New York Times*, 30 April 1998.

42. Schlozman and Tierney, *Organized Interests and American Democracy*, 88–106; and Graham Wootton, *Interest Groups: Policy and Politics in America* (Englewood Cliffs, N.J.: Prentice Hall, 1985), 221–22. According to John T. Tierney, the NRA has "a

huge budget and a large, excitable membership." "Organized Interests and the Nation's Capitol," in Petracca, *Politics of Interests*, 207.

43. "NRA: More Bang for the Buck," *Washington Post*, 4 March 1986. See also Jonathan D. Salant, "Analysis Ties Vote, NRA Money," *Syracuse Post-Standard*, 9 May 1991, which reports on findings from Public Citizen's Congress Watch. *Common Cause* offers the same kind of analysis. For example, it reported that among House members who supported an NRA-backed amendment to water down a bill criminalizing the use of weapons parts to make assault-style semiautomatic weapons (the amendment exempted domestic-made parts), 93 percent received NRA PAC contributions within the previous five years. Sixty-nine percent of those who did not receive NRA PAC money voted against the amendment. The amendment passed 257–172 on 4 October 1990. *Common Cause News*, 17 October 1990.

44. Laura I. Langhein and Mark A. Lotwis found that money was important in influencing votes on the Firearms Owners Protection Act of 1986 in the House of Representatives. They found not only NRA contributions but those of HCI to be important, along with lobbying and grassroots efforts, especially those of police organizations in conjunction with HCI. Yet these findings do not necessarily contradict the prevailing view that money does not normally buy votes because Langbein and Lotwis found that representatives' votes on this bill had no effect on their home constituents, making it a relatively low-visibility issue—that is, one in which money is more likely to be important. In addition, the study found lobbying to be an extremely effective counterforce. Finally, these patterns may be quite different for the Senate. "The Political Efficacy of Lobbying and Money: Gun Control in the House, 1986," *Legislative Studies Quarterly* 15 (August 1990): 413–40.

45. Frank Sorauf comes to this conclusion in part by specific examination of the case of the NRA. Sorauf even questions the solidity of the link of money to access. See *Money in American Elections* (Glenview, Ill.: Scott, Foresman, 1988), 307–14. See, more generally, Michael J. Malbin, ed., *Money and Politics in the United States* (Chatham, N.J.: Chatham House, 1984); Larry J. Sabato, PAC Power (New York: Norton, 1984); Richard L. Hall and Frank W. Wayman, "Buying Time: Moneyed Interests and the Mobilization of Bias in Congressional Committees," *American Political Science Review* 84 (September 1990): 797–820; and Robert Biersack, Paul S. Herrnson, and Clyde Wilcox, eds., *Risky Business: PAC Decision-Making and Strategy in 1992* (New York: M.E. Sharpe, 1994). Laura I. Langbein examined the impact of gun PAC spending on the Firearms Owners Protection Act of 1986, and noted that "NRA donations to pro-gunners clearly prevented many from switching away from a pure pro-gun position." "PACs, Lobbies and Political Conflict: The Case of Gun Control," *Public Choice* 77, no. 3 (1993): 569.

46. Keller, "Powerful Reputation Makes National Rifle Association a Top Gun in Washington," 799; and Steven V. Roberts, "Rifle Group Viewed as Key to Gun Law," *New York Times*, 5 April 1981.

47. James Q. Wilson, *Political Organizations* (New York: Basic Books, 1973), 33–35. For more on purposive incentives, see Jeffrey M. Berry, *The Interest Group Society* (Glenview, Ill.: Scott, Foresman, 1989), 53–54.

48. Wilson, *Political Organizations*, 35. This concern is reflected in the NRA's stated purposes, the first of which is "to protect and defend the Constitution of the United

States, especially with reference to the inalienable right of the individual American citizen guaranteed by such Constitution to acquire, possess, transport, carry, transfer ownership of, and enjoy the right to use arms, in order that the people may always be in a position to exercise their legitimate individual rights of self-preservation and defense of family, person and property, as well as to serve effectively in the appropriate militia for the common defense of the republic and the individual liberty of its citizens." The NRA's other four stated purposes are promoting "public safety, law and order, and national defense"; training others in the use of weapons; promoting shooting sports; and advancing hunter safety. See "The NRA Member Guide."

49. Ronald J. Hrebenar and Ruth K. Scott, *Interest Group Politics in America* (Englewood Cliffs, N.J.: Prentice Hall, 1990), 103.
50. Berry, *Interest Group Society*, 60. NRA grassroots activity is described in Tom Loftus, *The Art of Legislative Politics* (Washington, D.C.: CQ Press, 1994), chap. 7; and Ronald G. Shaiko and Marc A. Wallace, "Going Hunting Where the Ducks Are," in *The Changing Politics of Gun Control*, ed. John M. Bruce and Clyde Wilcox (Lanham, Md.: Rowman and Littlefield, 1998).
51. "Consumer Product Safety Agency Created in 1972," *CQ Almanac, 1972* (Washington, D.C.: Congressional Quarterly, 1972), 141–50.
52. "Testing, Testing, Testing," 60 *Minutes*, aired 20 March 1994; and Jeff Brazil and Steve Berry, "Federal Safety Law Targets 15,000 Items, but Not Guns," *Los Angeles Times*, 1 February 1998.
53. Quoted in Harrington, "Politics of Gun Control," 148.
54. The armor-piercing capabilities of such bullets are derived from replacing soft-metal lead tips with hard metal, such as bronze, that is coated with Teflon.
55. "Kill the 'Cop-Killer' Bullets," *New York Times*, 29 August 1983.
56. Stephen Kleege, "Brookhaven Eyes Bullet Ban," *New York Times*, 15 August 1992. For more on the Brookhaven case, see Jervis Anderson, *Guns in American Life* (New York: Random House, 1984), 102–4.
57. Davidson, *Under Fire*, 88–95. The revised bill included exemptions for target shooting and sporting ammunition. See P.L. 99–408 (100 Stat. 920).
58. Quoted in Carol Matlack, "Under Assault," *National Journal*, 22 April 1989, 978.
59. "Letter-Writing and Campaigns," *CQ Weekly Report*, 9 March 1991, 605. See also Stephanie Saul, "NRA Takes Aim at Brady Bill," *Newsday*, 16 April 1991.
60. Ian Brodie, "High Price to Pay for Defying the Gun Threat," *The Times of London*, 18 October 2000.
61. Davidson, *Under Fire*, 36. See also pp. 30–36.
62. This fierce intraorganizational struggle between a moderate faction seeking a broader, more pragmatic, and outer-directed approach and a more extreme inner-directed faction seeking greater purity and homogeneity on the gun issue is remarkably similar to the "broad" versus "narrow" bifactional splits that have characterized the internal struggles of single-issue minor parties in American history (including such third parties as the Liberty, Free Soil, Prohibition, Greenback, and Right to Life parties). Each arose from single-issue social movements that paralleled many of the traits of the NRA. See Spitzer, *Right to Life Movement and Third Party Politics*, 29–31, 51–52, 70.
63. Davidson, *Under Fire*, 101–7.

64. Matlack, "Under Assault," 981. The NRA has also battled such police chiefs as former Los Angeles police commissioner Daryl Gates, and Baltimore County's chief, Neil Behan. Most established police organizations, including the National Fraternal Order of Police, the International Association of Chiefs of Police, the International Brotherhood of Police Officers, the Law Enforcement Officers Association, the National Sheriffs Association, the National Association of Police Organizations, the National Organization of Black Law Enforcement Executives, and the Police Executive Research Forum, have broken with the NRA on the gun regulation issue. The NRA has sought to counter this by producing police officers who say that these groups do not represent most of the rank and file. See Carolyn Skorneck, "Group of Beat Cops Backs NRA Opposition to Semi-Auto Gun Ban," *Cortland Standard*, 7 June 1989; Davidson, *Under Fire*, 98–100; and "Again, the NRA Beats the Cops," *New York Times*, 16 September 1988.
65. "NRA Reportedly Threatens Bennett's 'Political Future,'" *Syracuse Post-Standard*, 18 March 1989; and Matlack, "Under Assault," 979–80.
66. Patrick B. McGuigan, "Loose Cannons," *Policy Review*, Summer 1989, 54–56; Richard Lacayo, "Under Fire," *Time*, 29 January 1990, 20; Davidson, *Under Fire*, 177–78; and Michael Fleeman, "National Rifle Association Meets, Group Suffers Declining Members," *Cortland Standard*, 8 June 1990.
67. Peter H. Stone, "She's Gunning at Legislation," *National Journal*, 25 June 1994, 1531.
68. Anderson, *Inside the NRA*, 25.
69. Richard Willing, "NRA Duo's Aim: Hard Line, Softer Image," *USA Today*, 19 January 1996. The NRA has also made a concerted effort to recruit women into its organization, and even to cultivate NRA identity among children. See Bob Herbert, "Targeting Women For Guns," *New York Times*, 7 December 1994; "Why Johnny Can Shoot," *Mother Jones*, January/February 1995, 15; "Taking Aim at the Youth Market," *Harper's Magazine*, March 1995, 16; and Katharine Q. Seelye, "Gun Association Is Trying to Lure Children, Its Foes Say," *New York Times*, 19 November 1997
70. John Mintz, "Ideological War Pits NRA Hard-Liners Against More Moderate Staff," *Washington Post*, 29 May 1995; Butterfield, "Aggressive Strategy by N.R.A. Has Left Its Finances Reeling"; and "Bush Quits the NRA in Outrage," *Syracuse Post-Standard*, 11 May 1995.
71. Stephen Labaton, "House Kills Sweeping Provisions in Counterterrorism Legislation," *New York Times*, 14 March 1996.
72. Fox Butterfield, "Questions Raised on Report of Agents at Racist Outing," *New York Times*, 27 August 1995; and Jane Fritsch, "N.R.A. Criticized for Its Aggressive Tactics," *New York Times*, 30 July 1995.
73. David Johnston, "Waco Witness Says N.R.A. Consultant Posed as a House Aide," *New York Times*, 17 July 1995; David Johnston, "Republican Attacks Use of N.R.A. Consultant in Raid Case," *New York Times*, 19 July 1995; and Fritsch, "N.R.A. Criticized for Its Aggressive Tactics."
74. Neil A. Lewis, "N.R.A. Takes Aim at Study of Guns as Public Health Risk," *New York Times*, 26 August 1995; and Bob Herbert, "More N.R.A. Mischief," *New York Times*, 5 July 1996.
75. Sam Howe Verhovek, "An Angry Bush Ends His Ties to Rifle Group," *New York Times*, 11 May 1995.

76. "Wayne LaPierre, on the Ropes," *New York Times*, 20 May 1995; and "The G.O.P. and the N.R.A.," *New York Times*, 12 May 1995.
77. Katharine Q. Seelye, "Close Votes in N.R.A. Elections Quash Hope for Internal Unity," *New York Times*, 6 May 1997; idem, "Heston Asserts Gun Ownership Is Nation's Highest Right," *New York Times*, 9 September 1997; Robert J. Spitzer, "Door No. 1: Muskets? Or Door No. 2: Free Speech?" *Christian Science Monitor*, 19 September 1997; Michael Janofsky, "N.R.A. Tries to Improve Image, with Charlton Heston in Lead," *New York Times*, 8 June 1998; Powell, "The Revival of the NRA." Jack Anderson argues that the NRA has alienated itself from most hunters and sportspeople in his book *Inside the NRA*.
78. The CSGV has taken a harder line on gun regulation than the Brady Campaign. In 1993 and 1994, CSGV worked closely with such broadcast networks as MTV and Nickelodeon, and with movie studios including Walt Disney Co., Paramount, Sony Corp., and Warner Brothers to produce and promote an antiviolence campaign (which would presumably include a strong gun warning component). MTV has provided free air time for public service spots sponsored by CSGV. See W. John Moore, "Lights! Camera! It's Gun Control Time," *National Journal*, 18 December 1993, 3007.
79. Pete Shields wrote about his experiences in *Guns Don't Die—People Do* (New York: Arbor House, 1981). Shields stepped down as chair in 1989 and died in 1993. When first founded, the organization was called the National Council to Control Handguns. See also "Leading the Call to Arms," *Time*, 20 April 1981, 27.
80. Robert Curvin, "Is the NRA in Trouble?" *New York Times*, 11 October 1982. Figures from data provided by the Federal Election Commission; Adam Clymer, "House Approves Repealing of Ban on Assault Guns," *New York Times*, 23 March 1996; Patterson and Singer, "The National Rifle Association," 69.
81. Wayne King, "Target: The Gun Lobby," *New York Times Magazine*, 9 December 1990, 82. The 1994 membership figure was obtained from the HCI national office. See also Michael Isikoff, "The Brady Bill: Success and Growing Pains," *Washington Post*, 31 May 1991.
82. Barbara Gamarekian, "Fighting the Fight on Gun Control," *New York Times*, 11 February 1987; Philip Shenon, "Wife of Aide Cut Down with Reagan Scoring Hits Against the Gun Lobby," *New York Times*, 25 May 1990; and King, "Target."
83. Lisa Girion, "Gun Violence Moves Moms to Action," *Los Angeles Times*, 3 April 2000; James Dao, "New Gun Control Politics," *New York Times*, 11 March 2001; James Dao, "Gun Control Groups Use N.R.A. Tactics for Fall Elections," *New York Times*, 24 July 2000; Homsher, *Women and Guns*.
84. Standard books on the 1988 elections do not even mention gun control as a salient issue that year. See, for example, Paul R. Abramson, John H. Aldrich, and David W. Rohde, *Change and Continuity in the 1988 Elections* (Washington, D.C.: CQ Press, 1990); Peter Goldman and Tom Mathews, *The Quest for the Presidency 1988* (New York: Simon and Schuster, 1989); and Gerald M. Pomper et al., *The Election of 1988* (Chatham, N.J.: Chatham House, 1989). The gun issue might have been important in swinging Pennsylvania to Bush in 1988, a state Dukakis lost by about 2 percent of the vote. Pennsylvania has the second-highest NRA membership of any state in the country. Even so, this one state would have made little difference in altering Bush's wide margin in the electoral college.

85. Noam Scheiber, "Gun Shy," *New Republic,* 29 January 2001, 15–16; E.J. Dionne Jr., "Guns and Votes," *Washington Post,* 13 February 2001.
86. Quoted in Worsnop, "Gun Control," 520.
87. Hazel Erskine, "The Polls: Gun Control," *Public Opinion Quarterly* 36 (Fall 1982): 455.
88. This discussion relies primarily on Gallup poll results, as Gallup is generally considered the most reliable, accurate, and objective of the polling organizations. Even so, Gallup's results are consistent with those of other mainstream national and academic pollsters, such the National Opinion Research Center and the Institute for Social Research. Gallup poll updates cited in this section are from Gallup's website, *www.gallup.com.* Gary A. Mauser and David B. Kopel complain that polls sponsored by large media outlets are less reliable than those conducted by survey research organizations and tend to be "slanted, loaded, or technically incompetent." "'sorry, Wrong Number': Why Media Polls on Gun Control Are Often Unreliable," *Political Communication* 9 (April 1992): 86. They mistakenly lump Gallup and Harris polls together with all other media polls, failing to distinguish between polls conducted by these and other respected polling organizations as part of their regular polling and instances when these organizations join with one or more media outlets to pursue particular issues or questions. The explosion of media polling does indeed pose accuracy and reliability problems, but the problems identified with media polling extend to subjects other than gun control. Although Mauser and Kopel are correct in urging that media polls be interpreted with care, their selective analysis of such polls exaggerates problems that are endemic to all polling, and they fail to take into account the broad range of such polling, which finds general concurrence with what is known about public sentiment on the major features of the gun issue. For a balanced and detailed discussion of the virtues and problems of media polling, see Thomas E. Mann and Gary R. Orren, eds., *Media Polls in American Politics* (Washington, D.C.: Brookings Institution, 1992).
89. Erskine, "The Polls: Gun Control," 455, 460. This fact is well established in the public opinion and interest-group literature. See, for example, Robert Weissberg, *Public Opinion and Popular Government* (Englewood Cliffs, N.J.: Prentice Hall, 1976), 130; Herbert Asher, *Polling and the Public* (Washington, D.C.: CQ Press, 1992), 18; Wootton, Interest Groups, 317–18; and Schlozman and Tierney, *Organized Interests and American Democracy,* 36. Gary Kleck disputes the notion that opinion on gun control has been relatively consistent and supportive, calling it "very volatile." To support this argument, he cites some Massachusetts state polls taken in 1976 concerning a state gun issue. Aside from the very limited geography and time period he cites to support his conclusion, Kleck fails to recognize or appreciate the relative consistency of national gun opinions when compared to other key national issues across the last seven decades, as well as the inherent volatility of state polls concerning state issues. *Point Blank* (New York: Aldine de Grnyter, 1991), 363.
90. As V.O. Key noted, "markedly unimodal distributions of supportive opinion are associated with most public policies and services." *Public Opinion and American Democracy* (New York: Knopf, 1961), 31. Kleck considers these general data to be "meaningless" because there may be little concurrence between what citizens consider adequate gun control and the actual controls that exist. *Point Blank,* 361–62. While such a disjunction may exist, Kleck fails to note, first, that this principle ap-

plies to public opinion on virtually any policy issue, from health care to welfare to international trade. It is a truism of public opinion that "the level of political information of the mass electorate" is "abysmally low." David H. Everson, *Public Opinion and Interest Groups in American Politics* (New York: Franklin Watts, 1982), 59. Second, despite this, the durability and visibility of the gun issue as a federal, state, and local concern, as well as the prevalence of guns in American society, increase confidence that American opinion on this subject is as well informed as that regarding any policy issue. And third, the political and policy mandate of a citizenry that prefers stronger controls than currently exist is perfectly clear to officeholders and decision makers. That this preference has not been translated into more policy enactments is a function of the myriad political forces that intervene between the citizen and the state. See Bernard C. Hennessy, *Public Opinion* (Belmont, Calif.: Duxbury, 1970); and Robert S. Erikson, Norman Luttbeg, and Kent L. Tedin, *American Public Opinion* (New York: Macmillan, 1991).

Kleck also argues that "there was little long-term trend in support for gun control over the period 1959–1990" and that "there was little that could be described as a strong long-term trend" (p. 367). Yet even Kleck's own data contradict this false conclusion, as his data compilation shows national support in favor of gun purchase limits to range from 67 to 79 percent and support for federal handgun registration to range from 66 to 80 percent during the 1959–90 period (p. 378). The short-term fluctuations that prompt Kleck's comments are ubiquitous in American public opinion.

91. "Large Majority Favors Handgun Registration," *Gallup Report*, June 1985, 15; George Gallup Jr. and Dr. Frank Newport, "78% Support Gun Control," *Syracuse Post-Standard*, 28 September 1990; Lawrence L. Knutson, "Poll Finds Wide Support for Gun Control," *Cortland Standard*, 30 December 1993; and George Gallup Jr. and Alec Gallup, "Handgun Waiting Period," *Syracuse Post-Standard*, 11 November 1988.

92. Carol D. Foster, Mark A. Siegel, and Nancy R. Jacobs, eds., *Gun Control—Restricting Rights or Protecting People?* (Wylie, Tex.: Information Plus, 1993), 71–73.

93. "Sentiments on Gun Issues," *New York Times*, 12 March 1992; "A Little Gun Control, a Lot of Guns," *New York Times*, 15 August 1993; and Knutson, "Poll Finds Wide Support for Gun Control." The *Times* survey asked respondents if they favored a waiting period without citing any other conditions or circumstances. Except for the post–Brady law survey, the Gallup polls just quoted asked if respondents favored a waiting period "in order to determine whether the prospective buyer has been convicted of a felony or is mentally ill." The citing of this condition probably explains why the Gallup support numbers are 3 to 10 percent higher than those of the *Times* surveys. Regardless, the degree of support is extremely high.

94. Jill Smolowe, "Go Ahead, Make Our Day," *Time*, 29 May 1995, 21.

95. Leslie McAneny, "Americans Tell Congress: Pass Brady Bill, Other Tough Gun Laws," *Gallup Monthly* 330 (March 1993): 3. Percentages of respondents supporting a handgun ban, from 1980 to 1993, were 31, 38, 39, 41, 42, 41, 43, and 42 percent, yielding a positive correlation coefficient of .69. Gallup did not ask this question from 1994 to 1997.

96. Felicity Barringer, "Majority in Poll Back Ban on Handguns," *New York Times*, 4 June 1993; Benjamin I. Page and Robert Y. Shapiro, *The Rational Public* (Chicago: University of Chicago Press, 1992), 94–96.

97. U.S. Bureau of Census, *Statistical Abstract of the U.S.:* 1992 (Washington, D.C.: Government Printing Office, 1992), 241 See also "Guns in America: Who Owns Them," *New York Times*, 9 March 1992; and Tom W. Smith, "The 75% Solution," *Journal of Criminal Law and Criminology* 71 (Fall 1980): 307–9.
98. Pauline Gasdow Brennan, Alan J. Lizotte, and David McDowall, "Guns, Southernness, and Gun Control," *Journal of Quantitative Criminology* 9, no. 3 (1993): 289–307. The authors also provide an excellent synthesis of the literature on this variable. Robert M. Jiobu and Timothy Curry, "Lack of Confidence in the Federal Government and the Ownership of Firearms," *Social Science Quarterly* 82 (March 2001): 77–88.
99. Richard L. Berke, "Fears of Crime Rival Concern over Economy," *New York Times*, 23 January 1994.
100. "Majority Supports Stiffer Handgun Laws," *Gallup Report*, August 1983, 4. A 1 percent difference in support of a seven-day waiting period was also found between gun owners and the population as a whole in a 1993 *New York Times*/CBS poll.
101. Wootton, *Interest Groups*, 320, 326.
102. Gerald M. Pomper with Susan S. Lederman, *Elections in America* (New York: Longman, 1980), 168–69. The analysis covers platforms from 1944 to 1976.
103. Dennis S. Ippolito and Thomas G. Walker, *Political Parties, Interest Groups, and Public Policy* (Englewood Cliffs, N.J.: Prentice Hall, 1980), 136.
104. All references to the content of party platforms are drawn from copies supplied by the national party committees.

Chapter 5. Institutions, Policymaking, and Guns

1. For example, Peter Woll says that "American bureaucracy is an independent force, and from its independence it draws much of its strength and prestige. It is a powerful and viable branch of government, not properly subject to complete control by Congress, the President, or the judiciary." *American Bureaucracy* (New York: Norton, 1977), 248. Douglas Yates says that "it is widely agreed—even among those who disagree on most other political issues—that something must be done to get the bureaucracy under control." *Bureaucratic Democracy* (Cambridge, Mass.: Harvard University Press, 1982), 149. Francis E. Rourke chronicles "the extraordinary influence bureaucrats now exert on policy decisions." *Bureaucracy, Politics, and Public Bureaucracy* (Boston: Little, Brown, 1984), 10. See also John J. DiIulio Jr., Gerald Garvey, and Donald F. Kettl, *Improving Government Performance* (Washington, D.C.: Brookings Institution, 1993), 18–19. The nature of bureaucratic power is nicely detailed in Kenneth J. Meier, *Politics and the Bureaucracy* (Pacific Grove, Calif.: Brooks/Cole, 1993), 57–79, although Meier points out, apropos of my analysis, that bureaucratic power varies according to the kind of agency.
2. This discussion is drawn from Carol Skalnik Leff and Mark H. Leff, "The Politics of Ineffectiveness: Federal Firearms Legislation, 1919–38," *Annals of the American Academy of Political and Social Science* 455 (May 1981): 48–62; Franklin E. Zimring, "Firearms and Federal Law: The Gun Control Act of 1968," *Journal of Legal Studies* 4 (January 1975): 133–43; and Lee Kennett and James LaVerne Anderson, *The Gun in America* (Westport, Conn.: Greenwood, 1975), 201–13.

3. Submachine guns were differentiated from machine guns, as the former were less bulky and more portable. The first and best known of these was the Tommy gun, developed during World War I, then marketed and sold commercially after the war.

4. Roosevelt's attorney general in the 1930s, Homer Cummings, was a staunch advocate of national gun registration. In 1937, he was quoted as saying, "Show me the man who does not want his gun registered and I will show you a man who should not have a gun." Quoted in Leff and Leff, "Politics of Ineffectiveness," 53. Cummings's successor, Robert Jackson, recommended to Congress in 1940 that all firearms be registered, that all weapons transfers be recorded, and that each transfer be taxed. "A 1940 Proposal: Register Firearms," *New York Times*, 11 April 1989.

5. Leff and Leff, "Politics of Ineffectiveness," 61. The NRA was a prominent part of a broader coalition that included gun manufacturers, the American Legion, the American Wildlife Institute, the American Game Association, the Izaak Walton League, various pistol groups, and other similar organizations.

6. This observation is supported by Leff and Leff, "Politics of Ineffectiveness," 57–60; and by Kennett and Anderson, *Gun in America*, 213–15, 252–54.

7. "The Gun under Fire," *Time*, 21 June 1968, 14.

8. Standard aggregate means for measuring these accomplishments include the presidential box score (the congressional approval rate of presidential proposals to Congress) and presidential support scores (percentage of congressional support for proposals favored by the president). Johnson's average rating for the box score during his presidency, 57.4 percent, exceeds that of any president during the time that this score was kept (Eisenhower through Ford, 1953–75).

9. All presidents face similar influence cycles, and the final year of a president's term is invariably the low point of presidential influence, a fact especially true for Johnson because he had already announced his intention not to seek another term and was facing ever-increasing hostility over Vietnam. See Paul C. Light, *The President's Agenda* (Baltimore: Johns Hopkins University Press, 1982), 32, 202–6; and Robert J. Spitzer, *President and Congress: Executive Hegemony at the Crossroads of American Government* (New York: McGraw-Hill, 1993), 270–71.

10. This analysis is summarized in Robert J. Spitzer, *The Presidency and Public Policy* (University, Ala.: University of Alabama Press, 1983), 150. The presidencies studied were those from Eisenhower to Ford.

11. The bill that Johnson signed was studded with features he opposed, including mandatory emphasis on riot control, removal of pressure to integrate local police forces, broad wiretapping provisions, the narrowing of limits on the rights of the accused, a change in the funding formula aimed at upgrading local and state police forces from direct grants to localities to block grants to states, and weakened gun control. See Spitzer, *Presidency and Public Policy*, 68; and "Congress Passes Extensive Anticrime Legislation," *CQ Almanac* 1968 (Washington, D.C.: Congressional Quarterly, 1968), 225.

12. "Gun Controls Extended to Long Guns, Ammunition," *CQ Annual Almanac* 1968 (Washington, D.C.: Congressional Quarterly, 1969), 552. The following discussion is drawn from this account.

13. See, for example, Woodrow Wilson, *Congressional Government* (New York: Meridian Books, 1956); Richard F. Fenno, Congressmen in Committees (Boston: Little,

Brown, 1973); Charles O. Jones, *The United States Congress* (Homewood, Ill.: Dorsey Press, 1981), 196–97; and Steven S. Smith and Christopher J. Deering, *Committees in Congress* (Washington, D.C.: CQ Press, 1990).

14. Spitzer, *Presidency and Public Policy*, 116–18.

15. Ibid., 120–25. When the 165 bills are categorized by the four policy areas, and averages of roll-call votes are calculated, the figures are as follows: in the House, 1.5 roll calls for constituent bills (37), 1.8 roll calls for distributive bills (40), 2.2 roll calls for redistributive bills (57), and 3.1 roll calls for regulatory bills (31); and in the Senate, 3 constituent, 3.3 distributive, 8 redistributive, and 11 regulatory. Thus the Gun Control Act's total of 5 roll calls in the House exceeds the regulatory average, and the 11 in the Senate ties the regulatory average. For more on this analysis and its justification, see pp. 115–29. The controversial nature of the gun bill is even more notable when one considers that Congress also considered a prodigious array of controversial and landmark bills during this time, dealing with such areas as civil rights, education, welfare, and Vietnam.

16. "The Gun Control Controversy," *Congressional Digest*, May 1986, 130; and "A Question of Guns," *Newsweek*, 24 June 1968, 81–85.

17. Zimring, "Firearms and Federal Law," 149–70. See also Jervis Anderson, *Guns in American Life* (New York: Random House, 1984), 86. A careful analysis of the legal and implementation-related consequences of this and subsequent legislation is found in William J. Vizzard, *Shots in the Dark* (Lanham, Md.: Rowman and Littlefield, 2000).

18. The repeal was enacted in the form of a rider attached to a tax bill. "Equalization Tax, Ammunition," *CQ Almanac, 1969* (Washington, D.C.: Congressional Quarterly, 1970), 334–36. The effort was led by Senator Wallace Bennett (R-Utah).

19. "Federal Gun Law," *CQ Almanac, 1985* (Washington, D.C.: Congressional Quarterly, 1986), 228–30; Steven V. Roberts, "Senate Votes Sweeping Bill To Loosen Control of Guns," *New York Times*, 10 July 1985; and Paul Duke, "Bill to Loosen U.S. Gun Law Passes Senate," *Wall Street Journal*, 10 July 1985. All accounts of Senate action emphasize the considerable impact of the NRA's efforts.

20. The last successful discharge petition was in 1983. The two bills so petitioned that were enacted into law were in 1938 and 1960. Randall B. Ripley, *Congress: Process and Policy* (New York: Norton, 1988), 135; and "Congress Relaxes Federal Gun Control Laws," *CQ Almanac, 1986* (Washington, D.C.: Congressional Quarterly, 1987), 83.

21. Steven R. Weisman, "Reagan Tells of Initial Pain and Panic after Being Shot," *New York Times*, 23 April 1981. Reagan reversed himself after his presidency, coming out in support of the Brady bill in 1991. While the substantive consequences of Reagan's change of heart on this modest measure were very small, its symbolic impact was significant. Steven A. Holmes, "Gun Control Bill Backed by Reagan in Appeal to Bush," *New York Times*, 29 March 1991; and Ronald Reagan, "Why I'm for the Brady Bill," *New York Times*, 29 March 1991. Reagan also came out in favor of banning assault weapons after his presidency. Osha Gray Davidson, *Under Fire* (New York: Holt, 1993), 201.

22. Linda Greenhouse, "House Adjourns Gun Control Debate to Cut Costs," *New York Times*, 10 April 1986. Greenhouse also noted, referring to the bill, that "the episode

was testimony to the power of the National Rifle Association, one of the best organized and most feared lobbies in Washington." "The N.R.A.'s Lobbying Is as Effective as Ever," *New York Times*, 13 April 1986.

23. Linda Greenhouse, "House Passes Bill Easing Controls on Sale of Guns," *New York Times*, 11 April 1986.

24. Ibid. That the NRA viewed these two provisions as serious reverses is evidenced by the fact that one day after McClure-Volkmer was signed into law, NRA Executive Vice President G. Ray Arnett fired all fifteen members of the NRA's public education division, who were then given two hours to clean out their desks and leave the building. Several explanations have been offered for the firings, but anger over McClure-Volkmer was at least one, if not the primary reason. Arnett himself was later forced out. Davidson, *Under Fire*, 187–88.

25. See, for example, John Herbers, "Police Groups Reverse Stand and Back Controls on Pistols," *New York Times*, 27 October 1985; and Philip Shenon, "An Alliance Is Slain over Gun Control," *New York Times*, 9 April 1986. See also "House Votes to Weaken U.S. Gun Control Law," *CQ Weekly Report*, 12 April 1986, 783. As Linda Greenhouse noted, "If the police lobbying was unusual, even more startling was the extent to which it failed." "N.R.A.'s Lobbying Is as Effective as Ever."

26. Quoted in Davidson, *Under Fire*, 65.

27. Laura I. Langbein and Mark A. Lotwis, "Political Efficacy of Lobbying and Money: Gun Control in the U.S. House, 1986," *Legislative Studies Quarterly* 15 (August 1990): 413–40; Laura I. Langbein, "PACs, Lobbies and Political Conflict: The Case of Gun Control," *Public Choice* 77, no. 3 (1993): 551–72; and Richard Corrigan, "Hunters Help NRA Win Showdown," *National Journal*, 19 April 1986, 954.

28. Robert Reinhold, "Effort to Ban Assault Rifles Gains Momentum," *New York Times*, 28 January 1989; and "Bush, a Lifetime NRA Member, Opposes Semiautomatic-Gun Ban," *Syracuse Post-Standard*, 17 February 1989. One clear indication of this is the author's clipping files: that for assault weapons for the year 1989 was by far the thickest.

29. Clifford Krauss, "House Resoundingly Defeats Ban on Semiautomatic Arms," *New York Times*, 18 October 1991. The massacre occurred on 17 October. Hennard used a Glock 9-mm semiautomatic pistol and a Ruger P89.

30. Nancy Herndon, "Moves to Make Assault Guns Illegal Matched by New Wave of Buying," *Christian Science Monitor*, 27 February 1989; and "Deadly Decision on Assault Rifles," *New York Times*, 26 July 1990. The most common of these assault weapons include (in order of popularity) the TEC–9, the AR–15, the Uzi, the MAC–11, the MINI–14, the AK–47, the MAC–10, the SPAS–12, the HK–91, and the HK–93. About fifty weapons fall under the assault weapon category, but these ten account for nine-tenths of all assault weapon crime. Jim Stewart and Andrew Alexander, "Assault Weapons Muscling in on the Front Lines of Crime," *Atlanta Journal and Constitution*, 21 May 1989; and Robert J. Spitzer, "Assault Weapons Ban," *Christian Science Monitor*, 16 April 1998. Title XI of the Violent Crime Control Act (108 Stat. 199; PL103–322) defines assault weapons, including both rifles and pistols.

31. Gerald M. Boyd, "Bush Opposes a Ban on Assault Firearms but Backs State Role," *New York Times*, 17 February 1989; Charles Mohr, "U.S. Bans Imports of Assault Ri-

fles in Shift by Bush," *New York Times*, 15 March 1989; and Bernard Weinraub, "Bush Considers Calling in Guard to Fight Drug Violence in Capital," *New York Times*, 21 March 1989. Sensing the mood of the public and the government, Colt Industries voluntarily suspended the sale of its copy of the military M–16 rifle. Charles Mohr, "Impact of Curbs on Guns Debated," *New York Times*, 16 March 1989. The ban immediately affected the import of about 113,000 assault-type weapons. Charles Mohr, "Federal Agency to Begin a Survey on Use of Semiautomatic Weapons," *New York Times*, 23 March 1989. Imported assault weapons accounted for about a quarter of those owned in the United States.

32. Douglas Jehl, "Clinton Undertakes His Drive on Guns and Crime," *New York Times*, 12 August 1993; and John M. Broder, "Clinton to Impose a Ban on 58 Types of Imported Guns," *New York Times*, 6 April 1998.

33. Clifford Krauss, "Senate Approves Ban on Manufacture of Military-Style Weapons," *New York Times*, 18 November 1993; and Clifford Krauss, "Senators Back Ban on Selling Guns to Minors," *New York Times*, 10 November 1993. The measure prompted surprisingly little opposition and passed 99–1.

34. Katharine Q. Seelye, "In Gun Vote, an Odd Hero for Liberals," *New York Times*, 7 May 1994.

35. Seth Mydans, "Freshman Withstands an N.R.A. Fusillade," *New York Times*, 9 May 1994. The representative was Steve Horn (R-Calif.).

36. "Gun Curbs Stall on Hill; Some Imports Banned," *CQ Almanac,* 1989 (Washington, D.C.: Congressional Quarterly, 1990), 262.

37. Katharine Q. Seelye, "G.O.P. Gains Allies in Move to Repeal Assault-Rifle Ban," *New York Times*, 26 January 1995; Katharine Q. Seelye, "Gingrich and N.R.A. to Delay Bill on Gun Ban," *New York Times*, 28 January 1995; and Jerry Gray, "Dole, in a 2d Nod to Right, Pledges to Fight Gun Ban," *New York Times*, 18 March 1995.

38. Adam Clymer, "House Approves Repeal of the Ban on Assault Weapons," *New York Times*, 23 March 1996; and Alan Greenblatt, "Repeal of Assault Weapons Ban Unlikely to Go Beyond House," *CQ Weekly Report*, 23 March 1996, 803.

39. "Legislative History, Violent Crime Control Act, PL 103–322," *U.S. Code Congressional and Administrative News* (St. Paul, Minn.: West, 1994), IV, 1821; David E. Sanger, "Chinese Arms Seized in Undercover Inquiry," *New York Times*, 24 May 1996; and Spitzer, "Assault Weapons Ban."

40. Gwen Ifill, "Hot Debate Magnifies a Modest Gun Law," *New York Times*, 12 May 1991.

41. "NRA Showed It Still Had What It Takes to Overcome Gun-Control Advocates," *CQ Almanac,* 1988 (Washington, D.C.: Congressional Quarterly, 1989), 100–101. For an example of the NRA's "hassle factor" at the state level, see Tom Loftus, *The Art of Legislative Politics* (Washington, D.C.: CQ Press, 1994), chap. 7.

42. Gwen Ifill, "House Passes Bill to Set Seven-Day Wait to Buy Handguns," *New York Times*, 9 May 1991; "Gun Control's Red Herring," *New York Times*, 6 May 1991; and Gwen Ifill, "Cost Is Put in the Millions for Computer Gun Check," *New York Times*, 7 May 1991. The cost estimate was from the Congressional Budget Office.

43. "Anti-Crime Bill Falls Victim to Partisanship" and "Brady Bill Part of Stalled Crime Package," both in *CQ Almanac,* 1991 (Washington, D.C.: Congressional Quarterly, 1992), 262–70, 271–73; and "No Compromise Forged on Crime Bill," *CQ Almanac,* 1992 (Washington, D.C.: Congressional Quarterly, 1993), 311–13.

44. Clifford Krauss, "Gun Bill Freed from a Logjam; Passage More Likely," *New York Times*, 38 October 1993. The *Times* dubbed the bill's revival "political CPR." Sarah Brady compared it to the Dewey-Truman story, when predictions of Truman's political demise in the 1948 elections proved to be premature. Adam Clymer, "How Jockeying Brought Brady Bill Back to Life," *New York Times*, 22 November 1993; and Karen DeWitt, "Five Years of Struggle by Bradys Pays Off," *New York Times*, 22 November 1993.

45. Fox Butterfield, "Brady Law Halts Permits for 45,000," *New York Times*, 12 March 1995; "Stricter Standards Decrease Ranks of 'Kitchen-Table' Gun Dealers," *Syracuse Herald American*, 19 May 1996; and "Law on Gun Buyers," *New York Times*, 5 September 1997. For more on the federalism consequences of the Brady law, see Carol J. DeFrances and Steven K. Smith, "Federal-State Relations in Gun Control: The 1993 Brady Handgun Violence Prevention Act," *Publius* 24 (Summer 1994): 69–82. For a discussion of the limitations of the Brady law, see James B. Jacobs and Kimberly A. Potter, "Keeping Guns Out of the 'Wrong' Hands: The Brady Law and the Limits of Regulation," *Journal of Criminal Law and Criminology* 86 (Fall 1995):93–120.

46. Ifill, "House Passes Bill to Set Seven-Day Wait To Buy Handguns." Prominent defectors from the NRA included Reps. Les AuCoin (D-Oreg.) and Susan Molinari (R-N.Y.). See Steven A. Holmes, "Rifle Lobby Torn by Dissidents and Capitol Defectors," *New York Times*, 27 March 1991.

47. Voting patterns were similar in the Senate, but regional analysis is more statistically variable for Senate votes because of the smaller number of senators. The eleven southern states send only twenty-two representatives to the Senate.

48. "President's Jump in Favor of Gun Control Startles Aides," *Syracuse Post-Standard*, 10 December 1993.

49. For example, the NRA publication *American Rifleman* featured a cover story in its January 1994 issue (the first to come out after passage of the Brady law) under the banner ANTI-GUN FRENZY. The cover article's reference to passage of the Brady law was this: "When Bill Clinton signed the Brady bill into law November 30, a drop of blood dripped from the finger of the sovereign American citizen." Oddly, the only photo on the cover of the issue was that of Hillary Clinton, whose role on the gun issue was less prominent than were the roles of other members of the Clinton administration. The lead article was entitled "Line Up and Shut Up. Face Forward. Stay in Line. State Your Name. Last Name First," 32–33.

50. "Brady Bill Part of Stalled Crime Package," 271.

51. Frank Bruni, "Senate Votes Gun Curbs, Hours After Georgia School Shooting," *New York Times*, 21 May 1999; Frank Bruni and James Dao, "Gun-Control Bill Rejected in House in Bipartisan Vote," *New York Times*, 19 June 1999; "Gun Control Agreement Eludes Conferees, Derails Juvenile Crime Legislation," *CQ Almanac* 1999 (Washington, D.C.: Congressional Quarterly, 2000), 18:3–26.

52. Leslie Maitland Werner, "An Agency Steps Out of Obscurity," *New York Times*, 27 January 1985; and Wayne King, "A Bureau That Battled Bootleggers Is Tough Target for Budget-Cutters," *New York Times*, 1 February 1988. The Treasury Department first exercised jurisdiction over firearms when it was charged with collecting the excise tax on firearms sales in 1919. Josh Sugarmann, *National Rifle Association: Money, Firepower and Fear* (Washington, D.C.: National Press Books, 1992), 91.

53. " . . . Any Gun You Want," *New York Times*, 7 October 1981.

54. Quoted in Sugarmann, *National Rifle Association*, 124–25.

55. Peter Maas, "Can John Magaw Save the ATF?" *Parade Magazine*, 19 May 1996, 4, 6; "A Role for B.A.T.F.," *New York Times*, 4 May 1995; and Fox Butterfield, "Long Before Bombing, Gun Lobby Was Lashing Out at Federal Agents," *New York Times*, 8 May 1995.

56. "Gun Controls Extended to Long Guns, Ammunition," *CQ Annual Almanac*, 1968 (Washington, D.C.: Congressional Quarterly, 1969), 552; Bill Keller, "Powerful Reputation Makes National Rifle Association a Top Gun in Washington," *CQ Weekly Report*, 9 May 1981, 801; Mary McGrory, "Pity the Poor, Suffering Gun Owners," *Ithaca Journal*, 15 July 1985; and B. Drummond Ayres Jr., "U.S. to Seek Rise in Fee for Gun Dealers," *New York Times*, 4 January 1994.

57. According to one account, "even inexperienced gun owners could make the change in a matter of minutes, using only a file." The weapon was first popularized in a 1974 John Wayne movie, *McQ*. Erik Larson, "The Story of a Gun," *Atlantic Monthly*, January 1993, 52. See also Larson, *Lethal Passage: How the Travels of a Single Handgun Expose the Roots of America's Gun Crisis* (New York: Crown, 1994).

58. "U.S. Aides Find Gun Smuggling Is a Low Priority," *New York Times*, 6 September 1985.

59. Charles J. Hanley, "America Is a Mother Lode of Firepower for World of Conflict and Crime," *Cortland Standard*, 6 April 1994.

60. Sugarmann, *National Rifle Association*, 122.

61. "Two Regulatory Units Facing Budget Cuts," *New York Times*, 14 February 1981; and Phil Gailey, "White House Planning to Kill Firearms Enforcement Unit," *New York Times*, 9 September 1981.

62. Davidson, *Under Fire*, 52–53.

63. "Treasury, Postal Funds in Continuing Measure," *CQ Almanac*, 1983 (Washington, D.C.: Congressional Quarterly, 1984), 273.

64. The agency was given jurisdiction over arson and explosives in the Anti-Arson Act of 1982.

65. King, "A Bureau That Battled Bootleggers Is Tough Target for Budget-Cutters." Higgins likened such arrests to ticketing jaywalkers, although the volume of improper gun exchanges suggests a more serious problem. See also Robert D. Hershey Jr., "Vigor Wins New Life For Firearms Agency," *New York Times*, 23 December 1985.

66. Stephen Labaton, "Firearms Agency Struggles to Rise from the Ashes of the Waco Disaster," *New York Times*, 5 November 1993; and Maas, "Can John Magaw Save the ATF?" The ATF was also rocked by repeated charges of sexual harassment and racial discrimination within the agency.

  Branch Davidian group leader David Koresh (his real name was Vernon Howell) had amassed an enormous quantity of arms and munitions, including machine guns and explosives. For more on this incident, see Ronald Kessler, *The FBI* (New York: Pocket Books, 1993), 418–29.

67. "Firearms Agency Bans Armor-Piercing Bullets," *New York Times*, 6 February 1994; Steven A. Holmes, "Treasury Imposes New Regulations on Some Shotguns," *New York Times*, 1 March 1994; and "Another Blow to the N.R.A.," *New York Times*, 2 March 1994.

68. In 1993 and 1994, the NRA focused much attention on the fate of the Branch Davidians in Waco and the case of Randy Weaver and his family, armed white supremacist extremists who lived in Idaho. Several family members were killed in an FBI–federal marshal assault on the Weaver home in 1992. The NRA has sought to depict both incidents as cases of innocent, law-abiding citizens set upon by the government because they owned weapons. There is good reason to believe that the government mishandled both cases (a conclusion the government has already reached about the Waco case), but in both instances it had ample cause to take action. The NRA's effort to elevate these individuals to martyr status and depict federal law enforcement officials as fascist tyrants can be seen in the *American Rifleman* issues of September 1993 (in particular Robert K. Corbin's "The President's Column") and November 1993 ("The Randy Weaver Case," 41–43), and in the *American Hunter*, October 1993, 43–44. The ATF played no direct role in the Randy Weaver case and did not participate in the final assault on the Waco compound.

69. Wendy L. Martinek, Kenneth J. Meier, and Lael R. Keiser, "Jackboots or Lace Panties?" in *The Changing Politics of Gun Control* (Lanham, Md.: Rowman and Littlefield, 1998), 24.

70. Richard Gid Powers, *Secrecy and Power* (New York: Free Press, 1987), 184–85.

71. Philip J. Cook, Stephanie Molliconi, and Thomas B. Cole, "Regulating Gun Markets," Journal of Criminal *Law and Criminology* 86 (Fall 1995): 59–91; and William J. Vizzard, "The Impact of Agenda Conflict on Policy Formulation and Implementation: The Case of Gun Control," *Public Administration Review* 55 (July/August 1995): 343.

72. Martinek, Meier, and Keiser, "Jackboots or Lace Panties?" 41–42. See also William J. Vizzard, *In the Cross Fire: A Political History of the Bureau of Alcohol, Tobacco, and Firearms* (Boulder, Colo.: Lynne Rienner, 1997); William J. Vizzard, *Shots in the Dark* (Lanham, Md.: Rowman and Littlefield, 2000); James Moore, *Very Special Agents* (Urbana, Ill.: University of Illinois Press, 2001).

73. E.E. Schattschneider, *The Semisovereign People* (Hinsdale, Ill.: Dryden Press, 1975).

Chapter 6. Gun Policy: A New Framework

1. See, for example, Martin S. Geisel, Richard Roll, and R. Stanton Wettick, "The Effectiveness of State and Local Regulation of Handguns: A Statistical Analysis," *Duke Law Journal* 4 (1969): 647–76; Glenn L. Pierce and William J. Bowers, "The Bartley-Fox Gun Law's Short-term Impact on Crime in Boston," *Annals of the American Academy of Political and Social Science* 455 (May 1981): 120–37; John Henry Sloan et al., "Handgun Regulations, Crime, Assaults, and Homicide," *New England Journal of Medicine* 319 (10 November 1988): 1256–62; and Colin Loftin et al., "Effects of Restrictive Licensing of Handguns on Homicide and Suicide in the District of Columbia," *New England Journal of Medicine* 325 (5 December 1991): 1615–20. See also Erik Larson, "The Story of a Gun," *Atlantic Monthly*, January 1993, 48–78; and idem, *Lethal Passage* (New York: Crown, 1994).

2. Basic issues and consequences of American federalism are summarized in William H. Riker, *Federalism: Origin, Operation, Significance* (Boston: Little, Brown, 1964); Michael D. Reagan and John G. Sanzone, *The New Federalism* (New York: Oxford

University Press, 1981); and David C. Nice, *Federalism: The Politics of Intergovernmental Relations* (New York: St. Martin's, 1987).

3. Lee Kennett and James LaVerne Anderson, *The Gun in America* (Westport, Conn.: Greenwood, 1975), 174–86.

4. Craig Wolff, "In New York, the Brazenness of Illegal Gun Dealers Grows," *New York Times*, 11 November 1990; and James Dao, "States Joining in Combating Illegal Guns," *New York Times*, 26 April 1993; Patrice O'Shaughnessy, "Guns on New York's Mind," *New York Daily News*, 16 May 2000; Hannah Glover and Erica Pearson, "Young Gun," *Village Voice*, 21–27 March 2001. The ease of gun purchases in Florida has made it "the hub of a booming illegal trade in arms" for criminals, terrorists, and others in Caribbean and Latin American nations. Guns purchased over the counter in Miami were used to assassinate three Colombian presidential candidates in 1989. According to ATF Director Stephen Higgins, "We have the reputation as being the No. 1 supplier of weapons in this hemisphere, and that reputation is probably well deserved." Larry Rohter, "From Brazil to Peru to Jamaica, Gun Smugglers Flock to Florida," *New York Times*, 11 August 1991. See also B. Drummond Ayres, "Virginia Aims to Shed Image as 'Handgun Supermarket,'" *New York Times*, 23 December 1992.

5. "One Gun a Month Is Plenty," *New York Times*, 10 February 1996; and Fox Butterfield, "Report Links Crimes to States with Weak Gun Controls," *New York Times*, 9 April 1997.

6. Kevin Sack, "Gun-Control Battles Reveal Gradual Shifts," *New York Times*, 13 June 1993; and Dirk Johnson, "In Heart of Gun Country, Utah Is Changing Its Mind?" *New York Times*, 14 October 1993. The gun issue figured in the 1993 gubernatorial elections in New Jersey and Virginia.

7. Larry Rohter, "In Wave of Anticrime Fervor, States Rush to Adopt Laws," *New York Times*, 10 May 1994. For more on state gun control efforts, see John M. Bruce and Clyde Wilcox, eds., *The Changing Politics of Gun Control* (Lanham, Md.: Rowman and Littlefield, 1998), chaps. 5–8.

8. "Come Armed," *Economist*, 10 October 1987, 31; Mary McIver, "A Lethal Lucky Charm," *Maclean's*, 12 October 1987, 59–60; "Even the NRA Can Have a Bad Day," *U.S. News & World Report*, 25 April 1988, 15; Andrew Kirby, "A Smoking Gun," *Policy Studies Journal* 18 (Spring 1990): 746–48; Richard L. Worsnop, "Gun Control," *CQ Researcher*, 10 June 1994, 517; and John Hickman, "Gun Control in the Georgia General Assembly," *Comparative State Politics* 16 (October 1995): 22–34.

9. John L. Gaddis, *The United States and the Origins of the Cold War, 1941–1947* (New York: Columbia University Press, 1972).

10. Many analysts have noted the need for more and better data on guns and the consequences of gun use. See, for example, James D. Wright, Peter H. Rossi, and Kathleen Daly, *Under the Gun* (New York: Aldine de Gruyter, 1983), 22; and Osha Gray Davidson, "Get the Facts on Gun Deaths," *New York Times*, 31 July 1993.

11. John M. Dawson and Patrick A. Langan, "Murder in Families," *Bureau of Justice Statistics Special Report*, July 1994; and Carol D. Foster, Mark A. Siegel, and Nancy R. Jacobs, eds., *Gun Control—Restricting Rights or Protecting People?* (Wylie, Tex.: Information Plus, 1993), 43, 44.

12. Andrew H. Malcolm, "From the Police Blotter: Eight Stories That End in Death," *New York Times*, 17 April 1989. The eleven deaths arose from eight instances.

13. "Seven Deadly Days," *Time*, 17 July 1989, 31.
14. Arnold Wolfers writes that "the insecurity of an anarchical system of multiple sovereignty places the actors under compulsion to seek maximum power even though this may run counter to real desires." *Discord and Collaboration* (Baltimore: Johns Hopkins University Press, 1962), 84. Herbert Butterfield describes this as a "Hobbesian fear—that you yourself may vividly feel the terrible fear that you have of the other party, but you cannot enter into the other man's counter-fear, or even understand why he should be particularly nervous. For you know that you yourself mean him no harm, and that you want nothing from him save guarantees for your own safety." *History and Human Relations* (New York: Macmillan, 1952), 21. Butterfield's description applies equally well to two strangers passing on a darkened street as to the behavior of nations.
15. Waltz emphasizes that anarchy is an "ordering principle" in international relations. Kenneth N. Waltz, *Theory of International Politics* (Reading, Mass.: Addison-Wesley, 1979), 88–89, 93. People often mistakenly assume that the "anarchy" of the inner cities, for example, reflects the absence of any codes of conduct and behavior. Such is not the case. Instead, it reflects the substitution of conventional civil norms with an intricate and different (and certainly more dangerous) "street culture" or "code of the streets." See, for example, Elijah Anderson, "The Code of the Streets," *Atlantic Monthly*, May 1994, 80–94.
16. Bruce Russett, *The Prisoners of Insecurity* (San Francisco: W.H. Freeman, 1983), 3.
17. William T.R. Fox, "The Uses of International Relations Theory," in *Theoretical Aspects of International Relations*, ed. William T.R. Fox (Notre Dame: University of Notre Dame Press, 1959), 35.
18. John H. Herz, "Idealist Internationalism and the Security Dilemma," *World Politics* 2 (January 1950): 157. See also Herz, *Political Realism and Political Idealism* (Chicago: University of Chicago Press, 1951).
19. Robert Jervis, "Cooperation under the Security Dilemma," *World Politics* 30 (January 1978): 169.
20. Recognizing this problem, the United States and the Soviet Union signed the ABM Treaty in 1972 to prevent both sides from developing and deploying antimissile missiles. See Russett, *Prisoners of Insecurity*, 78–79, 116, 155.
21. Herz, "Idealist Internationalism and the Security Dilemma," 173.
22. Russett, *Prisoners of Insecurity*, 47–66; and Walter S. Jones, *The Logic of International Relations* (Boston: Little, Brown, 1985), 377. John T. Rourke says that "there can be little doubt that arms both create a possibility of war and help create a climate of hostility and anxiety that is fertile ground for war." *International Politics on the World Stage* (Guilford, Conn.: Dushkin, 1991), 501. A study of the relations between powerful nations from 1815 to the present found that disputes between nations resulted in war 82 percent of the time when accompanied by an arms race. Conversely, only 4 percent of international disputes resulted in war when there was no arms race. The analysis was based on a total of ninety-nine "serious disputes" between nations. See Michael D. Wallace, "Armaments and Escalation: Two Competing Hypotheses," *International Studies Quarterly* 26 (March 1982): 37–56.
23. Rourke, *International Politics on the World Stage*, 503.
24. Waltz, *Theory of International Politics*, 88.

25. Quoted in Jervis, "Cooperation under the Security Dilemma," 201.
26. Conversation with John J. Mearsheimer, 25 April 1994. See his book, *The Tragedy of Great Power Politics* (New York: Norton, 2001).
27. Robert Jervis, *Perception and Misperception in International Politics* (Princeton: Princeton University Press, 1976), 89.
28. Foster, Siegel, and Jacobs, *Gun Control*, 10, 52. About 6.7 million violent crimes occur each year. Of those, 2.3 million involve weapons; 27 percent of those involve handguns and 8 percent involve other guns.
29. Larry Rohter, "Pistol Packs Glamour, Power and Reputation as a Menace," *New York Times*, 10 March 1992. According to a study of assault weapons use in crime by the Cox newspaper chain, such weapons were twenty times more likely to be used in crimes than other weapons.
30. Hunting enthusiasts point out that many standard hunting rifles are semiautomatic as well. But one can make strong arguments for differentiating such weapons from assault weapons (as recent legislation has done) in order to protect legitimate hunting purposes, and for barring large magazine clips. While the distinction between semiautomatic hunting and many assault weapons is mostly cosmetic, an arms-control approach, discussed later in this chapter, supports the principle of making such distinctions for the purpose of putting brakes on the domestic arms race.
31. This is the argument Alfred Blumstein makes about the proliferation of gun violence among juveniles. See "Youth Violence, Guns, and the Illicit-Drug Industry," *Journal of Criminal Law and Criminology* 86 (Fall 1995): 10–36. An apparent contradiction to this assertion is the case of Kennesaw, Georgia, which passed a local ordinance in 1982 requiring every household to maintain firearms and ammunition. The town's mayor claimed this action resulted in a decline in local crime without any rise in gun deaths. It turns out, however, that the law was not enforced and exempted those who did not believe in having or using firearms. In addition, claims that crime declined after the ordinance was passed turned out to be a statistical artifact (based on the small absolute number of crimes in a small town of about 9,000 people). In fact, the average crime rate in the four years following passage of the law was higher than in the four years preceding the law. David McDowall, Brian Wiersema, and Colin Loftin, "Did Mandatory Ownership in Kennesaw Really Prevent Burglaries?" *Sociology and Social Research* 74 (October 1989): 48–51.
32. Gary Kleck paints an idyllic picture of armed citizens serving as helpers or "complements" to police, providing "an additional option for dealing with danger." Kleck fails to consider the multiplication of danger in society from criminal, accidental, and suicidal gun use stemming from the introduction into society of "millions of people [who] are armed and dangerous to each other." *Point Blank* (New York: Aldine de Gruyter, 1991), 142–43.
33. Andrew H. Malcolm, "Many Police Forces Rearm to Counter Criminals' Guns," *New York Times*, 4 September 1990; Gary Pierre-Pierre, "Police Officials Are Said to Be Rethinking Rapid-Fire Guns," *New York Times*, 18 February 1995; and Clifford Krauss, "Police Plan More Training in 9-mm. Gun," *New York Times*, 5 June 1995.
34. Jervis, *Perception and Misperception in International Politics*, 83.
35. Sam Howe VerHovek, "In Killing of Repo Man, Law Shields the Killer," *New York Times*, 8 March 1994.

36. "'Make My Day' Law May Make for Homicides with Impunity," *Syracuse Post-Standard*, 22 August 1986.
37. David McDowall, Colin Loftin, and Brian Wiersema, "Easing Concealed Firearms Laws: Effects on Homicide in Three States," *Journal of Criminal Law and Criminology* 86 (Fall 1995): 193–206. See also the response of Daniel D. Polsby, "Firearms Costs, Firearms Benefits and the Limits of Knowledge," 193–220, and the response of McDowall and associates in "Additional Discussion About Easing Concealed Firearms Laws," 221–25, in the same journal issue.
38. Blumstein, "Youth Violence, Guns, and the Illicit-Drug Industry," 33; Fox Butterfield, "Cities Finding a New Policy Limits Guns," *New York Times*, 20 November 1994; Clifford Krauss, "Shootings Fall As More Guns Stay at Home," *New York Times*, 30 July 1995; James Q. Wilson, "Just Take Away the Guns," *New York Times Magazine*, 20 March 1994, 47; and Robert J. Spitzer, ". . . Maybe, but Not in Cities," *Los Angeles Times*, 19 February 1996.
39. According to the New York State Police, the average lifespan for guns on the streets is "less than 30 months." This high turnover rate is attributed to the tendency to lose or throw away guns used in crimes, and to their seizure by the authorities. Barnaby J. Feder, "Moynihan Wages Battle on Second Front of Gun War," *New York Times*, 20 March 1992.
40. Ronald Smothers, "A Debate in Congress Focuses on the Science of Destruction," *New York Times*, 7 November 1993; Adam Clymer, "Moynihan Asks Big Tax Increase on Ammunition," *New York Times*, 4 November 1993; "Company's Destructive New Ammunition Has Critics," *New York Times*, 27 December 1994; and Daniel Patrick Moynihan, "Just Bit the Bullets!" *Washington Post National Weekly*, 9–15 January 1995. The Winchester Ammunition Company voluntarily withdrew its Black Talon bullets from the market in the face of public criticism, although more than twenty other manufacturers continue to produce such bullets.
41. Russett, *Prisoners of Insecurity*, 189.
42. David Johnston, "Congress Never Even Got to Vote to Ban This Weapon," *New York Times*, 20 June 1999; James Dao, "In 80s, Afghan Militias Fought with U.S. Rifles," *New York Times*, 7 October 2001; "U.S. Gun Industry Armed Osama bin Laden's Terror Network," Violence Policy Center Press Release, 7 October 2001.

Index

About the Author

ROBERT J. SPITZER (Ph.D. Cornell University, 1980) is Distinguished Service Professor of political science at the State University of New York, College at Cortland, where he served as chair of the political science department from 1983 to 1989.

Professor Spitzer's books include *The Presidency and Public Policy* (1983), *The Right to Life Movement and Third Party Politics* (1987), *The Presidential Veto* (1988), *The Bicentennial of the U.S. Constitution* (1990), *Media and Public Policy* (1993), *President and Congress* (1993), *Politics and Constitutionalism* (2000), *The Right to Bear Arms* (2001), and *Essentials of American Politics* (coauthor, 2002). He has contributed more than 200 articles to a variety of journals, books, and other publications, and is often interviewed and quoted in national media on gun control and other subjects.

From 1986 to 1990, Spitzer served as a member of the New York State Commission on the Bicentennial of the U.S. Constitution. He currently serves as president of the Presidency Research Group. He has testified before Congress on several occasions, most recently in 1998 before the U.S. Senate Judiciary Committee on gun control.